Maitreya
on
Buddha Nature

Maitreya on Buddha Nature

a new translation of
Asaṅga's mahāyāna uttara tantra śāstra

by

Ken and Katia Holmes

with a comprehensive commentary based upon traditional
Kagyu explanations according to its contemporary masters

Khenchen Thrangu Rinpoché and

Khempo Tsultim Gyamtso Rinpoché

by

Ken Holmes

Copyright © 1999 Ken & Katia Holmes
All artwork by Master Artist Sherapalden Beru, of Kagyu Samyé Ling,
Scotland, and his students

First published 1999 by
Altea Publishing
Parkmount House, St Leonards Road, Forres IV36 0DW, Scotland

ISBN 0 9524555 8 7

Cover illustration: Future Buddha Maitreya teaching (detail from Gampopa thangka in shrine hall of Kagyu Samyé Ling monastery).

All rights reserved. No part of this publication may be reproduced in any form or by any means, including photocopying or any information storage or retrieval system, without written permission from the publisher.

Ken & Katia Holmes have asserted their rights under the Copyright, Designs and Patents Act, 1988, to be identified as the authors of this work.

A catalogue record for this book is available from the British Library.

Printed in Great Britain by Bell and Bain Ltd., Glasgow

This book is dedicated to the long life, good health and success in their work of all those striving for peace and understanding in this world. Their radiance is surely the most important factor in setting the tonality for the millennium to come. In particular, it is dedicated to HH the Seventeenth Gyalwa Karmapa, Urgyen Drodul Trinley Dorjé, to the Twelfth Tai Situpa, to the Twelfth Goshir Gyaltsabpa, to Dharma-Arya the Second Akong Rinpoché, to Khenchen the Ninth Thrangu Rinpoché and to Khempo Tsultrim Gyamtso Rinpoché, in gratitude for all the compassionate guidance they have given so generously over the years. It is also dedicated to the hundreds of unsung heroes and secret yogis whose devoted and often overlooked work has enabled the message of these great teachers to establish itself in the world.

The Twelfth Tai Situpa

FOREWORD

Arya Maitreya's Five Great Shastras constitute one of the major foundations of Mahayana Buddhism and it is with deep pleasure that I welcome this new translation into English of the Mahayana Uttara Tantra Shastra, Arya Maitreya's teaching on Buddha nature. His text not only elucidates the meaning of the Third Turning of the Wheel of Dharma but also serves as a bridge between the sutrayana and vajrayana levels of teaching. Thus, along with the Gyalwa Karmapa's "Profound Inner Meaning" and the Hevajra Tantra commentary, it provides the main theoretical basis, in the Kagyu tradition, for the actual practice of tantrayana. It is also the ideal theoretical grounding for the practice of mahamudra.

The beautiful poetry of the original root text is deep in meaning. It cannot be understood without the support of the traditional oral transmission, handed down through the lineage, and the use of commentaries. Ken Holmes, who has been my student for some twenty years, has based this 'meaning commentary' upon the explanations given by one of my own teachers, the erudite Kagyu scholar and supreme abbot of the lineage Khenchen Thrangu Rinpoche and the highly accomplished master and scholar Khenpo Tsultrim Gyamtso Rinpoche, according to the masterful commentary of Jamgon Kongtrul Lodro Taye the Great.

I pray sincerely that the true meaning of Lord Maitreya and Asanga, in explaining this most profound aspect of Lord Buddha's teaching, will serve to guide limitless beings towards true enlightenment.

The XIIth Tai Situpa

SHERAB LING
INSTITUTE OF BUDDHIST STUDIES
P.O. BHATTU   DISTRICT KANGRA   HIMACHAL PRADESH 176-125   INDIA

Contents

TRANSLATORS' INTRODUCTION   13

CLASSICAL INTRODUCTION   21
    The three major phases of the Buddha's teaching   21
      First phase   22
      Second phase   24
      Third phase   26
        A simple introduction to voidness   26
    The Buddha's own teaching or a *śāstra*?   29
    Source of this work   30
    The author   30
    Transmission of the text   34
    Subject matter   35
    Styles of explanation   37
    A bridge between sūtra and tantra   39

PART ONE: THE GOAL TO BE ACHIEVED:
THE THREE RARE AND PRECIOUS REFUGES   43

Introduction to the Seven Vajra Abodes   45

The Refuges   48
First Vajra Abode: buddha   50
    Homage   50
    Three qualities of self-fulfilment   51
      Not a creation   52
      Non-dual peace   53
      Non-dependent   55
    Three qualities which benefit others   57
    Three qualities of self-fulfilment, reflections   57
      Beginningless, centreless and endless   58
      Peace as spontaneity of dharmakāya   60
      Apperceptive nature   62
    Three qualities which benefit others, reflections   62

Second Vajra Abode: dharma   65
    Homage   66
    Context   67
    Relating content of homage to context   69
      Qualities of the truth of cessation   69

Inconceivability 69
Not two 73
Freedom from concepts 73
Qualities of the truth of the path 74
Stainlessness 74
Brilliance 74
Power to remedy 75

Third Vajra Abode: saṃgha 77
Homage 77
Context 79
Thusness jñāna 80
All-encompassing jñāna 80
Inner jñāna 81
What gives rise to these three 81
Relating content of homage to context 82
The way in which thusness jñāna is realised 82
The way in which all-encompassing jñāna is realised 83
Its special purity 84
They are a supreme refuge 85

General Points about the Refuges 86
Why it is threefold 86
What is the ultimate refuge? 87
Why are they called *ratna*? 88

PART TWO: THE BASIS FOR ATTAINING THE THREE RARE AND PRECIOUS REFUGES 91

General Comment on the Final Four Vajra Abodes 93
The final four vajra abodes only understood by Buddhas 93
They are inconceivable 94
Reasons for inconceivability 95
Causes and conditions for realisation 97

Fourth Vajra Abode: buddha nature 99
Brief Introduction: three reasons why beings possess *dhātu* 100
More detailed presentation through ten aspects of buddha potential 103
character and cause treated together, in brief 103
essential character 104
cause 105
fruition and function treated together, in brief 109

        fruition   110
        function   116
        endowments   118
        manifestation/approach   121
        phases   122
        all-pervasiveness   124
        changelessness   125
            in the impure phase   125
            in the partially pure phase   133
            in the completely pure phase   142
        inseparability from its qualities   145
Nine examples showing how buddha nature
remains changeless while concealed   153
        first example: buddha in decaying lotus   155
        second example: honey amid bees   156
        third example: grains in their husks   157
        fourth example: gold in filfth   158
        fifth example: buried treasure   159
        sixth example: seeds within a fruit   160
        seventh example: buddha image in tattered rags   161
        eighth example: future king in pauper's womb   162
        ninth example: statue inside its mould   163
        the meaning of these examples   164
The purpose of the buddha nature teachings   179

Fifth Vajra Abode: enlightenment   187
    The nature and cause of enlightenment   188
        treated together, in brief   188
        nature of enlightenment, in detail   190
        cause of enlightenment, in detail   192
    As a fruition   193
        in brief, as a summary of examples of stainlessness   193
        in detail   194
    Its function   198
        in brief, as twofold benefit   198
        in greater detail, as vimuktikāya and dharmakāya   200
    Its endowments   204
        in brief, listing fifteen qualities   204
        the fifteen qualities, in detail   205
    Actualisation   209
        in brief, the characteristics of the kāya   209
        in detail   213
            svabhavikakāya, five aspects and five qualities   214

sambhogakāya, five aspects and five qualities   217
nirmāṇakāya, the twelve deeds of the Buddha   220
Its permanence   231
   in brief, ten-point presentation   231
   the ten points in detail   233
Its inconceivability   237
   in brief   237
   in more detail   237

The Sixth Vajra Abode: the qualities of buddhahood   242
Synopsis: number of principal qualities and their relation to the kāya   242
More detailed explanation   245
   Introduction to the examples and their significance   245
   The qualities of freedom: the ultimately true kāya   246
     Ten powers of perfect knowledge   246
     Four fearlessnesses   251
     Eighteen distinctive qualities   254
   The qualities of maturity: the relatively true kāya   259
     The thirty-two marks of a perfect being   259
     Example for the marks   264
Scriptural source   264
Recapitulation of the examples   265
   The qualities of freedom   265
   The qualities of maturity   269

The Seventh Vajra Abode: enlightened activity   271
Summary   271
   Its spontaneity   271
   Its ceaselessness   272
More detailed explanation   273
   Its spontaneity   273
   It ceaselessness   274
Expanded explanation through nine examples   277
   Summary of the nine examples   277
   The examples   278
     The reflection of Indra: Buddha forms   278
     The divine drumbeat: Buddha speech   283
     Monsoon clouds: the all-pervading compassionate mind   286
     Brahma's emanations: emanation   291
     The sun's radiance: the penetration of primordial wisdom   293
     A wish-fulfilling gem: the mystery of mind   297
     An echo: the mystery of speech   299
     Space: the mystery of form   300

　　　　The earth: the application of compassion　301
　　　　Review of the purpose and significance of examples　302
　　　　Review of examples to show their sublime nature　306

PART THREE: CONCLUSION　311
The benefits of this text　312
How this śāstra was composed　320
Dedication　327

INDEX　331

Introduction

Buddhism is a living flame of truth, still burning brightly today, two thousand five hundred years after its first ignition. The lives of its great teachers, like candles lit one from another, have passed on the Buddha's initial wisdom from generation to generation. The Kagyu lineage carefully maintained this flame, first in India and then in Tibet, China and the Himalayan region. Due to the violent blows dealt Tibet in the last half of this century, the Kagyu teachings have left its lofty seclusion and spread throughout the world. It is through the living wisdom of the Kagyu oral tradition that we shall approach the teachings on Buddha Nature given to the world by bodhisattva Maitreya, around the fifth century, via the great master Āsaṅga.

A different approach to the study of this work might be that of some academics, who would build a hypothetical and well-labelled niche for these teachings, using linguistics, archaeology, fragments of texts found here or there and suchlike means, in the light of whatever fragments of historical knowledge they have of ancient India and its various traditions and religions. This may be informative and very fascinating, like detective work, but it is, in the end, often soulless, merely intellectual and, above all, highly speculative.

I am not at all against the academic approach: on the contrary. In this book, however, the intention is to pass on these teachings in a manner which reproduces, as closely as possible, the way they have been given, as an oral transmission, by some of our most distinguished lineage lamas. In practice, this has involved keeping as close as possible either to the explanations they gave in public or to clarifications of specific points given by them, to us translators, in private. In order not to detract from this direct transmission, personal forays into academic, text-based research have been intentionally shunned. The decision to do this has been made easier by the relatively recent publication of *The Buddha Within*,[1] in which Shenpen Hookham approaches this same text with admirable academic rigour and provides the reader with a wealth of food for thought, cross-references and bibliographic information.

To those actually practising these teachings, the oral tradition brings satisfaction and certainty, because one experiences the power of receiving the original meaning taught by the Buddha, kept alive through all these years due to the clarity of realisation of those who have transmitted it. Through the lineage we effectively travel back in time and participate in the vibrant power of these teachings just as they were millennia ago. This ancient text and its words has served, throughout this time, merely as a basis for the passing on of insight, within a system in which personal transmission, from master to disciple, was by far and away the main point. Its words are like the celluloid frames of a film, which spring to life when the bright light of a master's wisdom illuminates them on the screen of one's mind. In such a context, the living wisdom of the lineage master makes all the difference.

I mention these points because, in some countries, a certain chasm has opened between those translating dharma texts in universities and those doing so in dharma centres. Some academics feel that the devotee lacks the scholar's resources and critical impartiality, while the latter wonders how the scholar can approach such a work without the lineage blessing and close supervision. The devotee can also be suspicious, sometimes, of the scholar's need to create voluminous 'quotes and notes', in order for the thesis to be acceptable. This usually requires the latter to quote earlier Western academic authorities fairly extensively. The problem lies in the fact that their predecessors' understanding – albeit enshrined on untouchable pedestals of academic fame – sometimes bears little resemblance to the inner world of Tibetan Buddhist spirituality that they studied as external, often Christian, observers and that the present-day Buddhist has come to discover through intimate exposure.

The paradigm problems involved in bringing one's own cultural and intellectual preconceptions to the analysis of a situation is well-known. Most anthropologists will try to avoid it. Even so, it does not present too much of a problem for the pure anthropologist, who is reporting external, cultural customs in a 'language' the people of his or her culture can understand. It is, however, in my opinion, a significant and underestimated problem for the Western philosopher or religious anthropologist, whose work involves assuming what is happening in another people's inner, spiritual experience and who, like it or not, is equipped only with a Judæo-Christian, or classically Western, set of references with which to appreciate their world view.

The great contemporary Tibetan scholar Khempo Tsultim Gyamtso has pointed out that the best way for Buddhists of one tradition really to understand the philosophy of Buddhists of another tradition is to completely set aside their own preconceptions and put themselves fairly and squarely in the shoes of the other, so as really to see and feel the world as the other sees it. If this is valid advice, how much truer it must be for non-Buddhists or new Buddhists trying to understand Buddhism. In some ways, this having to 'stand in the shoes of the other' is a *sine qua non* for many people these days in dharma[2] centres, simply because of the sheer newness of Tibetan Buddhism. Those seriously interested in Tibetan Buddhist teachings and visiting these centres are still having to cross a significant number of cultural bridges to join Tibetan Buddhism on its side of the shore, until such time as translators and wise people will have brought it truly to these shores.[3] The experience of practising Tibetan Buddhism over a long term and under the guidance of a competent master does seem to have given many people a close appreciation of what Tibetan Buddhism is really saying about the world we live in and the way we live in it. Needless to say, the message of Buddhism itself is a universal one, far beyond questions of East or West, yet the accurate decoding of that message seems, at present, to require one to make the spiritual pilgrimage to the metaphysical place where it is well and thriving, in the minds of living Tibetan teachers.

My personal hope is that this unnecessary chasm between scholar and devotee will close. There is such a wealth of knowledge needing to be gathered from the imperilled Tibetan tradition that the more we all help each other to preserve it for the future, the better it will be. The present oral tradition should, in any case, be of great interest for the academic – be he or she anthropologist, philosopher or linguist – since it represents the real beliefs and customs of millions of people in recent times, no matter what was the bygone and, by now unascertainable, original meaning, a millennium and a half ago.

These are some of my reasons for presenting this translation and commentary as you will discover it in these pages. I feel a profound gratitude for having received the traditional explanations of these teachings. Part of this gratitude involves making them available, in book form, to those unable to receive them in detail directly from a lineage master, while at the same time providing a textbook for courses on this important text.

In the very last part of his life, Buddha Sakyamuni revealed the whole purpose of his forty-five years of teaching. Up until then, his instruction had taken place in two great waves, known by Buddhists as the first and second 'Turnings of the Wheel of Dharma'. In the few but highly significant discourses (*sūtra*) of the third and final Turning, he disclosed the one 'Rome' to which led all the many paths he had taught: *tathāgatagarbha*, now known commonly among Buddhists in the West as *buddha nature*. Centuries after the Buddha, when the world was ready to receive those teachings on a more popular level, Maitreya gave us this masterly text summarising the heart-meaning of those *sūtra*.

These teachings should be of interest to many people. Those intending to follow a life of meditation will need this information in order to be able to carry their practice to fruition. Those more interested in philosophy will be able to put so many of the Buddha's teachings into perspective once they have grasped the meaning of buddha nature. Anyone who has wondered about the meaning of voidness or the existence of God will find it interesting to discover what phrases like 'the Buddha within' really mean. More specifically, it is recommended that anyone following the Kagyu Buddhist tradition assimilate, in time, the meaning of this work as well as that of Gampopa's 'Gems of Dharma, Jewels of Freedom'. I hasten to add that this is not said in order to promote the two books upon which my wife and I have spent much of our lives. It is the other way around. It is because they are such vital foundations for good understanding that we were asked by His Holiness the Gyalwa Karmapa, in the late 1970s, to give priority to their translation into English.

My personal motivation for publishing what the Tibetans would call a 'meaning-commentary' to Maitreya's work is twofold. First is a sense of timeliness. Through my work in Kagyu Samye Ling[4] and constant contact with the evolving world of Tibetan Buddhism in the West, it seems apparent that many people practising Buddhism – particularly *vajrayāna*[5] Buddhism – and the world at large are ripe for as much reliable information as they can get about buddha nature. Without an understanding of buddha nature, someone might consider *vajrayāna* or tantric Buddhism as some ancient mumbo-jumbo. The uninformed observer could view it as an almost theistic form of Buddhist practice, and suspect some influence of other Indian or Tibetan non-Buddhist religions. This would be far indeed from the truth. In the light of these buddha nature teachings, *vajrayāna* is discovered to be the most intelligent system of transforming the human mind that one could ever evolve: light years removed from the primitive emotional chemistry and philosophical naivety of popular religions.

My second reason for working on this text is a sense of duty to my own teachers. By the twists of fate, or *karma*, and thanks to the guidance of His Holiness the 16th Gyalwa Karmapa,[6] my wife Katia and I had been fortunate enough to study this text at leisure, several times over, under two of the greatest Kagyu scholars: Khenchen Thrangu Rinpoché and Khenpo Tsultim Gyamtso Rinpoché.[7] This happened in the 'good old days' when such lamas could spend months working word by word through a dense scripture such as this. Nowadays, with literally hundreds of centres to care for, their time is always at a premium and they no longer enjoy such freedom. Through these lamas' kindness, and the invaluable help of the late Acarya Tenpa Négi,[8] a first translation of the root text was presented to HH the 16th Gyalwa Karmapa, who gave it his blessing and encouraged us to work on it further.

For almost twenty years, the teachings given by eminent teachers visiting Kagyu Samyé Ling have thrown much light upon points first brought up in those first word-by-word explanations. My own teaching experience in Scotland, where I have helped future retreaters understand the meaning of this text, has also been important. One never studies a work so well as when one has to explain it to others. Somehow students have an innate knack of finding the weak areas of one's knowledge.

All in all, Maitreya's work feels as though it has been maturing in me like a wine maturing in an oak cask. It now feels like the time has come to open the barrel and share this particular vintage that our kind teachers first poured in all those years ago. I hope that, among other things, it will help deepen the link between the reader and Maitreya, who is one of the most significant figures in Buddhism, both through his key role in establishing the present Buddha's teachings and, in his own right, as the next Buddha for our world. Sakyamuni is considered to have been the fourth of the one thousand and two Buddhas who illuminate this planet during its existence, by coming to teach the universal truth in its fullness. Maitreya will be the fifth.

It is said that, on leaving the paradise of Tuṣita to take his historic birth on Earth, Sakyamuni appointed bodhisattva Maitreya as his regent in that celestial realm and predicted that Maitreya would be the fifth Buddha. Later, while Sakyamuni was teaching in India, Maitreya appeared on many occasions as either Sakyamuni's interlocutor or spokesman. During the five thousand year period subsequent to Sakyamuni's passing from this world, Maitreya emanates in many ways, nurturing the dharma, helping individuals and establishing the links that will draw people to him in the future, at the time of his own buddhahood and teaching. Probably the most important activity of all during this time occurred when he gave the world his five great treatises, through his disciple Asaṅga, of which this text is the most profound.

Many thousands (if not tens of thousands) of years will pass, in worldly time, between the disappearance of Sakyamuni's teachings and the run-up to Maitreya's buddhahood here. Somewhere in that period, a very dark and savage time is expected for the inhabitants of the blue island in space we call 'Earth'. However, this long story of inexorable working-out of bad karma need not be the future lot of everyone at present living on this planet. While the world labours through that sombre tunnel, those of good mind can be taking the short cut to Maitreya's future by other, much more luminous, routes. If such is possible, may this book make a strong bond of faith with Maitreya and help speed the reader into his sublime presence.

There is a remarkable amount of academic discussion about this text these days. There is also quite a lot of interest in the differences

1   SUNY Press 1991
2   *dharma* – the teachings of the Buddha.
3   The experiments of Chogyam Trungpa Rinpoché were interesting in this respect.
4   Kagyu Samyé Ling monastery and Tibetan Centre, in Scotland, where the author has been based since 1971.
5   vajrayāna or *tantra* is a special aspect of the mahāyāna Buddhism found in Tibet, China, Korea and Japan (other countries too as a highly secret doctrine). It uses powerful techniques which enable suitable people to advance extremely quickly upon their path, under the very close guidance of an accomplished master.
6   HH the Gyalwa Karmapa is the Supreme Head of the Karma Kagyu lineage of Tibetan Buddhism. It is mainly through his activity that Kagyu Buddhism became established in the West. Mentioned here is his sixteenth incarnation. The present, seventeenth incarnation, resides at Tsurphu monastery in Tibet. See my *Karmapa* (Altea 1996).
7   These two teachers taught many present-day Kagyu masters, while they were residing with HH the Gyalwa Karmapa at Rumtek monastery in Sikkim. Khenchen Thrangu Rinpoché, Abbot of Rumtek, is the ninth Thrangu reincarnation and an extremely eminent lama who is not only a great Khempo, in the Kagyu tradition, but also a Geshe Rabjam, the highest academic order within the Gelugpa tradition. Khempo Tsultim Gyamtso, a yogin as well as a scholar, is not only erudite but extremely gifted as a teacher. His students exhibit remarkable prowess.
8   A linguist with Sanskrit, Tibetan, English, Hindi and other languages, appointed as HH Karmapa's official interpreter in Europe.
9   *rang stong* is the rough English pronunciation of the Tibetan *rang stong*, meaning 'self-void'.
10 *shengtong* is the rough English pronunciation of the Tibetan *gzhan stong*, meaning 'devoid of other'.
11 Dr Akong Tulku Rinpoché is the co-founder of Kagyu Samyé Ling and founder of Rokpa Trust. His compassionate work has not only touched thousands of people through the Buddhist centres and activities he has established but also many others both through the many humanitarian projects he has established worldwide and through the system of psychotherapy he has created. For more information refer to http://www.rokpa.org which covers his various activities.

A Classical Introduction

The Three Major Phases of the Buddha's Teaching

Immediately after attaining enlightenment, Buddha Sakyamuni did not rush to tell people about it but kept silent, in meditation. This was in itself a great teaching, showing that he had realised something far too deep and extensive for mere words to express. He remained in silence until the *deva*[1] requested him to teach and thereby launch the world into a major cycle of truth and awakening. According to the Buddha,[2] this cycle will last for some five thousand years. At present, we find ourselves living at a truly pivotal time for the planet, just over halfway through this period, in the sixth of its ten 500-year phases. Despite the effort it takes to maintain pure ethics in this age, it is still possible to follow the Buddha's teachings and to realise for oneself what he had realised.

By first remaining silent, the Buddha also established an ethic. A Buddhist should not proselytise but only respond, as a friend, when requested for help and advice. This is not only an ethical position but also sound sense, since even the wisest of counsel is only of benefit when it falls on ears that want to hear. When the listener's mind is ripe and ready, receptive and respectful, he or she will relate to the teaching not as something imposed from the outside but as something really sought for, from within, at that particular time.

The Buddha went on to teach for some forty-five years, addressing a remarkable variety of audiences. The India of his day was highly civilised and rich in culture. It was also a time of spiritual intensity: an epoch when – in India, Greece and China – thought systems were being evolved that would influence the world for millennia to come. It was the age of Confucius, Lao Tzu, Zarathustra and Socrates. In particular, many meditative traditions thrived in India, where there was also a keen intellectual interest in the nature of reality. Religious debates at the time used methods similar to differential calculus to speculate upon the nature of the smallest building-blocks composing the universe. Some of their notions, such as time's dependence upon events and the relation between perceived reality and consciousness, are only just being taken on board by Western science. Their theory of the elements postulated five omnipresent components called earth, water, fire, wind and space. Today we would call them mass, attraction, energy, motion and space. Their meanings, as defined in the texts of the time, are surprisingly close to those of the physics of this century.[3] As well as addressing these intellectually advanced audiences, the Buddha also taught everyday people and, as time went by, the large community of monks, then nuns, who accompanied him.

In retrospect, we can distinguish three major phases in his teachings. These are known to Buddhists as the Three Turnings of the Wheel of Dharma. The image of the wheel suggests a repetitive nature, something returning again and again to the same point. Dharma, the word generally used to denote the Buddha's teachings, can simply mean 'the way things are'.[4] Buddhas, who appear in 'golden ages' when the world is ready, repeat the timeless laws of universal truth, showing the ways things really are, for the benefit of the generations of that age.

The wheel of dharma is the counterpart to another wheel: that of existence. Time and time again, in life after life, beings are caught up by their habits and whirled through the processes of passion and anger, crying and laughter, birth and death. This 'whirling firebrand' turns incessantly but the wheel of dharma turns rarely. Thus, from time to time – be it in one's personal life or in the history of a planet – a rare light pierces through the fabric of illusion.

❋ **Phase One** established the foundations common to all his teaching. It revealed much about the nature of worldly existence, using ideas and a language which made sense to the common perception of reality. Its analysed happiness and suffering in a way which did not demand blind faith and allegiance but instead encouraged those who wished to put the Buddha's teachings to the test to do so by uncompromising investigation.

The absolute priority of this First Turning was to help people to eliminate, or at least reduce, suffering: the great shortcoming of this extraordinary universe. Hearing some religions' messages of joy and paradise, one may well wonder why Buddhism speaks first and foremost of suffering. Is it a pessimistic, gloomy faith? Not at all: it is a loving, compassionate and, above all, very realistic one. It should be clearly understood, by those of Christian background, that suffering is not at all viewed as a quality by Buddhists. It is not considered to have any intrinsic spiritual value. It is simply because Buddhism really cares for beings' *happiness* that the very first thing to be dealt with are the sufferings which, like poison in food, time and time again spoil would-be joys.

Many humans, animals and other beings have a very sorry lot, their existences being totally dominated by physical or mental suffering. Even the more fortunate can find their relative happiness easily marred by just a small amount of suffering. It is hard to enjoy assets, no matter how many they be, while the tooth is aching or the heart is broken! If one is truthful, most pleasures of this world come with a fairly expensive price-tag. And, beyond its relative ups and downs, all worldly existence is a suffering compared with the true bliss of enlightenment, the summit of all.

Thus the Buddha, the greatest physician, targets suffering from the very outset. Just as when sickness is cured, health comes naturally, likewise once suffering and its causes are removed, profound happiness is the natural lot of the mind. This natural happiness, which deepens as each layer of suffering is shed, is different from an artificial happiness, maintained by false optimism or carefully-contrived thoughts. Many are the religious or psychological ploys which can create artificial joy. They are relatively easy to implement. But as long as one does not treat the underlying pains and weaknesses of life, they are like sweets given to a sick person by someone who does not know which medicine can cure the sickness.

The essence of the First Turning is contained in the famous Four Noble Truths.

- The first truth is the Buddhist description of the cosmos, portraying the different life forms which inhabit it and their various sufferings and happinesses.
- The second truth points to the causes of their sufferings. To simplify, it says that through not recognising the true identity of

mind – voidness – an illusion of persona develops. Feeling one area of experience to be 'self' automatically defines the remainder as 'other'. The illusory ego develops its desires, aversions, jealousy, pride and so forth in relation to the illusory other. Known as *klesa* (defilements), these desires and so forth often motivate harmful actions. The actions (*karma*) generate suffering both for others in the immediate present and for their doer in the longer term, by the way they imprint and condition his or her mind. The chain reaction of suffering is therefore: ignorance ▷ ego ▷ duality ▷ defilement ▷ action ▷ suffering.

Whereas the first two truths are a cause-and-result pair dealing with suffering, the final two truths are a cause-and-result pair dealing with freedom from suffering.

▸ The third truth describes the states wherein suffering is no more.
▸ The fourth truth examines the causes of those states – the famous 'path' of Buddhism.

* * *

✽ **The second phase** The first phase had dealt mainly with what was tangible and conventionally true. For those who still wanted *to be*, it showed how to act wisely and create better future lives, with a minimum of suffering. For those who longed *not to be*, it showed the way to universal peace. Having taught, for many years, this way out of suffering, and having many disciples who had already managed truly to free their minds, Buddha Sakyamuni introduced the second phase of his teaching. This phase entered more profoundly into the absolute truth. It extended the understanding of voidness of ego, taught in the first phase, into an understanding of the voidness of all perceived phenomena. Hand in hand with this unveiling of the illusory nature of everything came the teachings on great compassion. Compassion and total voidness are the crux of this turning.

Over the years, his teaching had established a very complete scientific and psychological language, enabling all things material and mental in the relative world to be clearly defined and distinguished one from another. Just as, in the present day, our scientists' penetration of the minutest details of the atom is permitting us to understand and master many things in the material world, so also does the fine Buddhist analysis of mental processes enable mind to be understood and mastered. It can seem almost paradoxical at times that the finer and more precise the means of investigation, the greater is the discovery and power achieved.

Using the key terms developed in the First Turning's clear analysis of mind and its functioning, the Buddha revealed, in the Second Turning, all these elements of experience to be de*void* of any ultimate reality. Thus, having shown his disciples, in the first phase, how to dismantle the million cogs in the mechanism of ego-illusion, he went on to show, in the second phase, how even the cogs themselves and the names of the cogs are illusions.

The need for the second phase of his teaching is sometimes presented through a medical analogy. When constipated, one needs a laxative. However, to continue taking the laxative once the blockage is cleared would turn the laxative from medicine to potential poison. In order to destroy the illusions of ego, and all the harm they cause, the Buddha had given his disciples the analytical means to look into their own lives, their own minds, and see the truth of non-ego. This medicine cleared the blockage. The second phase of teaching was to clear out the medicine itself, by realising its voidness.

The second phase of his teachings was embodied in the teachings on *prajñāpāramitā* or Transcendent Perfection of Wisdom. Whereas the first phase spoke to everyone, the second phase only made sense to those possessing a certain spiritual maturity, acquired from previous lives and principally manifest as loving compassion and courageous strength of mind.

In the second phase, the Buddha made the omnipresence of voidness perfectly clear. Its teachings dismantled all illusions of fixed reality and even illusions of non-reality. However, they did not elucidate the actual nature of ultimate voidness, beyond the illusions. The sickness was removed as well as the side-effects of the medicine; now the true nature of real health was to be revealed.

* * *

❋ **The third phase** of the Buddha's teaching revealed the ultimate nature of voidness itself: the truth which remains when all the illusions have been dispelled by properly understanding the voidness of the relative world, as expounded in the second phase. What remains is not simply an *absence* of illusion. It is not an emptiness. It is not voidness as some vast cosmic space. On the contrary, it is the total, perfect *presence* of the love, compassion, wisdom, powers and all the other qualities of enlightenment. Most importantly, Buddha Sakyamuni showed that every single sentient being has this ultimate voidness as his, her or its true nature. Thus the Third Turning of the Wheel of Dharma teaches *buddha nature*: the fact that the wisdom and perfection of enlightenment is profoundly present in everyone, all the time.

Following this, over the centuries, various learned and enlightened teachers wrote treatises – *śāstra* – on *buddha nature*. Maitreya's work is the greatest of these classics.

A simple introduction to voidness

The Sanskrit term *śūnya* has been translated as voidness or emptiness: words which conjure up visions of hollow, empty space. To hear of a great master 'realising voidness' must make many people imagine some sort of absorption in vast, inky-blue cosmic expanses. These are pretty ideas, with some symbolic truth, but in reality such notions have little to do with the Buddhist *śūnya*.

Voidness is not blankness but wisdom: a bright, clear light of wisdom which renders illusions powerless. A master who has realised voidness knows illusions to be de*void* of the reality they seem to have. Thus a simple, everyday example of voidness would be to look at a mirage but know that there is no water really on the horizon. Wisdom understands that there is no water even though what the eyes see would suggest otherwise.

The 'voidness' of the distant shimmering lake is the wisdom in the mind of the perceiver, no longer tricked by delusion. 'Voidness' does not make the mirage become blank space and disappear. The wise person still sees it. But voidness-wisdom saves an awful lot of trudging through sand, in a useless attempt to assuage thirst! Realising the voidness of illusions does not necessarily stop them manifesting: it changes the way in which one relates to their manifestation.

Let us now go further than this simple example. Voidness is also very much related to limitlessness. It is an unconstricted freedom which refuses to be duped by this or that restricted view put forth by the babble of the intellect. What does this mean? Any person's moment-by-moment experience always depends upon (and is restricted by) specific factors. Humans, for instance, see only what humans see and hear only what humans hear. Different beings, such as dogs and bats, hear other things of which we are not even aware. And it is not just the senses which are limited. The specific nerve messages sent by the senses go on to be heavily filtered by the brain. Only a few are actually selected and perceived on the central screen of mind's awareness. Furthermore, these perceived sights and sounds are instantly cross-referenced with memories and past conditioning, which immediately colour the perception. The end result of all this is for each being to have a unique and highly subjective appreciation of reality. Yet in each being's mind, the restricted, subjective movie in the brain is, more often than not, taken to be a truthful direct perception of an existing outer reality.

Whatever the universe is, it is much more than any individual's perception of it. It is de*void* of that limited definition. Thus, in spite of what the eyes see and how the thirsty mouth salivates, the wisdom of the mind tells someone looking at a mirage that there can be other possibilities than a distant lake producing the vision of water.

Perception of reality is heavily coloured by past karma. Let us imagine three people in the same room. One has good karma and experiences it as a paradise. Another has fairly ordinary human karma and feels indifferent about the surroundings. The third has terrible karma and is psychotic, experiencing that very same room as hell. Perception depends upon the state of mind. The state of mind is the consequence of past karma.

Let us take another arbitrary example, that of fish. A man with rare and expensive fish in his pond may look at them with great love and pride, perceiving them primarily as a beautiful possession. A passing heron may view them as food. Another species of fish may jealously consider them as ugly; not beautiful at all. The fish will feel like themselves, neither as possessions nor a meal. A worm in a fish's stomach may just experience it as an enormous dwelling, with characteristic warmth and a certain smell. A passing god may perceive the fish as a naga water spirit. Some spirits may see it as a vicious sea-monster. Which one is the real fish? A wise mind understands how each being projects its own interpretations onto reality. The wisdom of voidness knows true reality to be devoid of those projections and infinite in its possibility.

Furthermore, everything in the universe depends upon other things for its very existence. All are interlinked, closely or remotely, through time and space, in a vastly complex fabric of change and interdependence. As soon as one truthfully investigates the nature of any one thing, one discovers the presence of everything. The limited labels with which we define the world around us are incredibly simplistic.

The above would just be useless toying with ideas of consciousness, were our perceptions of one another not the very source of all the joys and miseries throughout time. The limits of our views define us – as individuals, social groups and nations.

The main point is that any *thing* is infinitely more than simply the limited edition of it which we perceive. It has infinite possibilities and actualities. Their existence renders *void* our feeling that something is only what we think it is. Voidness, i.e. wisdom, recognises the difference between what *seems to be* and what *really is*. When one longs to shed delusions and experience the 'really is', the truth gradually dawns that the true reality cannot be just a different limited edition, an alternative mental snapshot: a heavenly *there* rather than a worldly *here*. It has to be, and is, inconceivably infinite.

By developing the above sort of reasoning, one can approach voidness analytically, using the intellect. There is another approach, as we shall see below,[6] which approaches voidness through meditation.

By applying voidness – as wisdom that pierces illusions – the teachings of the First Turning enable meditation to destroy myths of persona. Likewise, the Second Turning enables meditation to remove myths of concrete reality and thereby stimulate great compassion. The Third Turning removes delusions not by pointing out the mistake but by showing the truth.

The Buddha's Own Teaching or a Śāstra?

The teachings given by the Buddha were recorded by his closest disciples after his passing from this world. They form the Buddhist canon, in its four parts of *sūtra, vinaya, abhidharma* and *tantra*. This is an enormous body of work, filling more than a hundred volumes of scripture. They record teachings first in this place, then that place, first to this and then to that audience. The totality of the Buddha's teachings on any one given topic, such as karma, is scattered throughout these volumes.

Since the time of Buddha, various great Buddhists have written śāstra, treatises, in order to make the original canon more accessible. Sometimes they draw together the various elements of instruction on a particular topic. Sometimes they explain themes which are hard to penetrate.

This work comes from Maitreya, who not only will be the next Buddha of this age but also is presently the bodhisattva empowered to represent Buddha Sakyamuni in this period of time. The Buddha speaks through him. Thus some see his work as Buddha Speech, like the message of a king conveyed by an ambassador. However, as it elucidates the teachings of the Third Turning, it is more appropriate to consider it as a śāstra.

Source of This Work

Given the many traditions of Buddhism, we might rightly wonder to which trend of philosophy this text belongs and what message the author is trying to convey through his particular interpretation of the Buddha's teaching. This would be a very legitimate enquiry, since the stance of this particular work has given rise to much learned comment and argument throughout the ages. However, our present survey will not even begin to enter into the complexity of detail of this debate. It suffice to summarise the view of our present-day lineage masters.

Although this work comes directly from Maitreya, it was propagated by his disciple Arya Asaṅga, one of the greatest Buddhists of Indian history (see below) and one of the two forefathers of mahāyāna Buddhism.[7] In the early days of Buddhism in Tibet, some classed him as a proponent of the *merely-mind* (*cittamātra*) school of thought. Nowadays, he is widely considered to be one of the greatest of all the *middle-way* (*madhyamaka*) masters. Middle Way refutes some key doctrines of merely-mind and it would be wrong to classify this work as cittamātra. It would be better to consider it as stemming directly from the Third Turning teachings and expressing their meaning by explaining points made in several major Third Turning sūtra[8] and brought together in one in particular: the *dhāraṇīrājeśvarasūtra*.

The Author

Traditionally, Buddhist treatises were only written by those endowed with exceptional qualities. Three categories are distinguished. Best are those authors with direct realisation of voidness. Second best are those who have had direct experience of a Buddha. Third best are erudite scholars who have mastered the five branches of Buddhist knowledge.[9] *Authors* less qualified than these cannot be considered *authorities*. It is interesting to compare these two words, each descendants of the Latin *auctor, augere* meaning

Maitreya teaching Asaṅga

to increase or originate. Maitreya, the source of this work, transcends even those three categories, being a great bodhisattva[10] who had reached the highest (10th) stage, on the threshold of Buddhahood. His actual teachings were brought to our world by Dharma Master Asaṅga, whose life and work were predicted by the Enlightened One.[11]

The Story of Asaṅga

Prior to Asaṅga's birth (which some sources give as 375 CE), during a period of religious tension, anti-Buddhists had caused a serious fire at Nalanda university and this had destroyed many precious works. At that time, all texts were manuscripts, sometimes existing as only one or two rare copies in libraries such as that at Nalanda. This fire caused serious losses and augured badly for Buddhism. A nun, named Ethic of Clarity, very concerned by all this, had a vision that she should have two sons, to be brought up with the specific task of restoring strength to the dharma. Handing back her vows of celibacy, she carried out her mission, finding a different father for each child, and gave birth to Asaṅga, who later greatly benefited mahāyāna Buddhism, and Vasubandhu, who greatly benefited first the hinayāna and later the mahāyāna.

She sent the young man Asaṅga into retreat to meditate on Maitreya. After three years without tangible result, he became quite depressed and left his hermitage. Looking up he saw a pigeon leaving its nest in the rock face and noticed how the entrance hole had been worn smooth by the feathers of generations of pigeons. Inspired to diligence by this example of continual application, he returned to retreat. After a further three years without result, he again felt despondent and left, this time encountering a man removing earth from the top of a high hill. 'Hello, what are you doing?' 'Well, see my house down there, in the valley. It never receives any sunlight, on account of this hill. So I'm shifting the hill.' Nonplussed by this great perseverence, Asaṅga realised that he should take the encounter as a teaching telling him to persevere more and return to retreat.

After yet another three years without result, he again felt despondent and left, this time encountering a man rubbing an iron bar with a cloth. Fascinated, Asaṅga enquired what he was doing and was told that he was making a sewing needle! Once again impressed by so much diligent forbearance for such a small worldly end, he felt inspired to return to retreat.

After twelve years of meditation in retreat he still had no tangible signs of having accomplished anything. Extremely low, he gave up yet again. This time he left and encountered a wretched sick old bitch, her bones protruding and the bottom part of her body mangy and filled with sores. Furthermore, she was growling, full of anger. This pathetic sight sparked off great compassion in him. Looking more closely, he could see that the sores were infested with worms and that their presence was not only making the animal angry but could well prove fatal.

Reflecting long and hard, he tried to find a way in which he could remove the worms without harming them. Sticks or twigs would crush them. Eventually he realised that only his own body was sensitive enough to remove them safely and that only his tongue was really soft and skilful enough to remove them properly. Filled with a mixture of compassion and revulsion, he stooped to remove the first of the worms. He closed his eyes and nostrils, unable to witness what he would have to do.

He bent lower and lower until he touched the dust of the ground. Opening his eyes, he beheld Maitreya standing before him. Surprised, he exclaimed, 'At last, at last, but ... where have you been throughout all these twelve years of my ardent meditation?' Maitreya replied that he had been constantly with Asaṅga throughout the whole twelve years but that Asaṅga's mind had not been open enough to see him. The genuine heartfelt compassion evoked by the sight of the old bitch had completed his twelve years' hard and patient work of gradually removing mental obscurations. To prove the point, Maitreya suggested that Asaṅga go into the village, with Maitreya on his shoulder. Once there, Asaṅga asked people what they could see. Most saw nothing and thought he was crazy, except for one pious old lady who, puzzled, asked him why he was carrying a wounded dog on his shoulder.

Then Asaṅga's perception was transformed. He entered the pure land of Tuṣita – the realm of Maitreya. For many (some say fifty) years, Asaṅga received instruction on the entire mahāyāna from Maitreya. Depending upon one's view of things, this period can be seen as a time when he actually went elsewhere, to Tuṣita, and then returned to Earth, or else as Tuṣita being his meditation experience while here on Earth. He is reputed to have lived for 150 years, which could fit in with either thesis.

His subsequent activity in India was to propagate mahāyāna Buddhism and in particular Maitreya's teachings, condensed into the Five Great Dharma of Maitreya, one of which is this text. Asaṅga wrote his own commentary to it and was also a great teacher and author in his own right. He is considered to be a bodhisattva on the third of the bodhisattvas' ten levels of enlightenment.

Maitreya's five teachings are

- the 'Ornament of Definite Realisation',[12] which teaches absolute truth through the Middle Way view but in a concise way,
- the 'Ornament of Mahāyāna Sūtra',[13] 'Discerning Middle and Extreme'[14] and 'Discerning Dharma and Dharmata'[15] which develop it much more fully and
- this 'Mahāyāna Treatise on the Ultimate Continuum' which clearly and strongly elucidates the meaning of the various buddha-nature sūtra.

Transmission of the Text

Asaṅga composed commentaries to each of these five texts and Vasubandhu also made commentaries to 'Discerning Middle and Extreme' and 'Discerning Dharma and Dharmata'. Three of these texts – the two 'Ornaments' and 'Discerning Middle and Extreme' – were taught quite widely, notably through the work and subsequent lineages of Vasubandhu, Dignaga and Sthiramati. The remaining two texts, more profound in content, were taught through an oral tradition involving only gifted disciples. Several hundred years later, when the dharma became well established in Tibet in the 8th century, the first three texts were taught widely.

The two latter works were concealed, for future removal by Buddhist saints. One instance of this took place in the eleventh century when one day Maitripa saw celestial lights radiating from a crack in a stupa.[16] On investigation, he discovered the two Maitreya texts hidden in the stupa's base. He could read them, but doubted that he understood their meaning totally clearly. He prayed earnestly to their author, Maitreya, who appeared to him in a vision, gave him the verbal transmission of the text and inspired confident knowledge of its true meaning. Maitripa instructed many great scholars in the meaning of the Uttara Tantra and from them the teaching of it went to Tibet. Two streams of transmission emerged: the *explanation lineage* and the *meaning lineage*.

The explanation lineage has its main origination in Ngog Loden Sherab,[17] a Tibetan scholar who spent much time in India and who received teachings in Kashmir (from Guru Sajjana?) on these two less widely known śāstra of Maitreya, which he translated into Tibetan according to the madhyamaka standpoint. One of his contemporaries, Tsen Kawoché[18], had received special meditation instruction in this text from Guru Sajjana[19] and favoured a meditative approach to the meaning. From him comes the meditation lineage. The main difference between these two traditions is in their approach to voidness. To over-simplify this, one could say that the meditative approach can enable one to experience voidness first-hand as being the intangible, untainted plenitude of enlightened qualities. The explanatory approach only enables one to master an intellectual model of voidness, with the nature of enlightenment being merely speculative, not experiential. These two sometimes have very different views concerning what a Buddha may or may not be and what a Buddha can or cannot do.

There developed a tradition in which the Kagyu mahāmudrā[20] system of meditation was used as the meditative mainstay for understanding the subject-matter of the Uttara Tantra Śāstra. This meditative tradition of receiving the five great teachings of Maitreya, and in particular those of this text, eventually reached the third Gyalwa Karmapa, Rangjung Dorjé, who composed a summary of its meaning. Through the Karmapa lineage it reached all the renowned Kagyu lamas such as the eighth Shamarpa Chöji Döndrup, the eighth Tai Situpa Chöji Jungné, Jamgön Kongtrul Yönten Gyamtso and so forth, down to the present day lineage masters.

Subject-Matter

The essence of the teachings of all three dharmachakras is the same: to show the voidness of illusions of self-entity. Some religions postulate the existence of a god (or gods) who rewards with happiness and punishes with suffering. Buddhism explains happiness and suffering as natural results of past actions. Just as the seeds of sweet grapes and the seeds of deadly berries each bring forth their respective fruits with unerring genetic certainty, so do our actions imprint the 'genetic coding' of our future happiness and suffering. In time they bring forth their characteristic consequences. If one can grasp the natural laws governing these processes, there arises a real possibility of liberation from otherwise ever-continuing circles of existence created by action in ignorance. All the forms of ignorance have a common root: not recognising the voidness of illusions.

Phenomena in general or individuals in particular are totally devoid of any real self-entity, yet the normal delusion is to believe in a 'self' – in an 'I' – and hence in 'other'. Once there is a 'self' there emerges the need to keep it happy. When the happiness is threatened, it must be protected – hostility arises. 'I' likes 'I' – pride emerges. Then we are afraid of others matching our qualities and there is jealousy.

The way to remove ego-belief is through direct investigation. Using refined tools of meditation, one searches body and mind in an attempt to find this thing which feels so intimately like 'me'. Like gradually shaking free from the power of a hypnotist, one emerges from the power of suggestion of fickle, wandering 'I' thoughts. Nowhere can a real self be found. The non-finding of 'I' brings a natural understanding of non-ego, just as an audience understands that the hypnotised person on the stage, who thinks he is a dog and barks, never was a dog at all.

Besides illusions of self, deluded beliefs in the existence of 'phenomena', i.e. everything else, may also be removed by similar accurate inspection. One investigates things which can appear at first to be so independently and finitely real. After close inspection they are known to be dream-like and similar to a water-bubble.

The whole point of the teachings presented in the three dharmachakras is to provide, from a great variety of angles, all the help we need to realise absence of self (voidness). As we have seen above, voidness understands the illusions but is not duped by them. It recognises the infinite within the seemingly finite. This absence of limited entity and the presence of infinite wisdom is described as the *indivisible union of voidness and clarity*. Clarity here means lucidity – clear, vivid intelligence. This union *is* the very essence of the Buddhas. It is present in everyone's mind. If one can unveil it, buddhahood will manifest.

As this primordial union of voidness and clarity is present in *all* beings, anyone who puts the teachings into practice can liberate it to achieve enlightenment, regardless of their sex, race or background. Yet most people do not realise it, due to the presence of veils of ignorance in their mind. It is the degree of presence or absence of these veils which determines three main cosmic situations:

- impurity (ordinary beings), where there are strong veils due to karma, defilements (the global name for desire, hostility, jealousy etc.), deluded thinking etc. ,
- partial purity (great bodhisattvas) in which there remain slight, but no longer harmful, habits of deluded thinking and
- total purity (that of buddhas).

This system of Buddhist understanding pivots around the notion of there being a same enlightened essence in all things and all beings. The essential enlightenment is called *tathāgatagarbha*: the *garbha* (core or essence) of the *tathāgata* ('Which has become That' – buddha). It is also called *hridaya* (heart or essence). The essential nature of enlightenment, or 'buddha-nature' as it is widely called now, is the principal topic of the Uttara Tantra.

Styles of Explanation

There exist various ways of presenting this text, from the intellectual approach based on the explanation lineage from Ngog Lo Loden Sherab to a very direct spiritual approach where the meaning is grasped through mahāmudrā meditation. It will be presented here according to the way Khenchen Thrangu Rinpoché and Khempo Tsultim Gyamtso Rinpoché chose to present it in their first visits to the West. My personal feeling is that one could do no better than follow the example set by these two most senior tutors of the Kagyu tradition. Thus, this work should carry something of the tremendous blessing of the Kagyu lineage to its readers.

There have been extensive academic investigations into Maitreya's *mahāyānanottaratantraśāstra* and some fascinating modern works have been written containing a wealth of useful information.[21] Some writers and teachers present this work as being either a *rang stong*[22] or *shengtong*[23] classic. Here, we will not enter into the subtle and complex arguments concerning these two levels of Middle Way philosophy, for the following reasons.

Lord Buddha left us with a wealth of teachings. They form an encyclopædic whole that provides guidance for everyone. People vary enormously and their teaching requirements likewise. Even one individual needs different teachings at different times, as he or she progresses along a unique path to liberation. This is why the scriptures compare the Buddha's teaching to a great pharmacy, a wise teacher to a skilful doctor, the disciple to a patient, liberation to health and suffering to sickness. Just as no one medicine will cure everyone, and what is excellent for the one may be harmful for another, so it is with the dharma.

One can, of course, take an overview of dharma and recognise some teachings as being subtler than others, just as some medical treatments are far more sophisticated than others. Insofar as this book's topic – voidness as buddha-nature – is concerned, there do exist traditional analyses describing the various Buddhist views on voidness. They are presented as a graduated, deepening series of philosophies. Unfortunately, this can make the pride in some readers assume that only the deepest, finest view is good enough for them – be they ready for it or not. Some people's intellects devour information about teachings, practices and views of reality which are far too advanced for them, given their relative mental, emotional and spiritual immaturity. Hence the great need for people to find a good teacher, just as when sick one needs to turn to a good doctor rather than buy off-the-shelf medication with the most attractive packaging or highest price.

I have no doubts that the *shengtong* view is the highest and noblest that the intellect can attain. However, as far as I understand, a good meditator needs long and deep experience both of stable tranquillity (*samatta*) and subtle penetrating insight (*vipyasana*), such as that acquired through following the graduated instructions of *mahāmudrā*, before the terminology and the points of difference between rang stong and shengtong make real sense. They can seem to make sense – in a sort of algebraic way, to the intellect – long before that. But beware of delusion.

The algebra example is an interesting one. Any child can work out the sum that 500 apples + 600 bananas = 1100 fruit. But when, in reality, you have that many items to squeeze into your larder, and their smell pervades the house, and they have to be eaten before they rot, the reality proves to be much more than the simple equation suggests. Intellectually, we can make neat sets of abstract inter-relationships between thoughts like *voidness* and *buddha-nature* and so forth. Exploring their real relationships, once they are experienced, is quite different.

In this too-short life, there is no time to waste in fruitless intellectual speculation. If one has a good teacher, he or she will surely give the correct instruction when the time is right. Thus, past Karmapas have at times taught their followers the rang stong view and at times taught the shengtong view. It is not that the Karmapas switched their allegiance or had a breakthrough in understanding and upgraded their own view of reality. They were simply giving the level of abstract teaching needed by their followers at that time and place in history. The Eighth Gyalwa Karmapa, Mi-chö Dorjé, gave us an excellent summary of the whole question: relative reality is *rang stong* and ultimate reality is *shengtong*. This shows the two views to be clearly complementary and not in conflict. Therefore, I hope that the reader will trust in the good judgment exercised by our present-day lineage-holders and experience the value of the way in which they have decided to introduce Maitreya's wisdom to the Western world.

A Bridge Between Sūtra and Tantra

The term sūtra can be used loosely to mean all three areas of the Buddhist canon – the famous 'Three Baskets'[24] – *sūtra, vinaya* and *abhidharma*. The sūtra level of teachings covers everything that can be presented through theory whereas the tantra teachings are principally concerned with practice.

Despite their multiplicity, the Buddha's teachings are all designed to bring us to one final realisation. In that respect, they are like the many roads that all led to Rome – the desert roads of North Africa, the luscious roads of the Northern Mediterranean shores and the rainy windswept roads of Northern Europe: so many different routes travelled by such different people yet all meeting up in Rome. The 'Rome' to which all Buddhist roads lead is a recognition of the true nature of mind: primordial enlightenment. The practices of tantra enable one to realise this innate nature in a remarkably short time, i.e. one, three, seven or sixteen lifetimes, as opposed to the duration of three cosmic aeons,[25] which is the time one would expect the finest of the *sūtra* paths to take.

Some people may associate the word *tantra* with the outer manifestation of Tibetan Buddhism – its vivid iconography, sometimes erotic, sometimes wrathful, its visualisations, mantras, rituals and so forth. Those used to its practice know these things to be extremely sophisticated tools for psychological transformation. However, the word *tantra* itself does not refer to these aspects but to an inner meaning. *Tantra* means thread or continuity. All tantric practice is a way of carefully laying aside one's daily personality and linking up with the enlightenment which is *continuously* present within one. The thousand forms of tantra are the thousand faces of this enlightenment, like the many beautiful facets of a jewel.

This text, which is the highest point of sūtra, as its name suggests,[26] introduces us to the continuum which is enlightenment: the changeless thread of timeless purity which underlies our changing, time-space, impure illusion. The teaching of this work is fundamental to the practice of tantra. Were the diamond of innate enlightenment not there, all the ritual attempts to experience its many facets would be futile. They would be like twiddling the dials on a radio set when no station was transmitting.[27] Thus, Maitreya's text is spoken of as being the bridge between sūtra and tantra. It takes us, very accurately, as far as words and intellectual understanding can carry us. From there onwards, one must place one's trust in sincere and diligent meditation practice, under the guidance of a truly-qualified teacher, to enter the experience beyond words.

Notes

1   Deva – a god, in this case the gods Indra and Brahma.
2   The 5,000-year period given here is the way the Buddha's predictions are understood in the Karma Kagyu tradition. There is some debate concerning the overall length of the ten periods.
3   The physics of the first half of this century, immortalised by the famous $e=mc^2$, related matter to motion and energy (i.e. earth to wind and fire). This has been extended, by the quantists, to incorporate gravity (attraction, i.e. water element). Space is the constant backdrop. Consciousness (the subjective observer), presently under serious scientific consideration, was the sixth element in the Buddhist list. It will be interesting to see developments in this correlation.
4   See note 1 to chapter on Dharma.
5   Kun.rtsob.bdan.pa
6   See 'Transmission of the Text' later in this introduction.
7   The other being Nagarjuna, who was inspired by the tenth-level bodhisattva Mañjuśri.
8   Kongtrul explains these as being four profound sūtra, such as the laṅkāravātara and the avatamsaka, understood by realised bodhisattvas, and eleven extremely profound sūtra, such as the śrimālādevi and dhāranīrājeśvara, understood fully only by the buddhas.
9   The five branches of extraordinary knowledge are: interdependence, healing, language, reason and inner knowledge. The five branches of ordinary knowledge are: grammar, terminology, poetry, dramatic art and astrology. The XIIth Tai Situpa's book 'Relative World, Ultimate Mind' (Shambala 1992) explains these in further detail.
10 Bodhi is enlightenment: the ultimate personal achievement and that which helps others more than anything else. Sattva means courageous mind. A bodhisattva is some who has the determination and courage to work towards total enlightenment so as to fulfil his or her existence and help other beings.
11 The Mañjuśrīmālatantra predicted that a bhiksu called Asaṅga would be erudite in the meaning of these explanatory texts. He would be elarned in the scriptures dealing with both the absolute and relative levels of truth. In the world, he would be known as a great master and would compose treatises. He will compose a concise explanation of buddha-nature in order that the teachings on it endure in this world. He would live for 150 years.
12 abhisamayālaṃkāra
13 mahāyānasūtralaṃkāra

14 madhyantavibhaga
15 dharmadharmatavibhaga
16 Stupa – Buddhist monument, enshrining relics, representing the body, speech and mind of enlightenment.
17 rngog, the great translator (Lo for short) blo ldan shes rab
18 btsan dri med shes rab
19 Sajjana received these teachings from Anandakirti, in Kashmir. Anadakirti had received them directly from Maitripa.
20 Kagyu mahāmudrā The Kagyu lineage comes from the great Indian masters, Saraha, Nagarjuna, Shawaripa, Maitripa, Tilopa and Naropa. Taken to Tibet by Marpa the Translator, it was perpetuated there by Milarepa, Gampopa, Rechungpa and, since that time, by the seventeen incarnations of the Karmapas, assisted by the Tai Situpas, Sharmapas, Gyaltsabpas and Kongtrul Rinpoché, among others. Mahāmudrā is the central meditation tradition of the Kagyupa system.
21 See bibliography of Shenpen Hookham's *The Buddha Within*, in particular Ruegg and Takasaki's works.
22 Tib: rang stong, the 'self-void' school of Buddhist Madhyamaka philosophy.
23 Tib: gzhan stong, the 'devoid of other' school of Buddhist Madhyamaka philosophy.
24 tripitaka
25 The time from the inception of our universe until its final demise is one great cosmic aeon (great kalpa). The historical Buddha, Sakyamuni, took three cosmic aeons from the time of his first setting his heart on enlightenment until its total achievment.
26 See first verse of root text, in Introduction to the Seven Vajra Abodes which follows.
27 I have found this a very useful example in teachings. It shows how the character of a means can be quite different from that of the end. Radios or TVs are made of plastic, crystals, wires, vacuums and so forth. They are very material and not particularly pleasant. Yet without all their strange sophistry, one simply cannot pick up the beautiful concert or the wildlife programme. One small variation or fault in the set, and the image is spoiled or lost. In tantra, we assemble many seemingly unusual components, such as visualisation, chanting mantras, making mudras, using symbols and symbolic ritual objects. Without them being put together just as they should be, experience of the absolute becomes almost inpossible. When they are 'assembled' properly, a reality which transcends them manifests.

Part One

The Goal to be Attained:
The Three Rare and Precious Refuges

Introduction to the Seven Vajra Abodes

In Sanskrit, mahāyāna uttara tantra śāstra,
in Tibetan, the thek pa chen po rgyud bla ma'i bstan bcos,
in English, 'The Ultimate Mahāyāna Treatise on
the Changeless Continuity of the True Nature'.

The title of a śāstra tells the expert eye much about its content. One could easily devote a whole chapter just to the four words of this title. It could be the subject of a week of lectures. To put it very simply, this work is a śāstra or treatise belonging to the body of *mahāyāna* scripture. It is 'ultimate' both because it describes the ultimate truth and because it stems from the ultimate, i.e. final, phase of the Buddha's teaching.[1] It reveals the continuous presence of enlightened perfection to be the true nature of the changing, deluded realities which different beings experience, just as the awakened state is, relatively, the true nature behind all the varied dreams of a sleeper. The word *tantra* means continuum or constant thread.

Homage to all the buddhas and bodhisattvas.

Maitreya's first words are a homage. He pays respect to the teachings and lineages of transmission he has received from the Buddhas and bodhisattvas. He is transmitting their wisdom to us, not just conveying his own ideas. This greatest of masters starts with humility and thereby indicates how we should approach buddha-nature. If ever we have the privilege to explain it to others, we should follow his example and respectfully transmit traditional wisdom rather than propagate our own ideas.

1. *The entire body of this treatise can be condensed*
   into the following seven vajra abodes:
   buddha, dharma, saṃgha, buddha-nature,
   enlightenment, qualities and buddha-activity.

The overall structure of the text is very simple. It has three main parts: introduction, main text and conclusion. The main text has seven chapters, known as 'vajra abodes'. The first three deal respectively with the *buddha, dharma* and *saṃgha*. Together, they form the first part of the main body and describe the goal to be achieved through Buddhism. The last four chapters, dealing with *buddha-nature, enlightenment, enlightened qualities* and *enlightened activity*, form the second part and deal with the basis whereby it is possible to achieve this goal. They are called *vajra* abodes because they describe the ultimate truth that, like Indra's ultra-hard mythical weapon, the vajra, overcomes all yet itself can never be damaged by anything whatever. Ultimate truth is hard to penetrate even for meditative wisdom. It is impossible to penetrate using mere study or even profound reflection. Once attained, however, that truth pierces everything: no reality can resist it. It vanquishes all impurities.

The chapters are called vajra *abodes* because ultimate truth – primordial wisdom – abides in each. To use a simple analogy, we may gradually build up our understanding of someone by observing him first with his family, then at the office, then praying in a temple, then on the golf-course. We might also look at his DNA and x-rays, read his writings and so on and so forth until the picture becomes complete from every dimension.

Likewise, in trying to understand the ultimate nature, we examine it through *buddhas*, who *are* it and recognise it; through its expression as *dharma*, used by the buddhas to awaken others to it; through its presence in the *saṃgha*, who are partially awakened to it; through *buddha nature*, which is the way in which it dwells secretly as the true nature of each person and every thing; through *enlightenment*, which is its unveiling; through the *enlightened qualities* which are then revealed and the *enlightened actions* which flow from, and are part of, its ultimate truth.

2. *These are in a natural order and one should know the first three abodes to be derived from the introductory and the latter four from the Wise and Victors' Qualities chapters of the dhāraṇīrājesvarasūtra.*

The natural order of the seven vajra abodes is developed in the following verse. The points themselves have their major origins in various sūtra[2] and the order in which they are presented in this work is that found, first in the introductory chapter and then in the chapter on qualities, in the *dhāraṇīrājeśvarasūtra*.

3. *From the buddha comes the dharma,*
    from the dharma comes the realised saṃgha,
    from the saṃgha, the presence of the jñāna nature, the essence.
    Ultimately, when this jñāna has been made manifest,
    there will be supreme enlightenment. powers and so forth,
    endowed with every ability to accomplish
    the good of each and every one.

On an outer level, the *dharma* teachings, as a series of ideas conveyed by word of mouth or scripture, stem from the *Buddha* who first taught[3] them. The inner *dharma*, as an experiential journey of sacred realisations from here to enlightenment, arises directly from experiencing the buddha as the ultimate nature of mind. Through their own authentic mastery of dharma, we have the *saṃgha*. Because the realised saṃgha have understood voidness, and are its living embodiment, they let other beings know about *buddha nature*. Unlocking the potential of buddha nature brings *enlightenment*, which reveals a myriad of *enlightened qualities*. These marvellous qualities spontaneously enable *enlightened activity* to help all beings. This is the natural sequence of the seven vajra abodes.

The Refuges

When we take Refuge and become Buddhists, we learn to relate to the *Buddha* as a teacher, to the *dharma* as his teaching and to the *saṃgha* as the community which perpetuates the living lineage of his teaching. Such notions of *buddha, dharma* and *saṃgha* are called 'cause' refuges. They will be the causes for our liberation. The first three chapters of Changeless Nature leave the cause Refuges, which are well explained throughout Buddhism, to one side. Instead, it starts to penetrate the meaning of 'result' Refuges, presented through profound verses of praise.

Having first taken Refuge, our practice gradually deepens. Meditation and study unveil a more universal sense of the refuges. The Buddha, for instance, is no longer simply the historical person who taught in India all those years ago. Through visualisations, we become used to 'cosmic Buddhas', symbolising the various faces of enlightenment. In the detail of their imagery, things, such as the need to balance wisdom and compassion, are represented by, for instance, the two crossed arms of the Buddha holding a vajra and bell. Eventually, every aspect of these various visualised Buddhas is realised to be simply a symbol of living, meaningful qualities. Yet, for all their power and meaning, these mental images remain merely tokens: tokens not to be confused with the real thing. They are simply necessary symbols, representing the complexity and purity of our inner potential. Nevertheless, the power of using such symbols in our minds should not be underrated. As time goes by, these sacred – some may say archetypal – images can take up strong positions among our habitual mental iconography and play an important role in our transformation and development as human beings.

What do *buddha, dharma* and *saṃgha* mean when one attains realisation and evolves even further, moving from the icon to the reality? Does Maitreya, who is almost a Buddha, still seek his refuge in a historical personage called Sakyamuni or has he come to understand buddhahood within himself, rather than as an external object of mystery and mastery?

In the first three of the seven chapters of his work, he reveals the Refuges as being more than the external source of strength to which we turn in our struggle for liberation. They are the ultimate objective of all existence; the fulfilment of our relative journey through existence. They are the timeless, changeless, ultimate and inner nature of all things. They are the meaningful, perfect space of truth which always was ... and always will be.

It would be tempting to say that they are the timeless, perfect space in which all else is nought but swiftly-passing mist. But even that would underestimate them since, ultimately, there is nothing *other* than what they are. The 'devoid of other'[4] view of things portrays them in that way. However, it is a view that only a mind deeply immersed in the purest of meditations can penetrate and truly appreciate. Nevertheless, it is the king of views, and its words, as expressed through a *shengtong* interpretation of this text, come as close as words can to describing the ineffable ultimate truth. As close as words can. An expert winetaster may describe a wine as *long on the tongue, richly structured with a full body and a first taste of raspberry followed by an afterthought of hazelnut* ... and lead the imagination figuratively in the right direction. Merely hearing his words, however, is a far cry from the actual savour of the rare vintage as it travels the connoisseur's palate!

Buddha, dharma and saṃgha are often called the Triple Gem, or Three Jewels, although it would be more accurate to call them the Three Rare and Precious Things. This Sanskrit term *triratna* is well explained at the end of the third chapter. Let us stick with 'Triple Gem' for simplicity. They are presented collectively as the goal to be achieved, and the way in which they are described shows a certain permanence to each of them.

The last four vajra abodes – buddha nature, enlightenment, enlightened qualities and enlightened activity – are presented as the factors which form the basis for that goal to be achieved. To grasp the overall significance of these two sets of vajra abodes and their inter-relation demands considerable reflection. It can be taken on many levels and becomes gradually clearer when the subject-matter of the entire work has been digested intellectually and then is brought to life by meditation.

The First Vajra Abode
– buddha –

buddha, with a small *b,* is used here to distinguish timeless, universal, ultimate reality from *Buddhas,* with a capital *B*: beings who become that ultimate reality at specific times in specific places, as did Prince Gautama in India some 2,500 years ago and as will we all, one day. This chapter, on buddha, makes clear what it is that distinguishes buddha from all others, summing it up, as a 'result' Refuge, very precisely and beautifully through six distinct and unique qualities, in a verse well worth committing to memory.

4. *I bow down to the beginningless, centreless and infinite,*
to perfect peace, buddha,
fully self-awakened and self-blossomed which,
once purified and developed,
shows the fearless, permanent path,
to bring realisation to those with no realisation,
and which. wielding the supreme sword and vajra,
of knowledge and compassionate love,
hews down the seedlings of suffering
and destroys the walls of doubt
surrounded by the dense forests of mistaken views.

This verse, phrased as a homage, is the key to the meaning of *buddha.* The remaining verses of the chapter will refer back to it and develop its meaning analytically.

5. *Buddhahood is endowed with two-fold value.*
It is uncreated, spontaneous and

not to be realised through external causes.
It possesses knowledge, compassionate love and ability.

This verse uses a Tibetan term (*dön*) almost impossible to translate into English through a single word. At one and the same time, it means *value, meaning, point, purpose, benefit,* and *focus.*

What is the deepest *meaning* of one's existence for oneself? How can it be made *meaningful* for others? What is the whole *point* of existence, for oneself, for others. What is the *purpose* of life? What represents the highest *benefit* one can achieve, personally, or for others? And, away from the perpetual play of dualistic consciousness, what is the ultimate non-dual *focus* of deepest wisdom, the heart-nature of oneself and all beings, and of each and every thing? The answer to all these questions is *buddha.*

Maitreya takes us beyond popular stereotypes of Indian princes with haloes, beyond any idea of Buddha as someone and even beyond some Buddhists' conviction of Buddha being mere non-existence, 'like a candle going out'. He introduces us to the real inner *buddha*, as understood by his own crystal-clear awareness. This inner, formless buddha gives rise to all the outer forms of Buddha which manifest from time to time, just as the love in our heart gives rise to the smile on our face.

Buddhahood concerns two areas of key interest to us all:
- totally fulfilling one's own potential as a human being and
- totally fulfilling one's longing to be of use to others.

Each of these areas is treated through three main qualities, which merit much reflection.

Imagine being suddenly faced with the choice, 'What would be the three most fulfilling things you could ever imagine for yourself, on the understanding that they would remain with you forever after?' What would you answer? And likewise, what would you answer if someone asked you what three things you considered would make you the most useful person in the universe for others?

Maitreya gives us what are perhaps unexpected answers to these questions. The greatest fruition of one's own existence is liber-

ation: to be free, for ever, from the impurities and limitations which make one either a worldly being or, at a later stage, a saintly being, a bodhisattva. The three main components of this freedom are:
- not to be a creation,
- to be non-conceptual, at perfect peace and
- no longer to depend upon externals.

From these first three will automatically emerge the qualities of
- perfect omniscient wisdom,
- limitless, impartial compassion and
- true powers, strength and abilities

which fulfil the wish to help others.

Not to be a creation is expressed in verse 4 by the words *beginningless, centreless and endless*. This is not just a poetic way of praising the ultimate. It is full of meaning: a meaning touched on in this verse and further unfolded in the next.

Buddha is truly 'eternal and infinite' – words which seem to make sense until one thinks more about their meaning. Try to imagine time which never had a beginning – ever – no matter how far back one goes. Try to imagine space which just goes on and on, in which even trillions of our universes are an invisible speck because it has no end – anywhere. How immense these concepts are! Thinking of ultimate buddha's infinity, even in this elementary way, is quite different from thinking of a relative Buddha person, someone born in 623 BCE in Lumbini, becoming a Buddha in year 588 in Bodh Gaya and passing from this world in 544 in Kusinagara.

There is no starting-point for buddha. It never arose. It is never born. *Centreless* means that it has no one location. It cannot be pinned down to any one definition. *Endless* means that it knows no interruption. Being nowhere, it is everywhere. Being timeless, it is ever-present. Even in the darkest moment of the most desolate hell and in the most confused of minds, it is there. In contrast to this, all other things begin, exist and end. They are passing moments in time and space. They change. Change brings, among other things, inbuilt suffering. No created *thing* exists without some degree of suffering, albeit subtle. Buddha is nothing to do with any of that.

The good news in this, and the very foundation for all the practices of *vajrayāna* Buddhism,[5] is that timeless, changeless *buddha* is simultaneously present in every changing experience in time and space, just as the lasting silver on a mirror co-exists with every passing reflection. The primordial wisdom which is *buddha* is present in every thought, every feeling, every person we meet and every place we experience.

Vajrayāna Buddhism gives us the practical means to make this theory a reality. Its skilful psychological tools enable us to discover the great purity concealed within all *things*.

The freedom from creations, discussed above, focuses on the more evident sufferings of life – the birth, ageing, sickness and death that all living beings have to go through, and the foursome: not getting what you want, getting what you do not want, striving for, and then having to safeguard, what you do want. There is an English expression *You've made your bed, now you must lie in it*. The eight sufferings of human existence are the bugs in the bed we have to lie in right now. The irony is that we cannot even remember who we were in those past lives when we were making this bed.

Each type of existence in the cosmos has its typical creations and typical consequences of its creations. Animals are doing animal things, creating their sort of karma and experiencing the world as animals do. Likewise for humans and other beings. The motor force of all these existential situations in time and space is ignorance: ignorance of the changeless, ultimate nature. Buddha-wisdom is for ever free of ignorance and ignorance's creations and consequences.

To peace, to buddhahood are the words in verse four describing the second quality of liberation. This focuses less upon the karma and suffering mentioned above and more on freedom from thoughts and the dualistic way in which life is perceived. This is known as 'freedom from the *cognitive obscuration*'. Dualistic awareness – I-other, subject-object, perceiver-perceived – is a habit built up over thousands of lifetimes. Like it or not, most of us look out of our window of subjectivity onto a world that seems 'other'. Even in the quiet of meditation, there is a whisper of an observer experiencing the delight of a calm mind.

The personal, relative experience of oneself as an observing subject is unique. So also is the personal experience of the world observed. As far as we can tell, the universe on the other side of one person's mind's window is never exactly the same as that experienced by another person. We will, of course, never know, since we are unable to climb inside the mind of another and 'plug in' to their world. Conclusions have to be drawn through imagining someone else's reality, on the basis of what they say and how they act.

Our experiences of ourselves are unique and changing. Our experiences of the world and its inhabitants are unique and changing. Yet it is the stuff of these transient self-pictures and world-pictures – and their interaction – which defines the very quality of our lives. On the inside we can range from being like hell-dwellers to being like devas. The outer world can seem vary from being like paradise to being a painful hell. And there are endless bitter-sweet mixtures of such experiences. But always, no matter what, there are two sides: subject and object, me and you, us and them.

When we explore the reality of duality a little further, we realise that karma, i.e. all our actions, are really interactions between the subject one considers oneself to be and the objective world. Whatever fantasies, plans and actual actions engage subject with object, they all emerge from the way we define ourselves and others.

The threesome subject-object-interaction is known as *triplicity*. Buddha – enlightened wisdom – is totally free from duality and triplicity, for ever. Thus it is *peace, buddhahood*.

Let us explore this word *buddha*. Modern Buddhist translators have retained the Sanskrit rather than attempt an English equivalent. It is a rich word, with various simultaneous meanings but two in particular:

▸ awakening or emerging and
▸ reaching perfection or completion.

A correct, direct translation, according to the Tibetan tradition, would therefore give us something like *awakened and totally complete*. It might seem strange for us to say *I take Refuge in the Awakened and Totally Complete* rather than *I take Refuge in the Buddha* but it is worth reflecting that Buddhists up to the eleventh century, in India, were meaning just that as they said their prayers. Those were the resonances of the word *buddha* in their language. It is an interesting experiment to compare this meaning with personal associations one has already developed with the term. One can do this by closing ones eyes, thinking the word *buddha* or a phrase like *he became Buddha* and then observing the imagery which arises.

To be awakened from the sleep of ignorance implies that the consequences of ignorance – such as desire, craving, jealousy, confusion, pride, dualistic perception etc. – have come to an end, just as dreams and darkness disappear completely when we emerge from sleep. The state of buddhahood is to be awake: gone the confused limited sleep of not-knowing. Instead, there is the limitlessness of clarity in which the enlightened qualities are naturally, totally, complete. It is fulfilment. Just as the landscapes and personages of dreams have no place in the awakened state, so neither does any of the impurity of worldliness – ignorance, selfish emotion, karma, suffering etc. – have any place in buddhahood. Dream people and places do not go off to exist elsewhere when one awakens. Lucidity simply reveals their non-existence. Likewise buddha is not other than the world, but its true nature.

fully self-awakened and self-blossomed The third quality of liberation is that it does not depend upon anything. Most experience is dualistic. The quality of the subjective mind's experience is highly dependent upon the objective world. These days, the effort to make the mind happy by fine-tuning the objective world has reached a high level of sophistication. We surround ourselves with hi-fidelity sound, stylish decorations, all sorts of artificial odours and perfumes, textures and so forth.

Beyond this worldly dependence upon externals, even the spiritual journey is, for the main part, one of dependence. One depends upon teachers and their guidance. Furthermore, on a more subtle level, the meditative journey is one of understanding the relationship between subject and object in meditation and refining this relationship. One needs the guidance of an apparently 'other' Buddha or guru in order to disentangle the knots of confusion and habit tied in one's mind over thousands of lifetimes.

When the ultimate is attained, buddha is replete: by itself, in itself. The illusory knots of confusion having been untied, there only remains the wisdom that always was. Just as the knot of a knotted snake goes nowhere when it unravels itself, confusion disappears into wisdom.

In very simple, relative terms, we could consider that, if it takes three cosmic aeons to become a Buddha, one becomes, at that time, independent after three cosmic aeons of depending upon others and what is *other*. Buddha is independent. Worldliness is inter-dependent. The spiritual path itself is one of dismantling harmful interdependence by using subtle, harm-free, interdependent methods. This has been compared to rubbing two sticks together vigorously. Ignition occurs and fire eventually consumes both sticks. Spiritual skill interacts vigorously with harmful habit. The ignition is awakening to voidness, following which both habit and antidote go up in the flames of realisation.

The poem says *self-awake* and *self-blossomed*. These are the two implications of the word buddha, as explained above. Being awakened from the sleep of ignorance's impurity, there is purity. As all the enlightened qualities are self-present in that lucid awakeness, there will be the power to help others.

which, once purified and made manifest There are two main sorts of purity: innate purity and freedom from surface impurity. If one cleans and polishes a golden object or a precious gem, one does so in order to bring out the shining beauty innate to the material itself. One would not bother to clean and polish rubbish. Despite their innate purity, gold and gems can become encrusted superficially with dirt and their qualities are no longer visible.

Buddhahood is innately pure and resplendent with qualities. Unfortunately, most beings are completely unaware of its existence because it is covered by superficial impurity, which shuts out its radiance. Like a relic that has been ignored for centuries, it can become the archaeological 'find' of a lifetime for those who recognise it, clean off the impurities and gasp in wonder at its magnificence.

Those who complete the work of Buddhist practice achieve this twofold purity. Only then can enlightenment's qualities manifest, bringing great benefit for all beings. How? By *showing the path of fearlessness and permanence which will bring realisation to those with no realisation.*

'Realisation'[6] has a definite and powerful meaning. It is the wisdom which emerges from experience,[7] another term with which it is often paired. Life experiences and meditation experiences all come and go. The very character of experience is impermanence. This is why Buddhist meditation masters warn us against getting involved with experiences, even the profoundly 'spiritual' ones. One needs to learn how to relate to experiences skilfully. This is one of the great arts to be developed in this life. One may have little power to alter events but there is enormous scope for changing the way in which one relates to the experience of them. The many passing experiences of the Buddhist path give rise to lasting wisdom, in the form of an uncovering of truth. This is *realisation* which, unlike experiences, remains, deepens even, until it becomes the totality of truth.

In particular, there will be an unparalleled breakthrough at one stage, when one recognises the true nature of existence – buddha nature – for the first time. In fact, the term *realisation* is mostly used to refer to this authentic, lasting recognition of buddha nature, although it can be used more broadly to encompass all lasting awakenings to truth, either as the Four Truths or Two Truths.

The character of the path to realisation is fearlessness. One has first to overcome all the worldly fears due to the illusion of self: fear of loss, fear, change etc. This is the very heart of Buddhist renunciation and the point of strnegthening the mind through vows and precepts. Then, one has to overcome the fear of facing up to the awesome truths, about the nature of reality, that dawn through meditation. The reward of overcoming fear is fearlessness. As we will discover in Chapter Six, the Buddha possesses total fearlessness and is described as a lion of beings. He shows us how to face up to our illusions and overcome the fears they produce.

Buddha does this through *wielding the supreme sword and vajra of knowledge and compassionate love.* Although wisdom and love are compared here to two weapons, they are, in this ultimate sense, one and inseparable. This wisdom will be explained in later chapters as the various sorts of primordial wisdom.[8] The love is great, infinite love as described in many bodhisattva scriptures. *buddha's* omniscience could never be cold, selfish knowledge. Its loving care embraces all beings, equally and without exception. However, even *buddha* cannot liberate other beings but only guide them to their own liberation. We each have to liberate ourselves by developing the realisation and fearlessness mentioned above. How does this work? An awakening to the innate purity of buddha nature will *hew down the seedlings of suffering,* i.e. immediately stop the first thoughts of delusions of self from developing into karma and suffering. It *destroys the walls of doubt* like light which destroys darkness. Doubts, i.e. mental confusion regarding the truth, give rise to all sorts of *mistaken views,* compared here to something vast, *dense* and entangling, like a *forest.*

Having explored verse 4 – the main homage to the buddha – through the six qualities described in verse 5, the text furthers the exploration through verse 6.

6. *It is the uncreated because its nature is without beginning, middle or end.*

As explained above, all worldly creations are stamped with the characteristics of coming into being, existing and ending. buddha is nothing whatsoever to do with any of these. It is nothing like we have ever known. It is neither a physical nor a mental creation. It never began and will never end. It has no relative existence brought about by causes and conditions: it is not a result. The implications of this are far-reaching.

All we do as Buddhists – be it meditate, pray, care for others or whatever it may be – can never *create* enlightenment. Our Buddhist practices simply remove the tight, limited creations that define us as beings, so that the enlightenment, which was always there, can shine through. If enlightenment was a creation or result, it would begin, exist and then end and its very character would depend upon the causes which created it.

The process of creations coming into being is described through the coming together of *primal causes*, which have an almost genetic nature, and *secondary conditions*. To make this more easily understood, the example of a plant or tree is often given, although in reality we are talking about all mental and physical creations. The primal cause is the one which bears the quasi-genetic programming for the result to happen. This is compared to a seed, such as an acorn, which contains all the genetic information about its eventual result, the oak. No other seed or anything else in the universe has quite that programming. Only the acorn is the unique, irreplaceable, source of an oak tree. The secondary conditions which enable its genetic potential to be expressed are the likes of rain, sunlight, warmth, soil nutrients and so forth. These are general circumstances.

The general circumstances may vary considerably, yet the acorn will probably still manage to grow into a tree. With one or more conditions depleted, it may become a rather poor, sickly oak but it is still an oak tree. Excellent conditions will produce a superb tree.

Developing the spiritual skills of Buddhism causes one to progress along its famous 'path'. This path is often seen as being the cause of the result, enlightenment. It can seem to be the case because the quasi-genetic programming of enlightenment is present, in the form of buddha nature, which is like a primal cause. Gathering positive virtues and wisdom into one's changing being seems like gathering the auxiliary circumstances. The final result, the mighty tree of enlightenment bearing all its rich fruits, can appear to be an end result. Many Buddhists understand it that way. Yet it is not like that.

As explained above, the skilful means of Buddhism are merely antidotes to problems. We have ego-delusions. The antidote is to adopt a new identity: that of the bodhisattva. These two personae interact, combust in wisdom and disappear in a voidness in which the question of identity is not even posed.

One starts out with passionate desires. These are replaced by altruistic aspirations. These interact and disappear in a voidness in which there is no longer any need for someone to long for something.

In practising the six *pāramitā*,[9] the same applies. It is not so much a question of becoming more and more generous, for instance, but of destroying the habits of stinginess, fear of loss and the like, so as to let natural generosity express itself spontaneously.

These antidotes do not *create* voidness, wisdom and enlightenment, any more than pulling back a curtain *creates* sunlight in a room. The sun creates sunlight. Yet without the act of drawing the curtain – removing the obstacle – sunlight cannot enter the room. Enabling something to manifest its qualities by removing such obstacles is called a *result through removal*.

Sakyamuni Buddha's actions, in his previous lives as a bodhisattva progressing along the spiritual path during three cosmic aeons, never fabricated the qualities of his enlightenment, attained in the 'Highest Heaven' and demonstrated in that final existence in India. They simply undid, through goodness and insight, the ignorance of true reality which had been created by countless former lifetimes of ignorance. His bodhisattva actions freed, one by one and going from the grosser to the more subtle, a million knots of limitation to let the limitless become known.

> *It is said to be spontaneity since it is peace,*
> *possession of the dharmakāya.*

In our first exploration of peace, as no-concept, we discovered how buddha is without duality or triplicity. There is *peace*, i.e. freedom from the thinking and striving which an illusion of self produces and freedom from their disappointing consequences. Almost paradoxically, when striving for self-gain has completely ceased, the greatest wealth of qualities is obtained. This is called *dharmakāya*. *Dharma* means phenomena/things and *kāya* means embodiment. One attains the embodiment of everything.

All is perfectly present, with nothing that could be improved upon and nothing which needs modification. Every enlightened quality has always been there, effortlessly. Yet knowledge of that fact is covered up by effort. Thus buddha is the spontaneity of this universal wealth: the source of all the various relative dharma teachings.

There is a story of a huge and very fat man called 'Jewel in the Crown'[10] who, as his name suggests, possessed a very precious magical jewel, which he would sometimes tuck into one of the voluminous folds of flesh on his head for safe keeping. One day he panicked, feeling for his famous gem and not finding it. Desperate, he spent hours searching left and right, carefully retracing his steps and looking on the floor, behind furniture and anywhere it may have fallen. Desolate, he finally gave up and in tearful sorrow resigned himself to its loss. Lowering his weary brow into his hands in despair, he suddenly felt something hard. The jewel had been in the tuck of skin on the crown of his head all the time, deeper set than he thought.

Often what we are seeking is closer than we think. Humans and other beings do so many things in their desperate quest for happiness and fulfilment, yet – like this man's jewel – the greatest fulfilment has always been there. What is that fulfilment? In the traditional explanation to this verse, it is the presence of the *kāya* of enlightenment.

Kāya is the Sanskrit term for body, or embodiment. Perfect enlightenment is embodied in two ways: how it really is and how it can be perceived by those not perfectly enlightened. The *dharma-kāya*, mentioned above, is enlightenment itself, as only a Buddha can ever know it. It is formless. Through its grace and qualities, it can be experienced as forms, as we shall discover in Chapter Six, by those who are partially enlightened and those still unenlightened but with excellent karma. buddha could be experienced as buddhas in buddha-lands, as a human teacher, as a god, as an ordinary person, as symbols, as inanimate objects such as bridges or as almost anything. All these embodiments are known as form kāya. They are not real forms, simply the way in which our relatively impure minds interpret dharmakāya as forms to which we can relate.

This all happens spontaneously. Wherever beings are having their own meaningful experience of dharmakāya, dharmakāya itself is not having to make any effort. Effortless, it is peace.

The words, 'It is said ....', refer to a sūtra called, 'The Ornament of the Radiant Light of Primordial Wisdom, Penetrating the Field of All the Noble Enlightened Ones'.[11]

7. *Its realisation is not due to any external cause*
   since it has to be realised through pure apperception.

We have already seen that buddha does not rely upon anyone or anything for its realisation – its wisdom. More than this, its wisdom is non-dual. It has no object. It is aware of itself, i.e. apperceptive, but this awareness is not two-sided. This seeming contradiction cannot be explained satisfactorily with words. It has to be experienced, as the truth of the matter, in profound meditation. One should not confuse the apperception referred to here, concerning buddha *wisdom*, with the apperception described by cittamatrins concerning relative *consciousness*.[12]

For us, this verse means that, as and when we realise the buddha within, realisation will happen of itself and all by itself. It is sustained by nothing other than itself. Furthermore, it is not a self-contained, cosmic cocoon, far away somewhere. It embraces every thing, without being other than those things. This is why Milarepa said: 'Knowing this one thing liberates everything.'

It is knowledge since it has realisation of these three.
It is great compassionate love because it shows the way.

8. *It is ability because it removes*
   suffering and defilements by jñāna and compassion.
   Through these first three there is fulfilment for oneself
   and through the latter three there is fulfilment for others.

Having explored the three qualities of self-fulfilment a second time, the text now re-examines the three qualities of fulfilment for others. The three qualities of self-fulfilment were, as we have seen: not to be a creation, to act spontaneously rather than contrivedly and not to depend upon others. Many things may have qualities – a lamp is luminous, earth is supporting – but not necessarily be aware of them. buddha knows its own qualities. It knows itself to be the highest of all states: the ultimate truth. This gives it the wisdom to recognise, not conceptually but naturally and clearly, both the hidden buddha in every being and the limitations and sufferings which stop other beings from recognizing it. This primordial wisdom, known as *buddhajñāna* in Sanskrit, has two main facets, one embracing the ultimate truth itself and the other embracing all relative phenomena. These two will be explored in a later chapter as *thusness jñāna* and *all-encompassing jñāna*.

Innate to this primordial wisdom is limitless compassion. buddha cares for each and every being much more than the most loving mother cares for her child. Yet even ultimate wisdom, which understands the world's problems, and great compassion, which longs to resolve them, would be useless were there not also the innate power, within buddha, to interact with each being to guide him, her or it out of confusion and into the light of wisdom. The combination of these three qualities – primordial wisdom, compassion and power – makes buddha the greatest source of benefit for beings.

In this chapter we have explored three qualities of self-fulfilment and three qualities which ensure the welfare of others. That would normally make six qualities altogether. However, Tibetan commentaries often employ a particular way of counting which incorporates the identity of a group as well as those of its constituent parts. Thus the three qualities of self-fulfilment, as a whole, are added onto the three specific qualities to make four qualities of self-fulfilment. Likewise there are four qualities of fulfilment for others.

Notes

1 Third dharmacakra – see beginning of Classical Introduction.
2 In the introduction to his commentary on this text, Jamgon Kongtrul Lodro Taye mentions the *Tathāgatagarbhasūtra*, the *Mahāberī*, the *Aṅgulimāla*, the *Śrīmālādevīsūtra*, the *Dhāraṇīrājeśvara*, the

Mahāparinirvāṇa, the *Suvarnaprabhāsa*, the *Mahamega*, the *Ratnamega* and one for which the Tibetan title is *rab zhi rnam nges*. He also mentions four other sūtra, which are slightly less profound: the *Sandhinirmanocana*, the *Laṅkāvatara*, the *Ghanavyūha* and the *Avatamsaka*.

3   The Tibetans refer to the Buddha as *ston.pa* – the One Who Shows. See first page of Dharma chapter.

4   *gzhan stong*

5   *vajrayāna* is a special development of Mahāyāna Buddhism. It uses powerful techniques, such as visualisation and on-the-spot transformation of emotions, to help one progress more swiftly. Its practice requires a competent master, endowed with a lineage, and a disciple with great trust and diligence.

6   *rtogs*

7   *nyams*

8   *Jñāna*

9   The six *pāramitā*, or six transcendent perfections, are the six components of practice which leads to enlightenment. They are generosity, right conduct, forbearance, diligence, meditation and wisdom.

10   Skt: *Manikuda*   Tib: *gtsug na nor bu*

11   *Sarvabuddhaviṣayāvatārajñānālokālamkārasūtra*

12   Well explained in the Karmapa's 'Discerning Consciousness from Primordial Awareness'. This is available as a series of cassettes from Kagyu Samye Ling, as taught by Khempo Troru Tsenam Rinpoche.

The Second Vajra Abode
– dharma –

Once achieved, how does the state of buddha spontaneously help other beings to liberation? Does it radiate great blessing which immediately transports them to enlightenment? Not at all. Although buddha does radiate constant blessing, most beings are impervious to it. Some scriptures compare the grace of buddha to a hook. Faith and openness on the part of beings are compared to a ring. When the hook of blessing catches the ring of faith, extraordinary things are possible. But most beings lack the ring of faith and therefore even buddha is powerless to help them out of their trouble.

The only way in which buddha can help beings is by showing them how to acquire the faith needed to become open to the innate qualities of enlightenment. In fact, Tibetans refer to the Buddha as *ston.pa* – 'the One who Shows'. Some great lamas feel uncomfortable with this word being translated as 'The Teacher' – a commonly accepted title for the Buddha in many countries. Teaching implies having a curriculum of things to teach. It is a dynamic and person-based idea. *Showing* is closer to the truth as, in the presence of buddha, each person is automatically shown what he or she needs, rather like the way a mirror shows people their own faces and not one common face. As with the mirror, the process is without effort or intention. What is shown is called *dharma*, a word with ten different meanings.[1] Here we are concerned with *dharma* as what *buddha* showed and the teaching tradition to which this gave rise.

In this chapter, dharma is presented in three steps. The first verse is a homage, praising the principal qualities which constitute the content of dharma. The next verse reveals the underlying context: the last two of the Four Noble Truths. The remaining two verses link content and context.

Homage

9. *I bow down to the sun of dharma,*
which is neither existence nor non-existence,
nor a combination of existence and non-existence,
nor something other than existence and non-existence:
the unexaminable, beyond all verbal definition,
self-cognisant, peace,
stainless, brilliant with the light of jñāna,
which completely destroys craving for,
aversion to or dullness towards mental objects.

Let us first look briefly at the main points of this homage. The dharma is compared to the sun, because its light of buddha wisdom eliminates the darkness of ignorance. As was the case with buddha in the first chapter, here we are concerned with dharma as a result, or ultimate, Refuge and not as a causal, relative one. The result aspect of dharma has nothing to do with the four philosophical extremes of existence, non-existence and so forth which will be explained below. Beyond imagination or reason, it is inconceivable and ineffable. Being self-cognisant, it can never be 'known' by anything other than itself.

It is peace, being untroubled by any of the consequences of ignorance, i.e. dualistic thoughts, the defiled feelings they engender or the actions to which these lead. It possesses a twofold purity, since it is innately pure as well as being without any superficial pollution. This absence of impurity means that nothing blocks its innate light of buddha wisdom, the brilliance of which is the most powerful thing in the universe. Why so powerful? Because it, and it alone, is capable of totally eradicating the main poisons of the mind, which are all the consequences of ignorance mentioned above and represented in this homage by craving, anger and ignorance.

Eight principal qualities of dharma will be developed in the verses which follow. Three qualities will be attributed to the Truth of Cessation. Three will be attributed to the Truth of the Path. These six combine with the two truths themselves to make eight.

Context

10. *The dharma is that imbued with*
 the intrinsic characteristics of the two truths:
 that which is and that which causes freedom from bondage.[19]
 Inconceivable, not two and concept-free,
 purity, clarity and remedy.

Buddhadharma – the famous Buddhist Path of Peace – is the second Refuge. As we have seen, the Refuges exist as cause Refuges and result Refuges. Cause dharma consists of all the concepts which together make the Buddhist teaching. These concepts have been perpetuated through the spoken word and through writing. The latter consists primarily of the original canon received from the Buddha, consisting of *sūtra, vinaya, abhidharma* (the Triple Collection[2]) and *tantra*. To this must be added the principal treatises (*śāstra*), written by Buddhist teachers over the past 2,500 years, explaining this canon.

The Triple Collection represents remedies for the three main mind poisons. The sūtra, taken as a whole, are seen as the antidote to anger. The vinaya are the antidote to desire and abhidharma is the antidote to ignorance. Together, they discuss eighty-four thousand key types of experience. But, for all that and for all their precious value to the world, the Threefold Collection remains only concepts, and the sounds and letters which convey those concepts from one human being to another. Their great value is in enabling communication between those who have understanding and those who do not. Through their use – in teachings, personal advice, study and sincere reflection – attitudes and values can evolve, along with all that they determine in one's life. In particular, one learns to discern what ennobles life from that which poisons it. All these aspects of dharma are called *dharma as representations*.

Guided by these teachings and one's own growing discernment, one lives the life of a bodhisattva and meditates. This opens many doors of experience: those of overcoming desire and anger, feeling universal love, compassion, impartiality, sympathy, tranquillity in meditation and so forth. The words of dharma come to life. From a wide range of *experiences* emerges first-hand wisdom, known as *realisation*, as explained in the previous chapter. Whereas experiences come and go, realisation develops. In fact, although one can use the word realisation in this broader sense of a growing awareness of the Four Truths, its use in the scriptures is often confined to a specific and direct recognition of the void nature of things. The development of realisation is the result aspect of dharma, known as *dharma as realisation*.

Dharma as direct realisation is true dharma whereas dharma as representation is its reflection in the waters of the intellect. This *Uttara Tantra* is almost solely concerned with dharma as realisation, which has two functions. It has the power to eliminate all defilements and the power to bring about the full fruition of primordial wisdom. Intellectual knowledge – reason in any of its forms – cannot do this, just as the word 'candle' cannot illuminate a dark room. Words may tell us where the candle is and how to light it, but only the lit candle itself can shed light and dispel darkness. Only the practice of dharma can enable us to face up to our defilements and overcome them with the strength of peace and wisdom. Only such work on oneself will enable the light of wisdom to shine.

The dharma journey of personal experience and realisation is in fact a journey of liberation from that which binds us to a life spoilt by physical and mental suffering. There are three main types of bondage:
- the defilements (*klesa*): desire, anger, ignorance, pride, doubt and distorted views of reality, along with all their hybrid forms such as narcissism, jealousy, hypocrisy, frustration etc.[3]
- a deluded understanding, built of dualistic concepts and
- limitations and blockages in meditation.

These three are intimately related. Through inability in meditation, one is unable to rest easily and continuously in non-dual ultimate truth. In a darkness of ignorance, all sorts of confused dualistic perceptions and ideas occur. It is through them that desires, aversions and all the other grosser pollutions develop.

The Second Vajra Abode – dharma

Relating Content to Context

11. *'Freedom from bondage' applies to*
    the truth of cessation and the truth of the path.
    Each of these has qualities three, for each, respectively:

12. *It is inconceivable (because it cannot be examined by thought,*
    it is inexpressible and it is the knowledge of the realised),
    without the two and concept-free, peace.
    It is purity and so forth, these three being like the sun.

This journey of liberation from bondage holds two main areas of interest for us: the liberating process and liberation itself. The first is the Truth of the Path, described in this chapter as 'that which frees the bonds'. The latter is the Truth of Cessation (of suffering) which is described as 'freedom from bondage'.

The Truth of the Path shows us how to develop primordial wisdom by severing the three areas of bondage mentioned above. The Truth of Cessation is the resulting total freedom from bondage and perfection of wisdom. In the following verses, we will examine each of these two truths through the following points. The Truth of Cessation will be viewed as:

- inconceivability,
- not two and
- concept-free.

The Truth of the Path will be viewed as:

- purity,
- clarity and
- remedy.

The Qualities of the Truth of Cessation

Inconceivability is expressed by the following lines of the homage in Verse 9 above:

> *which is neither existence nor non-existence,*
> *nor a combination of existence and non-existence,*
> *nor something other than existence and non-existence:*
> *the unexaminable, beyond all verbal definition, self-cognisant,*

Many dharma students' hearts sink when they see this verse. The wording is heavy. But the meaning is crucial and liberating. It is the key statement of Middle Way Buddhism, distinguishing it from other religions and philosophies.

The Buddha's teaching dispels the darkness of ignorance, just as the rising sun dispels the dark limitations of night. Unlike other faiths, Buddhism does not attempt to proclaim ultimate truth by setting up dogma or credos and obliging its followers to adopt a set of conceptual beliefs. Instead, it simply invites one to explore reality. The beliefs of religions and philosophies can be complex, extremely subtle and sophisticated but, in a critical analysis, they all want to persuade the intellect that something either exists or does not exist. This verse shows Buddhism doing neither. By avoiding extremes of belief, it treads a middle way.

These days, most religious people on our planet adhere to a belief that a unique God exists, although each monotheistic faith has its own slightly different way of defining that God. Other faiths, such as Hinduism, believe in many gods. Many monotheistic and multitheistic religions believe in a personal soul, *ātman*[4] or ego. Non-religious people may believe that at least sub-atomic particles or energies exist.

Another facet of religious dogma is denial. It goes hand in hand with affirmation. If one thing *is*, that almost *de facto* defines some other thing as *is not*. But, before continuing, let us examine more closely these words 'exists' and 'is': they can lead to much misunderstanding. What they really mean, in these theological arguments, is 'exists absolutely', as opposed to 'exists only relatively'. Thus, in the Judæo-Christian traditions, people believe that God exists permanently and ultimately, independent of all the comings and goings of the worlds and our minds. In religions, words like 'eternal', 'timeless', 'all-powerful' are used to describe God, gods, soul or self. Furthermore, certain definite, eternal qualities are attributed to the absolute. It is these delusions about the ultimate that Middle Way Buddhism takes to task, particularly in its teachings of prajñāpāramitā. However, it must be stressed that *Buddhism has no problem with relative things existing dependently and impermanently.* Such existence – the world which is relatively real for any one of us – is not refuted.

Religions and philosophies make statements of existence, or non-existence, in their definitions of the absolute. It is their way of answering the most natural and fundamental question humankind can pose: 'In a final analysis, who are we and why?' Buddha's response to this question, through Maitreya's teaching, is to let us know that the intellect can never give an adequate answer and that reason alone cannot enlighten us on the subject. Utimate truth is inconceivable. This is the first – and extremely important – point about the dharma. Once it has been understood, precious time will no longer be wasted in fruitless speculation.

The famous Middle Way is a way of approaching the absolute yet avoiding the trap of the intellect, with its simplistic and extremist conclusions. The four principal extremes, or edges to be avoided (rather like the edge of a platform over which one can fall, if one strays from the middle) are:

▸ *existence* – belief that God, Buddha, gods, soul, ego (or whatever the absolute may be called) exists independently as an entity. Such belief usually targets something relative and impermanent[5] and credits it with ultimate, permanent existence.
▸ *non-existence* – beliefs that deny or under-rate the relationships between causes and effects which produce the experiences of the relative, impermanent world, and an innate moral power to actions.
▸ *existence and non-existence* – beliefs which try to combine the two views mentioned above and
▸ *neither existence nor non-existence* – beliefs which consider that an ultimate reality could be something other than the first two extremes.

To go deeper into this topic requires a highly disciplined and accurate use of words. It leads into an almost endless wealth of debate which taxes the intellect to its limit. In former times, truly remarkable dialogues took place between non-Buddhists and Buddhists, the latter using the subtle and skilful arguments of the prajñāpāramitā to point out the flaws in the logic of their adversaries. However, the point of Maitreya's text is not one of dismantling wrong beliefs: that was the task of the Second Phase of the Buddha's teaching. Here we move on to the Third Phase in which, having evacuated misconceptions, one establishes the true nature of reality. Maitreya makes it crystal clear that this is not a case of constructing other concepts but – in our personal quest for truth – reaching conviction in the fact that human reason alone will never unveil the ultimate.

What place does reason have in our Buddhist journey to truth? Clear correct thinking can be used to counteract confused, deluded thinking. Once the mind is free from the grip of deluded ideas, the way is clear for meditation to carry us to a direct realisation of the truth.

The verse continues to underline the point of inconceivability by stating clearly that the ultimate – i.e. the true dharma – is *beyond any verbal definition*. Thoughts consist of strings of words – specific mental sound patterns which we have learnt to associate with objects, actions, feelings and so forth. Many people consider the crowning glory of humanity to be its ability to observe, analyse and give names. The very basis of all education and study, even the act of reading this book, depends upon it. But those who have attained the absolute assure us that it could never be an object of intellectual observation and that it falls completely outwith the scope of reason. Of course, we can think *about* the absolute but those thoughts will never *be* or *behold* the absolute.

In practice, one gains indirect knowledge of the absolute through clear logical reflection. Then one meditates to obtain direct knowledge of it. The absolute becomes known as the experience of, and then realisation of, voidness: not voidness in the sense of empty space but as the potential of mind to produce experience. As one prayer[6] says,

Nothing whatsoever, it manifests as anything whatsoever.

When the absolute is realised, it is not as something observed. In the perfection of meditation, it is aware of itself, by itself, in a domain in which thought is unimportant. This 'dimension' of understanding is known as *dharmadhātu*, which translates literally as 'the true dimension of things'. Beyond all the limited, relative identities which we impose on reality, and de*void* of those limited views, there is clarity of mind, which understands all in a brilliant, naked freshness: a pristine awareness that words would only spoil.

When there is such pure, non-dual awareness, the true nature of all things is self-apparent. Through purity, everything appears as it is: Buddhas and Buddha Pure Lands, the play of mental clarity. Through impurity, i.e. conditioned thought-patterns and preconceptions, things appear distortedly as the various realms of worldly existence: the play of confusion. Thus, the true nature of all things is a crystal clarity devoid of conditioned, dualistic impurity. Hence so many vajrayāna texts speak of the *union of clarity and voidness*. Generally, they can be considered to be one and the same. More specifically, to be de*void* of confusion is the essential character of things[7] and clarity is their actual nature.[8] This innate quality of clarity is spoken of in the scriptures as the 'auto-cognisant primordial wisdom of the enlightened ones' or *buddhajñāna*.

The remaining two points concerning the Truth of Cessation are covered by the one word *peace* in the verse above. Unlike the suffering mind, Cessation is untroubled because it is:

not-two, meaning that it is not polluted by either defilements (kleśa) or actions (karma). The latter encompasses both virtuous and unvirtuous deeds – any action whatsoever based in duality. Virtuous actions lead to a relatively pleasant saṃsāra and unvirtuous ones to a life of suffering. But both are saṃsāra. Only non-dual primordial wisdom leads one out of saṃsāra.

free of concepts, as we have seen above, but in this context concepts are viewed as pollutions which trouble and limit the mind and gives rise to the karma and kleśa.

The Qualities of the Truth of the Path

stainless, brilliant with the light of jñāna,
which completely destroys craving for,
aversion to or dullness towards mental objects.

Stainlessness The great healing power of dharma lies in its two-fold purity. It is not only the innate purity of the ultimate but the purity that arises from awareness of that ultimate no longer being distorted by the presence of dualistic concepts, defilements and karma. A perfect diamond may be innately pure, yet if it is covered with mud, plaster and all sorts of less pure substances, no one will be able to appreciate its colour, geometry and other qualities.

Innate purity has already been described above – as the Truth of Cessation with its three main qualities. Dharma as the Truth of the Path is concerned with using the cleansing power of innate purity itself to remove transient, superficial impurities, gathered life after life. What better way to remove delusions than by confronting them with the truth? In fact, in these verses we could almost equate the words *purity* and *truth*. The crux of this path is to be found in the practice of meditation, under the guidance of a lineage master. This will awaken awareness of what is inexorably one's true nature, something resplendently pure.

At that time, there is realisation that dharma, besides being intrinsically pure, was never affected in any way by all the mess of saṃsāra. Just as space is unaffected by the clouds which have come and gone over millions of years in its expanse or just as gold is unmodified by whatever sort of filth accumulates on its surface, so is the primordial intelligence of mind unaffected by the actions of thousands of lifetimes of delusion.

Brilliant with the light of jñāna. In the growing light of that purity, all sorts of habitual illusions and actions will naturally be revealed as the limited sufferings which they are. This exposure and contrast with the peaceful sanity of wisdom robs them of their attraction. In the brilliant light of jñāna's purity, they can no longer exist, just as darkness cannot exist in full sunlight, which illuminates a myriad things spontaneously.

Let us explore this simile a little further. Imagine a dark night. One stumbles over objects, unable even to know what they are, it is so obscure. Bruised and battered, one makes one's way, just able to guess what is in the immediate vicinity through touch, guesswork and the comments of one's companions, also stumbling in the dark.

Dawn starts to break. The mysteries of the night's landscape begin to reveal themselves and the reasons for taking wrong paths, falling over things and mistaking a cliff-face for a house start to become apparent. Once the full light of day has broken and one has found high ground with a panoramic view, the entire landscape is obvious. What has taken all night to navigate could now be crossed in a half-hour.

In this analogy, we are considering things from the point of view of the traveller. As for the light which liberated the traveller – which here corresponds to dharma – it is evident that, in itself, it has nothing whatsoever to do with either his understanding or misunderstanding. Light is simply light. The paths, rocks and trees of the landscape also remain what they always were. What has changed is the accuracy and extent of the traveller's understanding.

As we shall discover again and again in this text, no analogy works satisfactorily when it comes to describing the absolute. In the above analogy, the problem would be that both the revealer (the light) and the revealed (the landscape) correspond to jñāna. The means and the end are the same in nature, at least, if not in breadth of compass.

Power to remedy As we have already seen in this chapter, this combined purity and clarity acts as the ultimate remedy for the three main mind poisons – desire, anger and ignorance – and all their derivatives.

Notes

1. *Dharma* - although ten meanings are given in all, the main ones are thing or phenomenon, quality, teachings, Buddhist doctrine.
2. *tripitaka*
3. Twenty-one main sub-defilements are mentioned in the *abhidharma:* wrath, resent, rage, irritation, jealousy, discontent, deceit, pretense, absence of dignity, absence of shame, dissimulation, avarice, narcissism, faithlessness, laziness, negligence, unmindfulness, unawareness, torpor, agitation and total distraction.
4. *ātman* the rough equivalent, in Hinduism, of the soul in Christianity. It means *essence, breath*, or *life*.
5. More details of this are found in the *abhidharma* where the 5 aggregates (*skandha*) are recognised as being the main targets for misinterpretation.
6. The *Short Prayer to Vajradhara* of Bengar Jampal Zangpo
7. Tib. *ngo bo*
8. Tib. *rang bzhin*

The Third Vajra Abode
– the saṃgha –

The saṃgha is discussed through two sets of three qualities, as were the buddha and the dharma. These six are expressed first through a homage, then in terms of their context and finally through a verse linking the content of the homage to the context.

Homage

13. *I bow down to those whose mind is no longer obscured,*
    the deeply-realised who have jñāna's perception,
    awareness of the total purity present in limitless beings.
    As the true nature of mind is lucid clarity,
    they see the defilements to be without essence
    and hence truly realise ultimate no-self –
    peace within all beings. Thus they know
    the all-pervading presence of perfect buddhahood
    in each and every one of them.

The saṃgha, as a cause Refuge, is the community[1] of beings capable of transmitting and perpetuating the Buddha's teachings. Through the purity of what they teach, their way of life and their intention, such beings truly deserve the epithet accorded in Refuge prayers: 'finest of companions'. They range from gatherings of monks and nuns, i.e. human beings who live mindfully and caringly by observing strict sets of precepts, to those saintly beings who have almost totally removed any impurity from their minds and whose wisdom is close to that of the Buddha.

This text is almost exclusively concerned with the saṃgha as a result Refuge. This is the *arya saṃgha* or realised saṃgha, composed of those who have unceasing, unreverting realisation of the true nature of everything. It is the presence of enlightened wisdom in them – rather than whatever personal details remain in their lives – which makes them a refuge worthy of this text's interest. Their qualities will be presented in terms of wisdom and purity.

As we shall see more fully in the following chapter,[2] Buddhism views the entire cosmos as containing three types of beings:

- *individuals*, i.e. the beings of the six realms of existence – devas, demi-gods, humans, animals, spirits and hell-dwellers – whose minds are under the sway of personality delusion. They are also called 'ordinary beings' or 'the immature'. Most have never even glimpsed ultimate reality. Technically, anyone who is not a realised being (see below) should be included in this category. Some very great Buddhists, famed for their kindness, purity and erudition, would belong to this group and remain in it until the power of karma and rebirth has been broken. They may have powerful experiences of voidness, but still do not have the stable, lasting control of it which characterises the realised being.
- *realised beings*, i.e. the mahāyāna saṃgha referred to in this chapter. They have definitively cast off personality delusions and hence will never again be reborn in the six realms due to the power of karma. They abide in the permanent presence of ultimate reality, which they realise through their primordial wisdom – jñāna. They develop their wisdom and purity until these are both absolutely perfect.
- Buddhas.

Through jñāna, the realised saṃgha know the ultimate nature of each and every being, without a single exception, to be the same ultimate nature they have recognised in themselves. Thus their vision of reality is a pure one. Instead of seeing fault and transient imperfection in others, they recognise the utter purity which is everyone's true nature. In particular, they clearly discern the ultimately-true clarity of mind, which they themselves realise, from the relative delusions of 'ordinary beings', just as someone awake knows who the sleepers around him really are, even though the groans and gasps of their dreams and nightmares reveal them to be under all sorts of strange, gripping illusions about themselves.

In particular, these realised bodhisattvas know the true nature of anything to be void yet lucid, i.e. not just blank nothingness but a limitless dimension of wisdom in which all can manifest. This manifests to them as being the true, changeless nature of everyone and everything, whereas the temporary delusions and sufferings in beings' minds are transient and devoid of any true quality of their own. The pivotal illusion, giving rise to all the others, is that of having a lasting ego.

Like the stuff of dreams or hypnosis, beings' illusions have no real basis and so never affect the true nature. Let us take, as a simile, a perfectly fit person. He or she may dream of being paralysed or be hypnotised to think so, but all the while possesses perfect muscles. Someone watching the dreamer or the hypnosis readily knows this. Likewise, the realised saṃgha understands us all to be Buddhas, all the time. The problem is that we ourselves do not recognise it. We ignore our true nature, peace: peace in the sense of freedom from dualistic delusion, defilement and suffering.

Context

14. *The saṃgha of the wise, who never regress, possesses insurpassable qualities through pure perception: thusness, all-encompassing and the inner.*

The three major qualities of the saṃgha's wisdom are to possess:
- primordial wisdom of how the true nature is,
- primordial wisdom of the true nature's full extent and
- inner primordial wisdom.

The global Buddhist term for wisdom – *prajñā* – covers all forms of wisdom, from the most banal of worldly understandings to highest enlightenment. *Jñāna* is a much more specific term. It means 'primordial wisdom' and is uniquely the highest summit of prajñā. Jñāna, wisdom as realisation of the ultimate truth, is presented in this text in its three main aspects as *thusness jñāna, all-encom-*

passing jñāna[3] and *inner jñāna*. In tantric texts, it is often found in a fivefold presentation.[4] Whether we speak of two, three, five or more jñāna, it makes no difference. These are just *our* analytical ways of trying to understand *the jñāna* which is the awareness of the Buddha.

Thusness jñāna is the self-awareness of the ultimate. This knowledge of the true nature, by the true nature, is a hundred percent present only in Buddhas. Bodhisattvas realise it to varying degrees. It could be loosely described as the ultimate truth of the ultimate, as opposed to the ultimate truth of the relative.

Consider the famous example of a coiled rope in a dark place being mistaken for a snake. The mistaken awareness brings the pain of fear and might make one do all sorts of things: faint, try to shoot the rope, spend minutes that seem like hours trying to creep slowly away from it ... all sorts of useless things. When light falls on the rope and it is seen for what it always was – simply a rope – all the relative delusion fades away.

Thusness jñāna is not concerned with relative delusions at all. It is constantly, lucidly, aware of the true nature – which is none other than itself: clear wisdom. In the example, it is only aware of the rope and not at all concerned with any relative delusion that could be projected onto the rope. This jñāna is unconcerned with any of saṃsāra's delusions but is the constant self-awareness present within dharmadhātu, the primordial space of mind. In particular, it is aware of the wisdom which *is* voidness. In the profound teachings of mahāmudrā, the wisdom of voidness is called *clarity, clear light* or *lucidity*.

All-encompassing jñāna This aspect of primordial wisdom pertains to the relative. Unlimited, it does not embrace a hundred or a thousand things but all beings and all things, knowing them for what they truly are – despite what they may seem to be to deluded beings. It is aware of each sentient being and of his or her motivation, attainment and subjective perception of reality. It also encompasses all objects, knowing their relative (i.e. apparent) colours, forms and other characteristics as well as their absolute identity. This knowledge clearly and properly discerns one thing from another, one quality from another, without either confusion or illusion.

Jñāna is irreversible clarity. To attain it, one must have reached the non-returner stage, as it is understood in the mahāyāna teachings, i.e. the first mahabodhisattva level or beyond. Because the understanding is so clear, return to delusion is impossible. There can be awareness of delusion but not delusion itself. This is like seeing the rope, knowing it unhesitatingly to be a rope, yet also being aware that it can be perceived as a snake in the dark by those who do not know there is a rope in that place.

All-encompassing jñāna is very important. Through it, realised beings understand the presence of dharmadhātu in everyone and everything. Thus they know the true nature of other beings to be dharmadhātu and this is the ground of spontaneous great compassion.

Inner jñāna The thusness and all-encompassing jñānas described above are not two isolated things but rather two facets of enlightened wisdom. Inner jñāna is the core which brings these two together. It is 'inner' because it is buddhajñāna belonging to the true nature itself. This inner, or natural, quality of wisdom will recognise the 'thatness of suchness', i.e. its own clarity and purity, and become thusness jñāna. It can also recognise itself within phenomena, and become all-encompassing jñāna. This latter knowledge is not simply restricted to awareness of the fact that phenomena (including beings) are devoid of their illusory qualities but knows them to be endowed with all the enlightened qualities.

What is it that gives the realised saṃgha such wisdom? It is purity – the absence of limiting conceptions and corrupting karma and suffering. This freedom is presented classically through three major qualities of purity:

- freedom from defilements,
- freedom from the cognitive obscuration and
- freedom from inferior motivation.

The first two of these were explained in the previous chapter.

Absence of lesser motivation means absence of selfish motivation. In order to be a Realised Being, personality delusions have to have been eradicated. There no longer remains a delusion of self but clear recognition of the universal identity which is voidness and clarity. Thus their compassionate motivation is not rooted in self-other dichotomies, in which one sacrifices oneself to help others, in an endless ocean of personalities. It is the motivation which comes from seeing through all the various personality delusions and knowing all beings to be Buddhas.

Relating content to context

The following verse shows:
▸ the arya saṃgha has thusness jñāna,
▸ it has all-encompassing jñāna,
▸ the purity it has achieved and
▸ why it is the supreme saṃgha refuge.

15. *They have thusness (jñāna)*
    because they realise the peaceful nature of all beings;
    their absolute purity of nature,
    and that all the defilements
    have been non-existent from the very beginning.

a: the way in which thusness jñāna is realised   The thusness jñāna of the bodhisattva saṃgha is direct wisdom, a crystal-clear lucidity in which the truth of any thing or any one manifests clearly and automatically. This truth is a perfect peace, inasmuch as it never even knew any of the aberrant projections of delusion. Besides having been, since beginningless time, devoid of anything to do with saṃsāra's dark misunderstandings, it is in itself great lucidity, or clear light.

If the snake, in the rope-snake example, were real, steps would have to be taken to avoid it or combat it, in order for the person to be saved. Because the 'snake' is merely a deluded perception, with no true basis in reality, it suffices that the observer understand what is really there for the danger to be over.

The realised saṃgha knows the lack of real substance in the six types of beings and the worlds which these latter perceive. Despite the pain and seemingly-endless darkness in which many of them live, none of what they experience has any basis in reality. Like nightmares, hallucinations and the like, none of it ever truly existed, yet belief in its existence causes pain, itself illusory.

16. *They have the all-encompassing, because their intelligence, which understands the ultimate object of knowledge, perceives that all beings have the nature of omniscience.*

b: the way in which all-encompassing jñāna is realised It is hard for our dualistic minds to comprehend non-dual wisdom. This verse mentions the 'ultimate object of knowledge'. We can understand ultimate both in the sense of final and in the sense of highest but we should not take the word *object* too literally. It just helps us to approach the incomprehensible.

In the normal process of knowledge, the observing mind focuses upon something and understands it, either through direct observation or reason. Even when this process becomes much more subtle, in meditation, with mind observing mind, there is the subject-understander and the object-understood. However, when one progresses from ordinary being to realised being (first mahabodhisattva level), the subject-object distinction becomes infinitely more subtle and, from the eighth mahabodhisattva level onwards, disappears completely.

The subject-object distinction is a habit of delusion. Once it has been vanquished, whatever appeared previously, as either 'other' beings or as an object of knowledge experienced by the intelligence of one's subjective mind, now appears as simply a phenomenon manifesting in the expanse of dharmadhātu. Whereas previously the knowing was accomplished through the direct experience of the senses, or by reasoned thought, now it is the self-wisdom of dharmadhātu which knows instantaneously all that is within its expanse. There is no distinction of nature between knower and known because each is the same, as the true nature of relative phenomena has now been recognised as dharmadhātu. This is why the term *auto-cognisant* is employed. The importance of this statement can be appreciated when one considers other religious beliefs in which the divine and the mundane are fundamentally different by nature and can never be the same.

Such wisdom transcends any wordly wisdom and simply cannot be grasped by the intellect. Hence, words which speak about it can sometimes seem senseless or like *haiku*. However, such words do have value and, in the light of meditation, their truth becomes more meaningful than anything else.

This transcendent wisdom is fully aware that the true essence of each and every sentient being is the omniscience of buddha, which knows all relative phenomena and every aspect of their ultimate nature. In the infinities of time and space, sentient beings are numberless. Whatever the extent of those beings' experience and the relative worlds of their projections, this wisdom knows all to be the auto-cognisant clarity of dharmadhātu.

17. *Such understanding is the seeing of self-cognisant jñāna.*
    It is completely pure because the 'stainless space'
    is free from hindrance and desire

c: its very special purity Possession of thusness primordial wisdom and all-encompassing primordial wisdom is something unique to those who have gone beyond the state of individuality and saṃsāric rebirth, i.e. to the mahābodhisattvas who form the realised saṃgha. Their understanding is quite different from the wisdom of the general Buddhist path. Although not as extensive as a Buddha's, it has the same nature, being auto-cognisant, clear perception of truth. As wisdom, it is pure in the sense of being:

▸ unpolluted by the obscuring power of defilements. This is because its thusness jñāna is dharmadhātu's infinite clarity of mind, which embraces all things and knows them to be itself, i.e. naturally stainless. Thus it is free from the cloying attachment of deluded involvement with specific phenomena, and all the hope, fear and so forth that such involvement creates and

▸ undeluded by the 'cognitive obscuration', which approaches things through dualistic conceptual filters. It is free of this through all-encompassing jñāna, which realises all things directly for what they really are.

The above wisdoms reveal all, like bright sunlight. To possess them is like directly 'seeing' the truth. It is very different from 'hearing about' truth, in saṃsāra's darkness, through Buddhist teachings.

18. *The never-regressing and deeply-realised are a refuge*
    for all beings because of their insurpassable buddhajñāna
    since they have exceedingly pure perception, through jñāna.

d: they are the supreme refuge   The wisdom and purity described above mean that the realised saṃgha are relatively close to the Buddhas' insurpassable qualities of wisdom and liberation. Their definite, lasting awareness of the true nature makes their path irreversible. Thus they are truly the finest of all the saṃgha refuges and excellent friends and guides for beings lost in confusion and suffering.

General Points About the Refuges

1. Why the Refuge is Threefold

19. *The refuges are presented as three,*
    through the aspects of teacher, teaching and those who learn,
    in relation to three yana and to three kinds of activity.

As the following verse makes clear, the only ultimate refuge is the Buddha. However, on a relative level, the three Refuges offer a variety which can be very helpful for the differing beings which constitute the Buddhist community. Although in theory all Buddhists turn equally to all three Refuges, in practice it seems to be the case that certain types of people find one of the three to be more attractive and more inspiring than the others.

Buddhas are the first and foremost of the refuges, through the supremacy of both their qualities and their deeds. Of the main types of Buddhist,[1] followers of mahāyāna Buddhism will find the Buddha's qualities particularly inspiring and will want to become Buddhas themselves so as to possess those qualities. Likewise, some people will find the Buddha's deeds to be the finest of all beings' and they will aspire to emulate them.

Some hinayānists, and especially pratyekabuddhas, are more attracted to the qualities of the teaching, rather than the teacher. For them, dharma is the most important refuge. They and others will want to accomplish deeds related to dharma, especially those of understanding and mastering the teachings on interdependence and cause-and-effect, through meditation.

Other hinayānists, and especially śrāvakas, are most attracted by the qualities of community – the Buddhist saṃgha. As for actions, they will enjoy striving to be fine monks or nuns and to nurture the saṃgha's strength or else, as lay people, they will feel most comfortable sponsoring monastic life and visiting temples from time to time.

Although the above three types of being are classical Buddhist archetypes, one can observe these different attractions quite vividly in the new Buddhists in the West. Some are most inspired by teachers, some by the knowledge itself and others by the saṃgha. The importance of one or another refuge can also vary with time in a single individual. Thus the three refuges provide succour for many different mentalities.

2. What is the Ultimate Refuge?

20. *Neither both aspects of dharma nor the deeply-realised saṃgha constitute a supreme refuge which will last for ever:*
because they are to be abandoned, one is inconstant,
one is nothing whatsoever and they (the saṃgha) fear.

For all their value as relative refuges which nurture beings and guide them to liberation, neither the saṃgha nor the dharma can be considered a truly ultimate refuge. A true, or ultimate, refuge needs to be constant and fearless. Only the Buddha fulfils these criteria.

The dharma cannot be considered an ultimate refuge for three reasons:
- it will be relinquished,
- it is inconstant and
- it lacks nature, being merely an absence.

The teachings of the 'dharma as representations' will be relinquished inasmuch as they are disposable stages of a path of evolution. They are often compared to a boat which only serves to carry one to the other side. The very nature of a path requires yesterday's position to be relinquished so that today's progress be achieved, otherwise one remains static. Dharma as representations is merely words and concepts. One idea gives way to another as the person evolves. Words and concepts are relinquished once the reality to which they led has been achieved.

Dharma as realisation is considered in two ways: the realisation of the Truth of the Path and that of the Truth of Cessation. The Path is a series of relative experiences, each of which gives way to another. Even the more constant wisdom that these experiences engender will change and evolve, until changeless buddhajñāna is achieved. Thus it is impermanent and inconstant.

The Truth of Cessation, as it is experienced by bodhisattvas in training or by arhats, lacks the qualities of the ultimate and is, primarily, merely the absence of suffering. An absence is not something in which one can take Refuge.

The samgha – even the realised samgha and arhats – still have fear, inasmuch as they have not removed every veil from their minds and thus cannot be a hundred per cent sure of knowing total truth. They could just be wrong. Only the Buddha has that absolute certainty of truth. It is one of enlightenment's unique qualities. Thus even the realised samgha take refuge in the Buddha and, from an absolutely critical point of view, cannot offer total assurance to limitless beings, as Buddhas can.

21. *Ultimately, only buddha constitutes a refuge for beings, because the great victor is the embodiment of dharma, which is the ultimate attainment of the samgha.*

Buddha is without the shortcomings mentioned above and is the only 'thing' in the entire universe which can offer a lasting, fearless refuge for any being. Furthermore, what is meant by buddha is in fact the expanse of dharmadhātu and its innate wisdom. This is the source of all dharma, hence buddha is the ultimate aspect of dharma. Likewise, the true character of the samgha is attainment of wisdom and qualities. The very end of their path of achievement is to become dharmadhātu. Hence buddha is the ultimate samgha. All three refuges are embodied by the buddha. Being beyond even the most subtle forms of birth, ageing, sickness or death, buddha is the eternal refuge.

3. Why they are called *Ratna*

22. *'Rare and Supreme' because their occurrence is most rare, they are stainless, powerful, the ornament of the world, the best possible thing and changeless.*

In the original texts, the three Refuges were qualified by the adjective *ratna*. This was translated into Tibetan as *dkon.mchog*, which sounds like *köncho*. These terms have been translated variously into English as *Jewels, Rare and Sublime, Most Precious, Gems* etc. The Sanskrit term *ratna* has six main significations, which would normally apply to a precious substance:

- *rare* – beautiful perfect gems are rarely encountered,
- *without imperfection* i.e. entirely composed of precious substance and flawless,
- *empowering* as they have the ability to purchase or bring about that which is needed and wished for,
- *adorning*,
- *supreme* being above all imitation, and
- *changeless* being noble in themselves and uninfluenced by subjective opinion.

We can apply these six qualities to the Refuges which are:

- *rarely encountered* as it takes so much goodness for them to manifest in a world and so much merit for someone to encounter them that entire cosmic aeons may elapse between times of sufficient spiritual openness in which buddhas appear,
- *without imperfection* as, by their very nature and definition, they are without the defilement and cognitive obscurations,
- *empowering* as they are endowed with unimaginable qualities such as clear cognition etc.,
- *adorning* the world since all wordly notions of virtue and wholesomeness stem from them,
- *supreme* being the finest thing in the world because they have transcended the world and
- *changeless* as they are not the creations of defilement and karma.

These implications pose a real problem in translating *ratna* into English. Rather than saying 'The Three Jewels', one should say 'The Three Rare, Stainless, Empowering, Adorning, Supreme and Changeless Ones'. Of course, this is too unwieldy. However, it does give us a clue to the respect felt when earlier Buddhists used this term. The Tibetan translation – the bisyllable *dkon.mchog* – takes up two of these meanings: Rare and Supreme.

Part Two

The Basis for Attaining the Three Rare and Precious Refuges

Some General Comments about the Final Four Vajra Abodes

The final four Vajra Abodes are only truly understood by Buddhas

23. *That these three rare and supreme arise from tainted suchness, untainted suchness, the qualities of immaculate enlightenment and the deeds of the Victorious Ones*
   is precisely the domain of those aware of the ultimate.

What gives rise to the Buddha, Dharma and Saṃgha discussed in the first part of this text? This question can only be answered by those fully 'aware of the ultimate', i.e. Buddhas themselves, because only they are directly aware of the whole process. Thanks to their teaching and in particular to this summary of their teaching by Maitreya, we can understand a little of the answer, which will be the topic of the remainder of this text and the last four vajra abodes. Although it deals with things subtle beyond our imagination and vast beyond description, we can have confidence in these teachings, just as we would have greater trust in the descriptions of someone who has travelled in a country than in the conjecture of those who have never left their own land.

Suchness is one of many words used to describe the ultimate. Although they all refer to the same ultimate, each highlights something different about it. Suchness indicates that it is the way things really are. *Buddha nature* means the same but lets us know that the way things really are is buddha. *Sugatagharba* – 'heart-essence of those who have become bliss' – tells us of its lasting happiness that is the quintessential nature of all things. There are many terms like these.

Untainted suchness is suchness as it truly is, undistorted by the illusions and blockages of the speculative mind. It is voidness and clarity. In the rope-snake example, it is simply the rope, without even a hint of snake projection. Or, to take another example – that of a jewel caked in mud – it is the innate purity which is the jewel, there to be uncovered and appreciated whenever anyone cleans it.

Tainted suchness is this true nature misinterpreted by mind's illusions. It is taken to be a self or a personality, nothing whatsoever, something other, God and so on and so forth. Although suchness retains all of its qualities, these are not recognised. This is like the rope being thought to be a snake, or the jewel remaining unfound and being thought to be a lump of mud. The harmless rope and the valuable gem remain there, as themselves, despite the deluded projections thrown upon them. The *fourth vajra abode* – buddha nature – will explore suchness in both the tainted and untainted phases.

By removing karma, defilements and delusions from one's life through the application of dharma, deluded projections are purified and truth reveals itself. This can be likened to realising the rope to be a rope or to cleansing the jewel but these examples are only partially satisfactory. When the purification has been achieved the untainted suchness will be fully recognised: this is enlightenment, the *fifth vajra abode*.

Due to enlightenment, all the qualities of suchness become manifest. They are the highest fulfilment for oneself, because suffering and its causes have been dispelled for ever and lasting, sublime happiness is attained. This is the topic of the *sixth vajra abode*. These qualities are also the supreme fulfilment of the wish to help others as they generate spontaneous and effortless activity to help every being, for as long as saṃsāra endures. The help is not just temporary relief from suffering but a showing of the way to end suffering definitively. This is the topic of the *seventh vajra abode*.

They are inconceivable

24. *The potential for the rare and sublime*
    is the domain of wisdom of the omniscient.
    In respective order, there are four reasons why
    these four aspects are inconceivable:

The potential for the three Refuges is, strictly speaking, contained in the prime cause: buddha nature. Here the term *potential* has a meaning extended to include the supporting conditions: enlightenment, qualities and activity. As we know, this very subtle causality is seen by Buddhas. The point of this verse is to stress the fact that, because *only* Buddhas see it fully through their two types[2] of auto-cognisant jñāna, it is inconceivable for other beings, who only have recourse to intellectual intelligence and dualistic observation.

Meditation, and in particular the insight stages of mahāmudrā meditation, will throw much light on the last four vajra abodes. But even the experienced meditator, not to mention the ordinary thinker, will save himself or herself a lot of unnecessary effort by simply accepting the impossibility of understanding it all. In particular, there are four paradoxes that the intellect finds hard to resolve and which can stymie those equipped solely with rational thought in their quest for understanding.

Reasons for their inconceivability

25. *it is pure yet accompanied by defilements,*
    and completely undefiled yet to be purified,
    it has truly inseparable qualities
    and is total non-thought and spontaneity.

This verse elaborates the four seeming paradoxes related to the remaining vajra abodes:

✗ **buddha nature** is spoken of as being pure yet also as being accompanied by defilements. These two notions seem, at first, contradictory as the presence of defilements is almost a definition of impurity. How can the perfection of suchness be simultaneously present in the most violent anger or jealousy?

✔ The resolution of this seeming paradox is found in the twofold purity discussed in the chapter on dharma. Buddha nature is perfectly pure as far as its real character, or essence, is concerned. The impurities, i.e. the defilements, are merely the outcome of a mistaken view concerning that nature and nothing to do with the nature itself.

✗ **enlightenment** is said to be completely free from defilements. Yet it is also spoken of as something to be purified by gradual practice. There is a seeming paradox between primordial purity and a need for purification, which implies impurity.

✔ **defilements** are a superficial impurity, not an intrinsic part of enlightenment, and therefore have never altered its actual nature, but simply obscured it. Consequently, removing them does not change its nature, which was always pure, but simply allows it to manifest.

✗ **enlightened qualities** are likewise spoken of as being innate to buddha nature, which we all possess. Yet those qualities only appear once the work of purifying the negative and nurturing the positive has been fully accomplished. At that time, it could seem to many as though the qualities appear for the first time as a direct result of the work of the path, and that they only exist in Buddhas.

✔ The qualities have always been an intrinsic part of buddha nature, in everyone, yet they cannot manifest due to the obscuring defilements and dualistic thoughts. This is similar to the sun which always radiates heat and light, yet is obscured from view by passing clouds. When the clouds go, the sun is seen afresh as doing what it has been doing all along: shining.

✗ **enlightened activity** is spoken of as being spontaneous and non-conceptual. This point is not a seeming paradox but something hard to comprehend. In most worldly activity, the quality of the end result depends much upon the amount and quality of forethought and planning that has gone into the action. How can a Buddha's actions respond so precisely to each being's specific needs without there being some thought about that being's circumstances, capacity and so forth?

✔ The Buddha's deeds to help specific beings are seen as the end result of the millions of good prayers and training while on the path when a bodhisattva. To take a very gross example, we could compare this to the spontaneous reflexes of an experienced driver and remember how much one had to think and condition one's actions when learning to drive. A more subtle example might be that of artists and writers, who have learnt how not to seize on the obvious but rather to leave space, into which novelty and inspiration can flow.

More detailed conceptual answers to the above conundra will be

The Final Four Vajra Abodes – general comments

found in the final four chapters, but these, and the answers above, are often more subtle than they at first seem. Even with deep reflection and meditation, it can take some time to grasp them properly. Perhaps, this is why Maitreya stressed, in the previous verse, the inconceivability of these topics.

The causes and conditions for realisation

26. *Since there is that to be realised,*
    the realisation, the attributes of realisation
    and that which brings realisation, then respectively
    the first point is the prime cause, that to be purified,
    and the remaining three points constitute conditions.

The Triple Gem discussed in the first three chapters can be considered as a result: not a creation or *thing* but a result by removal.[3] This result arises from one principal causes and three supporting conditions. These are respectively:

- *tainted suchness* – i.e. buddha nature, the fourth vajra abode,
- *untainted suchness* – i.e. enlightenment, the fifth vajra abode,
- *enlightenment's qualities* – the sixth vajra abode and
- *enlightened activity* – the seventh vajra abode.

The prime cause for buddha, dharma and saṃgha occurring and bringing their benefit to the worlds is the existence of buddha nature. This cause may be omnipresent but whether it produces its results or not depends upon the power of the supporting conditions, just as a seed may remain for a long while in the ground but will only produce its result once the warm weather comes and the rains fall. The supporting conditions are enlightenment, enlightened qualities and enlightened activity.

These four causes are all presented here in terms of realisation. That to be realised is buddha nature. To realise it is enlightenment. Buddha qualities are the qualities of the realisation itself: its fearlessness, uniqueness and attributes. Enlightened activity is that which will help others to accomplish the same realisation.

Notes

1   See 'Gems of Dharma', Chapter One on the five types of precious human being.
2   thusness and all-encompassing
3   See 'a simple introduction to voidness' in Translator's Introduction.

The Fourth Vajra Abode
— buddha nature —

Buddha nature is 'that which is to be realised'. It will be explained in this chapter through four points:
- a brief introduction to it, as *dhātu,*
- a more detailed exploration through its ten principal qualities,
- nine examples which help us understand how purification can make it manifest and
- an explanation of why this most subtle, ineffable reality needs to be taught through words and ideas such as this text.

A. Brief Introduction – Buddha Nature as Dhātu

*27. The buddha essence is ever-present in everyone because
the dharmakāya of perfect buddhahood pervades all,
suchness is without differences and
they have potential.*

*28. It is taught that all beings possess the essence of buddha
because buddhajñāna has ever dwelt in them,
the immaculate nature is non-dual and
the buddha-potential is named after its result.*

Dhātu is one of the most widely-used terms in Buddhism. It has a variety of meanings, many of which are conveyed by the English term *element*. Others are *domain, expanse, realm* and so forth. We study many elements in our analysis of reality, from the six prime elements – earth, water, fire, wind, space and consciousness – through to the eighteen elements of awareness and so forth. Here we are dealing with *the* element: the stuff of everything and everyone.

We shall explore buddha nature, as dhātu, through ten approaches in the next section. The main point to stress first is that all beings, from the tiniest insect to the greatest bodhisattva, possess it and possess it equally. The three reasons for this, given here by Maitreya and found in such scriptures as the *Tathāgatagarbhasūtra*, form one of the key points of Middle Way Buddhism and one of the pivotal statements of this work. Since the following is quite subtle and profound, the reader is recommended to consider the following 'reasons' more as topics of contemplation than logical arguments. The three reasons touch upon three facets of buddha nature which will be central to this chapter:

- buddha nature as dharmakāya, (line 2 in each verse),
- buddha nature as suchness (*tathatā*) (line 3 in each verse) and
- buddha nature as heart-nature (*gotra*) (line 4 in each verse) and hence ultimate potential of beings.

All beings possess buddha nature since:

1. *the dharmakāya of perfect buddhahood is all-pervading.* The actual nature of any 'thing' or any 'one' is voidness. This can be demonstrated through the cast-iron reasoning of Buddhist logic or through the direct experience of insight meditation. The teachings of the Third Turning make it clear that voidness is neither mere emptiness nor simply absence of suffering but the complete presence of enlightenment's qualities of perfect wisdom, compassion and power. These three are all facets of the enlightened primordial wisdom (buddhajñāna) mentioned in the second line of verse.[28] This universal embodiment of voidness-as-wisdom in all things is given the name *dharmakāya*: *dharma* meaning things and *kāya* meaning embodiment.

    Thus, whatever appears, through temporary illusion, to be a sentient being or a particular phenomenal reality is, in fact, the presence of dharmakāya. Dharmakāya *is* buddha. Thus all seeming 'beings' possess the very essence of buddha, at all times.

2. *Suchness has no differences.* Being true reality – present all the time whether recognised or not – this continual presence of wisdom, love and power is referred to as *thatness* or *suchness*. Being the only true reality, it is equally present in all things – 'all things' meaning in effect the six realms of existence: the entire spectrum of the non-real illusions that are projected onto true reality. It is the 'immaculate nature'.

    Actions continually re-shape, re-condition, the superficial experience of the mind. Its conditioning causes it to experience the world in a certain way. This process, called karma, operates over all sorts of timespans, depending upon the action. Many terrible actions can cause one, eventually, to experience life as hell. Many kind, generous deeds can make life, eventually, appear as heaven. Actions have been going on in such complexity for such a long time that each person has a unique and very complex experience of things. Whether these experiences take on appearances of being male, female or neuter as a god, demi-god, human, animal, spirit or hell-being, none of the myriad distinctions of species, race or sex or any other unreal projection of the mind ever affects buddha nature. It remains the same sole truth in all beings at all times. To return to our example, the fearful delusion of a terrified man does not affect a coiled rope.

3. *Sentient beings have the heart-nature / potential.* Compassionate, powerful buddhajñāna is equally present everywhere. Its presence gives all beings the potential to realise it to be the true reality, beyond and behind their illusions, just as the continuous presence of the rope creates the potential for recognising the diaphanous nature of one's snake illusion and the truth of what was always there.

The difference between buddhas and other beings is in their recognition (and subsequent realisation) of the truth. Even in saṃsāra's confusion, buddha nature's innate power is at work, giving a feeling of dissatisfaction with worldliness and a longing for truth. The power of truth to recognise itself (which we encountered in the previous chapters as auto-cognisant buddhajñāna) is always present but stifled to varying degrees. It is partially covered in bodhisattvas, quite heavily covered in Buddhists who have no meditation experience of voidness, and thickly stifled, but nevertheless still present, in those wreaking their own downfall at the darker end of the saṃsāra spectrum. But it works slowly and inexorably even in the latter, bringing them to enlightenment in the extremely long term. Gampopa explains in detail the five main manifestations[1] of this buddha-potential.

Another way of viewing this potential is to see it metaphorically as a genetic quality. We are all of the family, or stock, of Buddhas. Compassionate wisdom is our true birthright and genetic build, even if we have fallen upon hard times which no longer reflect our princely origins. Like an unalterable part of the DNA of our every cell, it is present throughout all the ups and downs of our life.

This potential is *named after its fruit*. One can apply both explanations given above, either understanding the potential to become buddha as being named after its result, just as

London Road, Oxford, is so named because it eventually leads one to London, or one can understand the continuous presence of a quasi-genetic coding of buddhahood within all things, just as the genes of a seed contain all the information of its fruit.

B. A more detailed exploration of buddha nature as *dhātu* through its ten principal qualities

29. *The meaning intended by 'ultimate domain'*
    should be known through its essential character,
    cause, result, function, endowments, approach,
    phases, all-pervasiveness, unalterability
    and the inseparability of its qualities.

This verse simply gives the ten main headings of the topics which will be the subject of the following sixty-five verses. They enter into the many aspects of purity of this 'ultimate truth which is the true domain of phenomena'. This purity is not easily understood, since it does not correspond to any of the daily situations of cleansing, detoxifying or refining to which we may be used. This is why these ten relatively profound angles need to be explored, through mature reflection, in order to appreciate the unique nature of this 'ultimate domain'.

Essential Character and Cause, taken together generally

30. *Like the purity of a jewel, space or water,*
    it is always undefiled in essence.
    It emerges through aspiration for dharma,
    highest prajñā, meditation and compassion.

The first two of these ten points are linked: the first shows us the purity which is to be realised and the second shows what does the 'purifying'. This is not in the sense of making pure a thing which was previously impure but in the sense of bringing recognition of a purity which was always there.

Three examples are used to emphasise the innate purity of buddha nature. The first is that of the mythical wish-fulfilling gem – a stone which is not only physically pure but the result of great virtue and hence charged with the power to fulfil one's pure wishes. The second is that of space, which is pure through being unobstructed, and the third is that of clear spring water.

What causes some beings to recognise this innate purity and others not to? There are four causes:

- aspiration for the mahāyāna dharma,
- highest prajñā which recognises the illusoriness of identities,
- limitless, blissful meditative absorption and
- great compassion towards sentient beings.

1. Its Essential Character of Purity

31. *Its qualities resemble those of a valued gem
because it is powerful,
of space because it is unalterable
and of water because it moistens.*

A precious worldly jewel has the power to dispel poverty. The wish-fulfilling gem is even more powerful, granting the wishes of those who physically come close to it. Likewise, buddha nature is powerful, since it brings ultimate happiness to oneself and greater benefit to others than anything else. It fulfils many lifetimes of sincere prayers, made while one was a bodhisattva, to completely purify one's mind and to relieve the endless sufferings of beings. The closer one comes to its true and total meaning, the more these wishes are fulfilled.

Like space, the ultimate domain of buddha nature is changeless. Nothing has modified it or ever will modify it. The earth changes, with the seasonal comings and goings of the elements. Entire universes come and go in space yet space itself is changeless. The myriad details of each world's story never affect space itself and likewise all the heavens and hells of myriads of beings' existences never alter one iota of buddha nature.

Water is wet and fluid, seeping and flowing everywhere. It brings life and enables growth. Moreover, the element water, rather than the substance H_2O, is cohesion wherever and however it occurs in the phenomenal world: the bonding between particles and between all sorts of realities. Water here symbolises the power of compassion innate to this ultimate domain. Embracing all, bringing growth and maturity and making the lifeline between enlightenment's liberation and saṃsāra's bondage, compassion is a vital part of the essential character of buddha nature.

2. The Cause for this Ultimate Domain being Recognised

32. *Hostility towards the dharma,*
the view that self-entity exists,
fear of saṃsāra's sufferings and
disregard for benefiting beings
are the four sorts of obscuration ...

There are four main obstacles which prevent one from recognising the buddha nature of all things. They are:
- *outright hostility towards the mahāyāna teachings*, or else a certain discomfort or lack of empathy with them. The mahāyāna teachings are the natural radiance of buddha nature. Antipathy towards them is ego's way of blocking the mind from recognising the clarity of truth from which they emanate.
- *belief in self-entities*, either of beings or of phenomena. The truth of anything is limitless, far from the limited identities and labels which beings project upon it. Blinkered, fixed views constantly take hold of the mind and prevent it from relaxing into a direct perception of the vastness of non-conceptual truth. Furthermore, on a grosser level, it will be hard for those with strong ego-beliefs to practise dharma and achieve its result: recognition of buddha nature, the wisdom of voidness of entity.
- *fear of the sufferings of saṃsāra*. Such fear in itself creates a veil

which blocks recognition of truth. Truth has the character of fearlessness since its compassionate wisdom recognises the void nature of suffering. On a more relative level, fear of saṃsāra prevents one from entering and practising the mahāyāna path which will carry one to such a recognition.
- *disregard for benefiting beings.* This lack of inclination to dedicate one's life to the welfare of others often comes from a preoccupation with one's own problems and situation. Sometimes it can come from an obsessive preoccupation with the development of one's own concentration meditation (śamatta).

33. *... of the desire-bound, the mistaken,*
śrāvaka and pratyekabuddha respectively.
The causes of purification are four:
strong aspiration for dharma and so forth.

Although the four obstacles mentioned above may be found to some degree in many persons, they represent the principal veil of four types of beings, respectively:
- *those with a selfish drive*, whose main priority is the gratification of their own senses. This is the antithesis of the selfless altruism of the bodhisattva whose mind has overcome the conditioning of sensuality. Desire and the other defilements form a driving force which carries the mind far from its true nature into delusion and all the consequent sufferings of saṃsāra.
- *the deluded*[2] are those with very rigid, but erroneous, beliefs in God, a soul or the like. Organised religion and life in a society, the values of which are based upon a long history of religious influence, often give people beliefs which are very strongly rooted, through indoctrination and conditioning from childhood onwards. Although the morality and outlook on life provided by most religions may contain some very positive aspects, leading to the betterment of humankind, their root premises are fantasies based upon something or someone which does not exist, and must necessarily lead to disappointment.

- *śrāvaka* are Buddhists following the way of the 'smaller vehicle'. They are defined as a psychological type, rather than as a geographical or historical group, and so could and do exist in any Buddhist country. Their chief characteristics are a sincere wish to go beyond worldly existence and achieve liberation and a preoccupation with overcoming their own emotions. They achieve the latter through an approach to meditation which, by its very nature, excludes the predominantly altruistic mind of the mahāyāna.
- *pratyekabuddha* are not buddhas but those who long for liberation (*buddha*) for themselves (*pratyek*). These are a special instance of the śrāvaka mentioned above. They are often śrāvaka who have taken their concentration meditation to an extremely high level of accomplishment during the times of former Buddhas. Thereafter, they meditate in solitude for many thousands of lifetimes and appear when later Buddhas manifest. Their meditational prowess tends to make them haughty, secretive and lacking in natural compassion.

34. *Those whose seed is aspiration for the supreme yana,*
    whose mother is prajñā, originator of buddha qualities,
    for whom meditative stability is a comfortable womb
    and compassion a nanny, are born as buddha's offspring.

The four obstacles mentioned above are removed by their four opposites:
- aspiration for dharma counteracts hostility towards it,
- great wisdom (prajñā) will remove illusions of personal or divine self,
- the clarity of meditative stability will dispel fear of saṃsāra, by revealing its sufferings to be illusions devoid of reality and
- compassion will naturally dispel lack of care for others.

The main emphasis of this entire text is one of *view*, a word used to describe one's understanding of reality and way of approaching it. On an intellectual level, this will take the form of a philosophical stance, be it formal or informal, while on a real-life level it determines the guiding dynamic of one's meditation, conduct and spiritual progress. Although some verses, such as this one and the former, are relevant to daily Buddhist practice, most are concerned with forming the clear view of reality that needs to underpin practice. This view is founded in a knowledge of the void-yet-lucid true nature of all things.

Thus, the four remedial qualities spoken of here are not to be taken as *separate things*, for Buddhists to practise, but as facets of the *natural* radiance of buddha nature itself. Devoid of concrete reality yet radiant with lucid intelligence which knows all, it naturally gives rise to aspiration for its cause (mahāyāna dharma), it is naturally wise, naturally the very body of deepest meditation and naturally compassionate.

We all have buddha nature yet only some people manage to recognise it and let its qualities shine. This is because of the four obstacles. In this verse, the relative birth of the bodhisattva is compared to a human birth. Sincere aspiration to the mahāyāna dharma is the initial sperm which fecundates the process. The fertilised seed needs to grow and be nourished in a propitious environment of wisdom, compared here to the body of the mother. Practically, this corresponds to the development of awareness of no-self and profound understanding of the nature of things. The womb in which this wisdom develops is stable, wise meditation.

Even when born, a baby still needs much care in order to develop healthily. The bodhisattva's 'nanny' is compassion, ensuring that spiritual growth happens as it should. Compassion deepens wisdom and fosters meditation. Athough the meditation referred to here is, in itself, mainly concentration meditation, it is intimately linked to compassion and wisdom, without which qualities it would be unable to sever the root of suffering and might lead one astray into rebirth in the deva realms.

Fruition and Function viewed jointly

*35. Its result has the transcendent qualities
of purity, identity, happiness and permanence.
Its function is revulsion with suffering
accompanied by an aspiration, a longing, for peace.*

Having looked into what buddha nature is and what causes it, the text now considers another two of its ten qualities: its full manifestation, as *fruition*, and the *influence* that such a fruition exerts. As a fruition, buddha nature embodies transcendental purity, identity, happiness and permanence. These are transcendental or pāramitā inasmuch as they transcend dualistic projections which can only conceive of purity as one end of a purity/impurity spectrum of values.

This is very interesting. In terms of an individual's progress along the path, there is a need to break progressively free from saṃsāra by changing the way in which one thinks. At the outset, saṃsāric beings make four great mistakes, by fostering concepts which make them believe:

- their bodies to be pure,
- some form of self to exist,
- their habitual experiences to be happiness and
- some things which are impermanent to be permanent.

For these saṃsāric habits and illusions to be remedied, they need to recognise the truth of the general Buddhist teachings on impurity, non-self, suffering and impermanence. These 'antidote' thoughts are like a laxative that clears constipation. They are very necessary and work well but are not in themselves the final healthy outcome. Health is not to take laxatives every day but to have both the sickness and its remedy cleared from the system. Thus, having rid onself of impure desires by contemplating impurity, one needs to move further along the path and rinse concepts of impurity out of the mind. Having rid oneself of ego by practising non-ego, one needs to move further along the path and rinse concepts of non-ego out of the mind. And so on and so forth.

Buddha nature has a natural, inherent purity which is transcendent because it has nothing to do with preconceptions of purity or impurity. Likewise it is the natural identity of everyone and everything, beyond conceptual projections of self or no-self. It is spontaneous bliss, beyond any notion of blissfulness or non-blissfulness and it is naturally permanent, nothing to do with conceptual time-frames.

This fruition, endowed with the above four pāramitā, functions in a very special way, giving rise to a feeling of being 'sick and fed up' with the limitations and sufferings of worldliness. On the positive side, it works from deep within the mind, producing a profound longing for peace.

3. Fruition – 'that which is to be attained'

36. *In brief the results of these*
constitute the respective remedies to both
the four ways of straying from dharmakāya
and their four antidotes.

The four misguided ideas that keep beings in the illusions of saṃsāra are the ones which, by their very definition, lead them away from the truth of dharmakāya. As explained above, the common level of Buddhist teachings counteract the four main pain-generating concepts of saṃsāra with peace-generating concepts of impurity, non-self, etc. From the resulting peace, it is relatively easy to progress to dharmakāya itself, which possesses the four non-conceptual pāramitā of purity, identity, happiness and permanence. These four pāramitā are only known by buddha's primordial wisdom and may be less easy to understand than they at first seem.

37. *This is purity because its nature is pure*
and all impurities of karma have been removed.

This couplet explains the pāramitā of purity. It is not purity as worldly beings conceive of purity. Nor is it the absence of impurity, i.e. absence of defilement (kleśa) and action (karma), that followers of smaller-vehicle Buddhism conceive of as their goal and nirvāṇa. The former is based in delusion and the latter is merely an absence, recognised conceptually. The purity of dharmakāya, i.e. buddha nature, arises from the immaculate nature of enlightened primordial wisdom itself. Buddhas and only Buddhas experience the natural purity of this wisdom, which does not depend upon any conceptual notion of purity or impurity.

They experience (although this is not really the right word) this purity as twofold. It is naturally pure: 'pure by its very nature'. It is also free from any veiling or distortion due to karma and kleśa. The relevance of this becomes clearer when one considers the overall task of unmasking buddha nature. Ordinary beings do not recognise it at all, due to heavy veils of karma and kleśa. Even realised bodhisattvas or arhats, who have rid their minds for ever of the grosser aspects of karma and kleśa and can never fall under their power again, still have very subtle imprinted thought-habits left by past karma and kleśa and these can generate extremely subtle forms of rebirth in bodies of light. Buddha nature itself, being free of karma and kleśa and any associated conditioning, has both innate purity and freedom from any veiling superficial impurity.

> *It is true identity because all complications of 'self'*
> *Or 'no-self' have been absolutely quelled.*

The final couplet of verse 37 explains the pāramitā of identity. Worldly beings have a notion of self in two ways: an innate feeling of self and a conceptual fabrication of self. The innate feeling is present from birth, due to lifetimes of habit. Humans, animals, spirits and so forth just automatically experience themselves as themselves, as opposed to other beings. The conceptual fabrication is acquired through thoughts and the complex play of life, through which a conceptual persona becomes structured. This can be taken to a sophisticated degree by personal, philosophical or religious beliefs which deify ideas of soul, ātman or ego. Both notions of self are delusions, inasmuch as the physio-psychological complex which constitutes a human being, and which is defined by Buddhists as the five aggregates, is an ever-changing fabric, within which no constant persona can be found.

The common teachings of Buddhism proclaim no-self in order to bring awareness of such delusions and to free beings from the personal sufferings they generate. Ideas of self are delusions. No-self is merely the conceptual recognition of an absence. Both are 'conceptual complications', a term used here for the difficult-to-translate Tibetan word *spros.pa*, pronounced trö-pa and meaning centrifugal – moving away from the centre. *Spros.pa* describes the mind when it leaves the spacious, limitless and peaceful domain of clear wisdom and thinks. Its thoughts attempt to describe, define, understand or comment upon things with mind-words which are but poor icons for true reality. They are stale whereas reality is ever-fresh.

Reality as dharmakāya has this quality of freshness. As the great mahāmudrā yogin Bengar Jampal Zangpo said,

Recognising it undistractedly is the very body of meditation.
May the meditator who can remain in the freshness
of the essence of whatever arises, be free of a mentality
which defines it as some object of meditation.

Ideas of *self* or *no-self* are both concepts which are unnecessary complications within the light of truth, in itself the true identity of us all. Just as the rope is the reality upon which snake ideas are projected, so is buddha nature the reality upon which mistaken notions of self, God, soul and the like are projected. It is our true identity both in the general sense of the word and in its etymological sense of being identical for us all. All beings and all things share the same ultimate identity. As we shall see later in the text, buddha nature was referred to by Maitreya as *mahatma*, the great self.

38. *It is happiness through the demise of the five aggregates, which are of a mental nature, and their causes.*

The pāramitā of happiness is beyond happiness as it is defined either by worldly illusions of happiness or by Buddhist concepts of happiness and suffering. Worldly beings undergo three types of suffering: the suffering innate to the five aggregates, the suffering of change and manifest suffering (physical and mental pain). These are well-explained in many Buddhist texts. However, most sentient beings are unaware of the extent of these sufferings and remain convinced that happiness can be found in their world: through human relationships, sense gratification and so forth. Yet life rarely lives up to their expectations.

General Buddhism points out the fallacies of their illusions, in order to help reduce unnecessary pain and misery. Yet, for all the relative truth of its teachings – not to mention the real benefit they bring – it remains an antidote and is not the final truth of the matter. The latter, which we are considering here as buddha nature or dharmakāya, has a natural bliss which is nothing to do with the transient happiness of the five skandhas or the conceptual satisfaction of no longer suffering in saṃsāra or even the bliss of Buddhist dhyāna,[3] etc. For this bliss to manifest, one must first employ the general Buddhist antidote thoughts of 'suffering'. This will bring the conditioned habits of worldly attachment to their end. Subsequently, once the antidote itself is removed from the system, the truth of the bliss pāramitā can manifest.

> *It is permanence since the sameness*
> *of saṃsāra and nirvāṇa has been realised.*

The pāramitā of permanence transcends worldly illusions of permanence and the Buddhist concept of impermanence. All creations, i.e. everything arising from causes and conditions, are impermanent. Worldly beings are unaware of this impermanence. They conceive of their bodies, health, physical prowess, mental ability and relationships with other beings and objects as though these would endure. They relate to them in that way. How many lovers have pledged themselves to each other for eternity. Yet, in fact, even within a second, things change.

In order to avoid the pain that comes through unexpected yet inevitable change, general Buddhism points out the delusions of permanence and teaches impermanence. Mature Buddhists with some realisation are very aware of the impermanence of worldly creations. The concept of 'impermanence' is deeply etched into the mental window through which they perceive reality.

Nirvāṇa is a negative term, inasmuch as it refers to an absence rather than an existence. It means 'without suffering' and refers to the liberated state in which karma's creations, due to ignorance, no longer manifest. As that state is itself an absence, it has no characteristics of its own. The notion of nirvāṇa is the conceptual satisfaction of knowing that a state exists in which impermanent aggregates or sufferings are no more. Thus nirvāṇa's only existence is as a concept projected onto an absence.

Those beings actually in saṃsāra or in nirvāṇa are, respectively, in a conceptual state with suffering and a conceptual state without suffering. As both states are conceptual, they have a sameness of ultimate nature but one should never underestimate their difference in relative character. A nightmare and a peaceful dream are both dreams, and similar in that respect, but so different in their detail and effect upon those who experience them.

There is more to the question of identity of saṃsāra and nirvāṇa than the simple fact that they are both conceptual. Buddha nature has always been, is and always will be whatever it is, no matter whether the mind is projecting ideas of impermanence or permanence, of nirvāṇa or saṃsāra. While worldly beings are creating karma and experiencing suffering, their true nature is buddha nature. While arhats are absorbed in the meditation of cessation, their true nature is buddha nature. To return to our analogy of dream, buddha nature is like the true identity of the person whether he or she sleeps and has nightmares or is in restful slumber once the bad dream is over.

There is another, even deeper, way of approaching the question of the sameness of saṃsāra and nirvāṇa, in which nirvāṇa is not the nirvāṇa described above, i.e. simply an absence of suffering or the peaceful withdrawal of the mind into a cessation of conscious activity, as practised in the hinayāna. If we consider 'non-abiding' nirvāṇa – described in more detail in the following verse – which is none other than buddha nature, then we realise that there has never been anything other than that: everything *is* it. What appears, from our present point of view, as 'saṃsāra' is, like all things, part of it. The identity of saṃsāra is nirvāṇa.

The actual realisation of the sameness of saṃsāra and nirvāṇa is a very high attainment. One should take great care not to fall into the trap of mistaking an accurate intellectual appreciation of the sameness of these two for a direct realisation of their sameness, due to skilful insight meditation. It is a trap which can lead to great danger. People who fall into it are called in the scriptures 'hopeless cases'. They can do a lot of damage to themselves and others, through good but misplaced intentions. Some think they are living out 'crazy wisdom' but it is really neurotic confusion.

These four pāramitā are not, in any way, in conflict with the classical Buddhist teachings on impurity, non-ego, suffering and impermanence. Here we are simply moving beyond the latter to describe the highest ultimate truth, for those capable of understanding it. The more generalised Buddhist teachings are dealing with what is relatively true, in a way which most people can easily understand. Each level of teaching has its appropriate time and place in an individual's spiritual journey, with most people needing to work intensively with what is relatively true in order to achieve a mind capable of realising what is ultimately true.

39. *Those of compassionate love have, through prajñā,*
    completely severed all self-cherishing.
    They will not want to enter a personal nirvāṇa
    because they dearly care for every being.
    Hence, by reliance upon these means to enlightenment,
    i.e. wisdom and compassion,
    the deeply-realised are neither in saṃsāra
    nor in the quiescence of a personal nirvāṇa.

This verse describes the bodhisattva way, profoundly rooted in buddha nature. It is a path of action which skilfully avoids the attractions of saṃsāra or limited nirvāṇa. Its result is the nirvāṇa of the Buddhas, called 'non-abiding' nirvāṇa. It abides neither in saṃsāra nor nirvāṇa.

'Those of compassionate love' are bodhisattvas, gradually uncovering the 'limitless, great, compassionate love'[4] of buddha nature. They avoid all the traps of falling into worldliness by avoiding their universal cause: belief in self. How? Through wisdom which pierces delusions of self and a subsequent activity which knows no self-interest.

Likewise, they avoid the temptation simply to bring their personal saṃsāra to an end. This could be achieved through concentration meditation, by entering into a personal nirvāṇa in which the habits of the six consciousnesses are radically severed. This gives a state free of suffering but one in which the qualities of buddha nature are not manifest. However, in such a personal nirvāṇa, subtle conditioning associated with the aggregates still persists in a latent form, in what is almost a great hibernation.[5] Bodhisattvas avoid this lesser nirvāṇa through a genuine care for all other beings, which leads them to dedicate their every faculty, such as the consciousnesses, and their every act to the welfare of other beings.

Thus the combined power of wisdom and compassion keeps the bodhisattva on the right track. The deep wellspring of this power is, in fact, buddha nature. Like a homing device, it ultimately leads the bodhisattva to a full realisation of buddha nature in a nirvāṇa which abides neither in saṃsāra nor in limited nirvāṇa.

4. Function – 'which makes it attained'

40. *Were there no such buddha-element,*
    there would be no discontent with suffering,
    nor desire, effort and aspiration for nirvāṇa.

This verse reveals the function – one could equally say action or influence – of buddha nature, by pointing out how things would be were it not to exist. It is an influence more and more strongly felt as the veils covering buddha nature are removed. Conversely, it is less and less in evidence in those who thicken their blockages. The whole range of beings, from those close to buddha nature to those furthest away, is well described by Gampopa[6] in his 'five types of potential.'[7]

What do beings feel as buddha nature's influence? A sense of spiritual awakening which gives a feeling of dissatisfaction with the limitations of this world and an intuitive knowledge that there is something far higher and nobler. These sentiments can be quite confused in what Gampopa calls 'the uncertain' and what we might well these days call 'spiritual seekers'. As he so rightly remarks, they get strongly involved with whichever valid religion, or school of Buddhism, they meet with first.

When buddha nature can function more strongly, it brings to life the Buddha's teaching, showing saṃsāra to be the mess it is and giving a deep-seated longing for the limitless peace, wisdom and compassion that one knows to be the real truth.

There are two ways of explaining this verse's negative justification of buddha nature's function. By describing what would happen were it not there, the text must either imply that some forms of existence do not possess it, or else point us to forms of existence which do have it but in which its power is suppressed or attenuated, as explained above. The first possibility takes a relative stance: sentient beings possess these two qualities of being sick of worldly suffering and longing for transcendental happiness, whereas inanimate objects do not. The second approach views it from an ultimate point of view: all phenomena are manifestations of buddha nature, referred to here as the 'buddha-element', and it is more a case of whether that nature is asleep or awakened[8] than one of having it or not.

41. *Awareness of saṃsāra's shortcoming, suffering,*
    and nirvāṇa's quality, happiness,
    are due to the existence of this potential.
    Why is this so? Without such potential
    they would not be present.

Buddha nature is described here through the Sanskrit term *gotra*, which can be translated as *seed, element, clan, nature* or *lineage*. It gives a certain sense of belonging, or an almost genetic potential, inasmuch as there are typical characteristics carried over from generation to generation. Ultimately, we are of buddha stock. Its innate qualities are etched into us throughout rebirth after rebirth. In one way, we are like the fairy-tale prince who spends a long time as a frog until the spell is broken and his true birthright is restored. Gotra can be taken both as a possession of certain innate qualities and as the potential that this possession creates, through the power it offers to generate its special results. It is at one and the same time like belonging to a family line and being able to reproduce it, through one's genetic inheritance. Ultimately, we have been buddhas from the very outset. Relatively, we have the potential to manifest the buddha qualities.

Thus we cannot remain contented with froghood when something deep inside knows we are princes. We long for the joys of the palace and the return of our beauty, so as to be able to ask for the hand of the fair maiden in marriage. As potential buddhas, we sicken of saṃsāra's petty joys, at a high price of suffering, and long for the peaceful, lasting happiness of nirvāṇa.

5. Endowments

42. *It is like a great ocean – an inexhaustible abode*
     containing precious substances of inestimable qualities.
     It is like a lamp-flame because this essence
     is endowed with inseparable qualities.

These examples show some of the qualities with which buddha nature is endowed. While buddha nature remains unrecognised and is hidden behind a fabric of illusions, it is called *basis* buddha nature. It provides the basis for purification, just as the coiled rope provides the basis for working through snake illusions and recognition of what is really there, on the barn floor. Basis buddha nature provides us with the cause for enlightenment. Result buddha nature is the fruit of Buddhist effort. In this and the following verses, we examine the *basis* qualities through the example of an ocean and the result qualities through the example of a candle flame.

43. *Because it contains the essence of dharmakāya,*
    the jñāna of the victors and great compassion,
    it has been taught as being similar to an ocean
    through being an environment, its gems and its waters.

Until it is made manifest, buddha nature is only a potential. As such, it has three quasi-genetic properties: the 'genes' of dharmakāya, those of buddhajñāna and those of great, universal compassion. These are indivisible. Dharmakāya is wisdom and that wisdom has compassion at its very heart. Here, the three qualities are compared to an ocean, the riches it contains and its waters.

Dharmakāya is omnipresent, hence vast beyond imagination, like the greatest of oceans. In Indian mythology, oceans were famed for the gems and rare things they contained. Many are the stories of adventurers setting off to distant oceans to make their fortune. The stunningly precious riches of enlightened wisdom are compared here to the varied, unimaginably valuable gems in the oceans. The waters of the ocean are the example for compassion which, as we have seen, has a fluid, bonding, lubricant quality.

While one is eliminating the veils covering buddha nature, aspiration for the mahāyāna dharma is the seed of future dharmakāya. Without it, enlightenment will never happen, just as a plant cannot grow if there is no seed. It is compared to an ocean because of its vast scope, embracing the welfare of all beings and the fullness of buddhahood. The seed for realising buddhajñāna is the wisdom (prajñā) which arises through skilful meditation. This seed grows to become the thusness and all-encompassing jñānas. The third seed is that of compassion, which develops from a limited, conceptual and emotional compassion to the non-conceptual, universal compassion of buddha. The wetness of compassion indicates that meditation and wisdom are not dry qualities but deeply humane ones.

44. *Since direct cognition, jñāna and freedom from stain*
    are inseparable within the immaculate ground,
    they are compared to the light, heat and colour of a flame.

The point emphasised about buddha nature's qualities at the time of fruition, when all obscuring veils have been removed, is that they are inseparable, like the light, heat and colour of a flame. The light of the flame represents the clarity of awareness when buddha nature is fully manifest. Clarity of cognition is a common Buddhist topic, usually described as a set of five (sometimes six) powers arising from purity of meditation. One encounters them also in the hinayāna teachings where they are described as the fruition of the various stages of the eight dhyāna. The five powers are:

- divine vision, which can see microscopic or extremely distant objects and things of other times,
- divine hearing, which hears extremely subtle or far-off sounds and sounds removed in time,
- knowledge of others' minds: their thoughts, intentions, capabilities, etc.,
- knowledge of past and future, which knows past lives, future lives and the origins and outcomes of actions and
- knowledge of miracles, enabling the body to be transformed into all sorts of things.

When present in meditators, arhats or bodhisattvas, this fivefold clarity is limited by the limits of their minds. When in its pure, unrestrained state, in Buddhas, it is an unlimited crystal clarity. As light dispels darkness, this unconfused and certain knowledge dispels the darkness of ignorance and confusion.

The heat is an example for thusness jñāna. The latter unmistakenly knows the true nature of everything and is the fire of truth which effortlessly burns up all defiling, veiling illusions. As fire is used to burn impurities and to disinfect, so does this wisdom remove belief in reality.

The colour of the flame represents the clarity of buddha nature, which knows the relative and ultimate simultaneously. Just as the yellow, blue and orange tinges of a flame are all inseparable from its heat, so is the knowledge of all the variety of phenomena inseparable from the vision of the ultimate.

6. Manifestation / Approach

45. *Suchness is approached in different ways*
    by ordinary beings, the deeply-realised
    and the completely-enlightened.
    This is how those who see the true nature
    have taught beings about this heart-essence of the Victors.

All beings possess this buddha nature. Ultimately, all beings are buddha nature – 'the heart-essence of the Victors'. Yet their approach to it varies tremendously, according to their degree of wisdom. What beings do about their buddha nature determines the way it manifests. In order that gifted disciples might understand it properly, Buddhas, who directly 'see' this one and only reality, have taught it as manifesting in three main ways. This classical threefold division will be the topic of many verses to come.

'Ordinary beings' are those still wandering in saṃsāra, from one life to the next, driven on by the dynamic power of ego-delusion and karma. Their approach to the nature of existence is quite mistaken. Mahabodhisattvas, free from rebirth and with deep realisation of voidness, approach it more correctly and the completely enlightened have an 'approach' (the word is not really adequate here) that is totally fitting.

46. *Ordinary beings distort,*
    those who see the truth correct the distortion
    and tathāgatas (approach it) just as it is,
    undistortedly and without conceptual complication.

Ordinary beings' approach to buddha nature is erroneous. They mistake it for a lasting personal identity and thus flounder in a hopelessly complex concatenation of dualistic, self-other situations. The things they do on account of these delusions and the suffering that they thereby engender keep them giddily turning on the saṃsāric roundabout. Realised beings who, through meditation, have developed stable insight into the voidness of self and phenomena, are systematically working on the correction and elimination of whatever is left of the debris of thousands of lifetimes' saṃsāric habits. They recognise much of buddha nature but still have not integrated its totality.

The completely pure, who have totally become *thatness*, i.e. buddha nature, without a single trace of saṃsāric confusion remaining, recognise it in all its splendour, with as many qualities as there are grains of sand in the Ganges. Because of their total, direct recognition of buddha nature, through auto-cognisant buddhajñāna, they do not need any sort of conceptual framework to approach it.

This gives us, effectively, three categories of buddha nature: unrecognised, partially recognised and totally recognised. The six points about buddha nature dealt with thus far have described it from various angles. The remaining four points are devoted to a detailed exploration of these three ways in which it is manifest.

7. Phases

47. *The impure, those both pure yet impure*
    and those absolutely, perfectly pure
    are known respectively as ordinary beings,
    bodhisattvas and tathāgatas.

The three categories explained in the previous verses are much more than a mere intellectual reflection. The tremendous differences between those caught up in wordliness and pure-minded bodhisattvas and, beyond these, the unimaginable horizons of purity which open up between bodhisattvahood and being a buddha, make these three manifestations of buddha nature of prime import.

This verse firmly establishes the names and defining criteria of these three types of beings, with their specific approaches to buddha nature. Worldly beings are 'the impure'. This may sound a very harsh judgement and therefore merits some reflection, in order that it be understood in context. If one of the main premises of this text is correct, i.e. that buddha nature is ever present but ever ignored by worldly beings, one can only conclude that, second-by-second, each and every moment of a wordly mind is a distortion. This, for a Buddhist, is in itself is a shocking truth to face up to. What, each second, ought to be the infinite, loving compassion and timeless wisdom of the mind (as it really is) is reduced to a self-centred, confused and dark vision of reality, which more often than not causes harm both to the person and to those around them.

Bodhisattvas – and here the word really means *maha-bodhisattvas*, i.e. those who have achieved the first great bodhisattva level and beyond,[9] have shed the most part of these impurities. They no longer act through self-interest or self-delusion. They have eliminated habitual patterns of desire, anger and ignorance from their mind-stream. They have fostered great stability in meditation and subsequent insight. They recognise buddha nature, to a certain extent. Thus they are very pure. However, the conditioning of past dualism remains (as momentary thoughts). Despite their subtlety and benign nature, these thoughts block off the manifestation of much of buddha nature's quality. Thus there is still some impurity, which is gradually lessened and refined through the ten levels of bodhisattva development.

When this process of purifying the defilement veil, the cognitive veil and the meditative veil has been taken to its absolute perfection, there is nothing left to obscure buddha nature. This is total purity: the domain of the buddhas, referred to here as *tathāgata*, those 'who have become that'.

48. *Buddha nature, summarised by the six points,*
    essence and so forth,
    is explained through three phases
    and by means of three terms.

What buddha nature *is* has been described by the first six of these ten points: essential character, cause, result, function, endowments and approach. How buddha nature *is viewed*, and related to, is described through the three phases – impurity, partial purity and total purity – and the three types of being defined by those phases – ordinary, bodhisattvas and buddhas.

8. All-pervasiveness

49. *Just as space, concept-free by nature,*
    is all-embracing, so also is the immaculate space,
    the nature of mind, all-pervading.

Space embraces all things. It would be impossible for something to exist outwith the bounds of space, as its very presence occupies space. Buddha nature – referred to here by one of its many epithets, the immaculate space – likewise embraces all things. Of the two inseparable characteristics of buddha nature, i.e. voidness and clarity, voidness is most akin to space and clarity makes that space immaculate. In other words wisdom is the true nature of mind, whether that mind be confused, partially liberated or totally liberated. Neither physical space nor the immaculate space has need to conceptualise in order to pervade.

50. *This, the general characteristic of all,*
    permeates the faulty, the noble and the ultimate,
    just as space permeates all forms
    whether lesser, mediocre or perfect.

In Buddhist logic, one defines two types of characteristics: general and specific. A general one would be the likes of impermanence, which applies to all compound creations. A specific characteristic would be the hot, burning nature of fire, which does not occur in other phenomena. Buddha nature is the general characteristic of all beings, irrespective of the qualities they possess. It is the general characteristic of our three main types of being who, respectively, are riddled with fault, have many qualities and possess every ultimate quality. This all-pervasiveness is likened to that of space, which is the same whether it is the space pervading an earthen pot, a copper pot or a golden pot.

9. Changelessness

> 51. *Since the faults are but incidental whereas*
> *its qualities are part of its very character,*
> *it is the changeless reality,*
> *the same after as it was before.*

This is one of the key verses of Maitreya's text. The faults are the myriad manifestations of relative reality, discussed as the Truth of Suffering, and their causes – karma and kleśa – discussed as the Truth of Origination of Suffering. These may continually cause beings to ignore the truth, but they never affect that truth itself, just as looking at something through distorting lenses does not warp the thing itself, only one's impression of it. The faults are described as 'incidental', being ephemeral distortions and nothing to do with the essential character. The qualities of buddha nature are, on the contrary, unchanging and part of its very character. Buddha nature is referred to here as *dharmata*, the real thing or reality. This term could be translated literally as *thinginess*, in the sense of being the true unique thing behind the multiple delusions.

True reality – buddha nature – is changeless. Although, from a bodhisattva's point of view, there will be an enormous difference between life before buddha nature has been realised and life after buddha nature has been realised, buddha nature itself never changes. It remains what it has always been, just as an object remains what it is while it is being looked at through distorting lenses and afterwards, when the lenses have been removed.

Changelessness of buddha nature in the impure phase

Verses 52-65 explore buddha nature in the impure phase by comparing it to space, which is not compounded, and by comparing the incidental impurities to the other four prime elements, which are compounded. The verses cover the main points first and then explore them in more detail, one by one.

52. *Space pervades all yet remains absolutely uncorrupted*
    on account of its extreme subtlety;
    likewise this, present in all beings, remains absolutely taint-free.

The element space differs from the other elements – earth, water, fire and wind. Space is uncompounded, i.e. it does not arise in specific forms due to various causes and conditions. It is constant. The other elements, however, are inconstant and compounded. Furthermore, there is not one of them that is not permeated by space. Space is the subtle, ever-present arena in which the other elements come and go. Be they oceans, deserts of sand, cosmic winds or fireballs like the sun, all come and go impermanently in space. Yet space is unaffected by them, no matter what form they take.

Likewise, buddha nature is the naturally intelligent domain of truth in which sentient beings arise and have their demise. It is the expanse in which they suffer and in which they liberate themselves from suffering. Nothing that happens, however horrible or divine, will ever taint buddha nature in any way.

53. *Just as universes always arise*
    and disintegrate in space,
    likewise do the senses arise
    and disintegrate in the uncreated space.

What at first appear simply to be Buddhist and Indian legends describing the inception of this and other universes turn out to have more significance than one might imagine. They describe wind first moving in space, and creating water, and the wind subsequently churning the water to produce earth. When we consider the real meaning of the elements, this signifies that movement (wind) in space produces various degrees of gravity, bonding and attraction (water) and that this gives rise to density and mass (earth). The subsequent stored energies and their potential is the element fire. This more or less accords with modern physics. Thus ancient diagrammatic representations of the universe show the earth mandala resting on the water mandala which itself rests on the wind mandala. All takes place in space. Universes arise and disintegrate in space but space itself never arises and never disintegrates.

Likewise, buddha nature remains the unchanging backdrop against which the five aggregates, the eighteen elements and the twelve gates of consciousness arise and perish. These thirty-five subjects – expressed here by the word *senses* – contain all the specific details of form, feeling, perception and so forth of which the various beings of the cosmos are constituted. Our Buddhist studies of interdependence show, with great finesse, how these details of existence constantly interact and generate each other, arising according to infallible patterns of causality. As they come and go within buddha nature, that nature itself remains the same.

54. *Just as space has never been consumed by fire,*
     likewise this is never consumed
     by the fires of ageing, sickness and death.

Fire is a great destroyer. The fire element even has the meaning of destruction, as it indicates the release of potential – of stored energy – which inevitably causes change of state. Various fires are described in the scriptures, all the way up to the great cosmic fires which occur as a universe burns itself out. Yet none of these fires ever singed space, let alone destroyed it.

Fire is taken here as a metaphor for the sufferings of ageing, sickness and death, which regularly destroy life's happiness. None of the pain, disappointment or mental torture that they engender has ever modified buddha nature by one iota.

55. *Earth is sustained by water, water by air and*
     air is sustained by space, but space itself
     is sustained by neither air, water nor earth.

In this and the following verses, we explore a fundamental relationship found in Middle Way philosophy: that between voidness and interdependence. Voidness is to be taken here as its highest form, i.e. buddha nature. Interdependence is the way in which the aggregates, elements and gates of perception generate each other. The relationship between the four dynamic elements and space will be used as a metaphor, to make the meaning easier to understand,

Earth is the material nature of something; its mass and solidity. More generally, it represents the constituent elements forming the body of any situation. Yet, were it not for the power of the water element – bonding, gravity and relational pulls – these constituent elements would simply fall apart. It is the cohesive power of the water element which keeps atomic particles revolving around each other, people in relationship with each other and so on and so forth, thereby maintaining earth's substantiality. Earth is sustained by water.

This fluid, bonding power is itself sustained by dynamic energy: the wind element, since it is movement (wind) which gives rise to gravitational pull. Water depends upon wind. Finally, movement depends on space for its very nature. Space, however, depends upon no other element. In Buddhism, as we explore these elements at work on physical, biological, meditational and many other levels, this order of dependency between them becomes apparent. To put it in modern terms, one might say that dynamics determine relationships and these shape the apparent reality of a situation.

In the world around us and within us, the earth, water and wind elements are in continual interdependent flux, giving rise to the play of phenomena. As we have seen, in the largest macro-cosmic sense, the universe is formed metaphorically by the wind mandala in space. Wind gives rise to the water mandala, which in turn gives rise to the earth. Yet unchanging space remains space, independent of these.

56. *In a similar way, the aggregates, elements and entrances*
are based upon action and the defilements.
Action and the defilements are always based
upon an erroneous way of using the mind.

We now apply the example of the previous verse. The building blocks of life in saṃsāra are the five aggregates, the eighteen elements of consciousness and the twelve gates of consciousness.

These are compared to the earth element. They are sustained by action (karma) and their motivating defilements (kleśa), compared here to the water element. Actions and defilements all occur through a false view of reality, compared to wind.

57. *This aberrant way of using the mind is based upon*
    the purity of the mind, yet mind's true nature
    is based upon none of the multitude of phenomena.

Just as the delusion of a snake is based upon the presence of a coiled rope, and would not occur if the floor were empty, so are the delusions making up the egocentric, dualistic way of using the mind based upon the presence of buddha nature: mind's true nature. Thus there is a whole and extremely complex build-up of errors, all based upon a misinterpretation of the true nature. The actions based on these errors end up fabricating the bodies of beings and the corpus of the universe. In this web of confusion, everything is interdependent, as vividly (if not necessarily accurately) described by the famous 'butterfly effect', whereby a butterfly beating its wings in a forest on one side of the world sets off a chain of events which indirectly causes a hurricane in on the other side. The true nature of mind does not, however, depend on any of these varied phenomena, just as a rope *is* a rope regardless of whether one person thinks it is a snake or another a piece of giant spaghetti.

58. *The aggregates, entrances and elements*
    should be known as being similar to earth.
    The actions and defilements of beings
    are to be known as similar to water.

The five aggregates are form, feelings, cognition, conditioning factors and consciousness. The gates of perception are the power to perceive, found in the five senses and mind, and the power to be perceived, of the five sense objects and mental objects. The eighteen elements are the three components – subject, object and interaction – of the five sense consciousnesses and mental consciousness. Together, these thirty-five make up the fabric of our lives and those of all sentient beings. They are the basis for pains and pleasures. As such, they are compared to the earth, which is the basis for terrestrial life. They also have a thick, dense quality.

Water spreads. It makes it possible for plants to grow from the earth. Our desires, needs, fears, jealousies, pride and other defilements spread to influence most of what we do. Water has a quality of instability, as do these karma and klesa.

59. *The improper way of using the mind is similar to wind whereas the true nature is like the element of space, having no basis and no abiding.*

All the dualistic thoughts – 'improper' both in the sense of not right and in the sense of not belonging – are like wind, subtle and invisible. Improper thoughts arise from basic ignorance of truth; of the true nature. They mistake it for a self or for solid realities and this inner 'movement' away from the centre of truth will stir up longings and fears which eventually lead to action and existence. They are the real flap of the butterfly wing that causes a hurricane.

The truth itself – buddha nature – is like space, inasmuch as it has no basis, i.e. no generating cause or supporting conditions, and it has no abiding. Abiding is the characteristic of all compounded things, which first come into being, then abide as something and finally disintegrate. Space and buddha nature are almost the only 'uncreateds' or 'uncompoundeds'.

60. *The improper way of using the mind abides within the true nature of mind. This improper way of using the mind gives rise to the defilements and to action*

The improper way of using the mind[10] is to ignore its true nature. The proper way to use it is to recognise it. In the rope–snake example, both delusion and correct perception are based upon the same input of visual data. The brain 'sees' differently due to the conceptual filters activated between the optic nerve and the final mental image. In regular life, beings use their five senses and the mind, yet all the incoming data is warped by habits of delusion, which filter the raw data and split it instantaneously into subject–object, I–other pigeonholes. If 'I' wants other: desire. If 'I' resents other: anger. If 'I' feels better than other: pride. And so on and so forth. From the desire spring actions to get what one needs. From anger spring actions to fight or flee from the enemy. From pride come actions designed to boost one's standing.

Were there not the truth, there would be nothing to distort. The improper exists because there is a proper.

61. *From the waters of action and the defilements*
arise the aggregates, entrances and elements,
occurring and disintegrating just like
all things that have beginning and end.

In this analogy, millions of tiny particles of earth swirl in the oceans. From time to time they come together in one place or another to make an island, which eventually crumbles back into the sea. Or, in terms of physics, the bonding and gravity in dynamic situations sometimes pull solid realities into being and, by a similar token, sometimes take them out of existence.

The actions of beings are determined by the way they think. Thoughts follow habitual tendencies which define personal needs and hates, and which reiterate all the other negative habits, such as jealousy and pride, on the one hand, as well as positive ones, such as generosity and loving care, on the other. The swirling ocean of the elements constituting the personal psychology causes one to become someone somewhere – a life here, a life there, a decade here as this, a decade there as that.

All compounded things have the characteristics of arising, existing and decaying. Beings' lives and life situations are the prime instances of this universal rule. As Buddha Sakyamuni so clearly pointed out, the comings and goings of beings are singularly marked by the sufferings of birth, ageing, sickness and death.

62. *The nature of mind is like the space element:*
    it has neither causes nor conditions
    nor these in combination,
    nor arising, abiding or destruction.

Something that arises through a prime cause and other circumstances is called a 'compounded' phenomenon. The true nature of mind – buddha nature – and space are not compounded. They arise from no single principal cause, nor from circumstances, such as immediate prevailing conditions. Thus they cannot be said to arise through the combination of prime and secondary causes, as is the case for all other phenomena.

Compounded phenomena all exhibit arising, abiding and disintegration. Space and buddha nature, being non-compounded, do not exhibit these characteristics.

63. *The true nature of mind, clarity, is, like space, unchanging,*
    never defiled by desire and so forth, the incidental ills
    which arise from an improper use of the mind.

The true nature of mind is clarity. Although confusion causes forgetfulness of clarity, it never defiles the clarity itself, which remains unchanged and unchanging, to be rediscovered whenever the drunkenness of confusion is over. Confusion and ignorance give rise to desire, the five other main defilements and the twenty subsidiary defilements, such as narcissism, hypocrisy and so forth. However far this snowballing effect takes one away from recognition of true reality and into the darker reaches of existence, the evils and harms it creates can never affect the true essence itself. For this reason, the defilements and karma are called 'incidental'.

It may seem callous to some to refer to the miseries of famines, holocausts, plagues and the like, or the inner sufferings of burning anger and jealousy, as 'incidental'. But that very reaction shows how far one has strayed from buddha nature and how much one ignores its truth and its magnitude. Dreamers and people under hypnosis may be having a terrible time, but that does not temper the fact that their apparent misery is a delusion and that they have, in fact, remained intact throughout.

64. *It is not produced by the waters*
 of karma, defilements and so forth,
 nor will it be burnt by the cruel fires
 of ageing, sickness and death.

Space is not produced by water and in no way depends upon it for sustenance. Likewise, buddha nature, the pure space of clear mind, is not produced by actions (karma) or the defilements or any of the saṃsāric realities that they generate. In no way does buddha nature depend upon them for its existence.

Besides not being a compounded production, buddha nature never disintegrates, deteriorates or disappears. Just as fire never even singes space, let alone consumes it, so neither do the cruel fires of ageing, sickness and death affect buddha nature in the slightest.

65. *One should know the three fires*
 of death, sickness and ageing
 to be similar, respectively, to
 the fires which blaze at the end of time,
 hellfire and ordinary fire.

Death, which brings a whole life to its end, is like the fire at the end of a cosmic age, when the entire universe burns out. Sickness is like hellfire on account of the intensity of suffering it produces. Ageing is the systematic deterioration of the whole system, like ordinary fires which gradually consume a stock of wood.

Changelessness of buddha nature in the partially-pure phase

66. *Free from birth, ageing, sickness and death,*
 they have realised the true nature, just as it is.
 On account of this, the wise
 have awakened compassion for beings and,
 even though free from the sufferings
 of birth and so forth, they demonstrate them.

Verses 66–78 will explore buddha nature in the partially pure phase, showing how the bodhisattvas in the ten levels of voidness realisation are completely beyond birth, ageing, sickness and death yet how, through compassion, they manifest these in order to help beings. Their buddha nature remains changeless throughout the play of these manifestations.

Those in the ten bodhisattva levels are described as being 'pure and impure'. They are pure inasmuch as saṃsāric suffering and its causes (action and defilements) have been removed by the root – the root being ego-delusion. They are eliminated for ever by constant contact with the truth of voidness. Yet they are impure inasmuch as subtle traces of ignorance and dualistic thought still recur, through habit. This verse introduces us to the main gist of what is described in more detail in the following verses.

67. *The deeply realised have radically removed*
    the sufferings of ageing, sickness and death.
    They are without them because their birth
    is not brought about by karma and what is defiled.

This verse underlines the fact that, despite appearing to others as being born and so forth, bodhisattvas' births and deaths in no way affect the innate clarity of their buddha nature.

Delusions, defilements and the actions they precipitate generate a powerful dynamic force of their own, carrying one from situation to situation of worldly existence. For as long as their repetitive cycles remain unbroken, they create rebirth after rebirth. Each of these lives will have its particular sufferings of birth, ageing, sickness and death, according to the karma one has created. As an 'ordinary being', i.e. an individual still caught up in karma, one can, thanks to the Buddha's teaching, systematically reduce these habits and progress along the spiritual path. One evolves through the *phase of accumulation*, in which negative habits are destroyed and good ones strengthened, and the *phase of integration*, in which one draws closer and closer to voidness. These phases are well explained, in greater detail, in the mahāyāna scriptures.[11]

The once-and-for-ever entry into direct realisation of the true nature of things is called the *stage of insight*. The first of the ten bodhisattva levels of deep realisation, it follows immediately after the moment when the last traces of karma and kleśa causing reincarnation are eliminated. The latter are like a final curtain over the light of truth. Their radical removal allows its radiance to shine through. From then onwards, through the remaining nine bodhisattva levels collectively called the *stage of cultivation*, one will be refining the realisation of voidness and removing subtle traces of saṃsāra – no longer strong enough to cause rebirth but still present as habitual thoughts. One then becomes a perfect Buddha – the *stage of no more training*.

In these last three phases – insight, cultivation of insight and perfect buddhahood – there is no rebirth in saṃsāra. Yet, to help other beings, Buddhas and bodhisattvas in those levels still appear to be born, to age, to be ill at times and to die.

68. *Since they have seen the truth, just as it is,*
    their compassionate nature shows
    birth, ageing, sickness and death,
    even though they have transcended birth and the rest.

The cause for their manifesting birth, ageing, sickness and death is the non-conceptual compassion innate to buddha nature, as opposed to the ego-illusions which produce saṃsāric birth. This topic alone merits considerable reflection.

Bodhisattvas' freedom from birth, ageing, sickness and death, and their recognition of the true nature of things, so magnificent, gives them a tremendous and spontaneous compassion for other beings. A rough metaphor for attaining the first bodhisattva level could be that of awakening from a bad dream to discover a beautiful, peaceful, starlit night, and naturally feeling compassion for others sleepers who are still writhing in terror from their own nightmares.

69. *Those blinded by ignorance see the Victors' children,*
    who have realised this changeless true nature,
    as though they were born and so forth.
    This is indeed a wonder!

This verse and the next highlight the particular quality these bodhisattvas possess of relating to other beings and inspiring them to set their hearts on enlightenment.

Let us continue the simile, and imagine that it were possible for the awakened person to manifest in the sleepers' dreams, in a way that would make sense in each of their delusions, so as gradually to ease their horrors and help them also to wake up gracefully.

Bodhisattvas manifest in the lives of sentient beings in ways which concur with the latter's particular perceptions of reality. It has to be that way, for these bodhisattvas are too subtle for our senses to perceive. The grossness of our minds' ignorance makes it impossible for us to perceive their worlds which are those of pure buddhafields. Fortunately, they can and do manifest in our worlds, appearing to be beings similar to ourselves, undergoing birth, ageing, sickness and death. This permits us to relate to them and receive their teachings – as formal teachings or an example to follow. They show us how to cope with life's ills, as well as with the practical aspects of meditation and compassion in action.

Just as one sighted person can lead hundreds of blind people to safety, so can one bodhisattva who possesses 'the eyes of primordial wisdom', i.e. who realises the clear-light nature of mind, lead many other beings out of mind's delusions and into a recognition of its clarity. Were their great compassionate help absent, the world would flounder in blind confusion forever. As it is, bodhisattvas manifest in all sorts of forms, as we shall discover later in this text, and bring the light of wisdom to ordinary beings. This is indeed a wonder.

70. *Those who have reached the domain of realisation*
    appear within the field of experience of the immature.
    Thus the skills and compassion of these friends for beings
    are truly excellent.

These bodhisattvas have extremely subtle bodies of light, invisible to the human eye. Their existence has none of the gross substantiality of existence in our world or the other worlds of the material cosmos. They have gone far beyond the five aggregates of which our lives are composed. Nevertheless, from that sublime state, they manage to appear within the gross fabric of existence in a way which (as far as our subjective experience is concerned) we can touch, see, hear and communicate with. They do this spontaneously, without planning and thought, and without having to fabricate the defiled chains of cause-and-effect which normally give rise to bodies.

In general, the saṃgha are referred to as the finest friends for beings, as they truly bring them happiness. Realised bodhisattvas are the very best saṃgha. The compassion and skill which well forth from their buddha nature, enabling them to be experienced by others, are excellent: excellent both in their nature and in the impartial and unlimited way they help beings.

71. *Even though they have transcended everything wordly,*
    they do not leave the world,
    acting within the world for the world
    but unblemished by wordly impurity.

The previous verses referred to the marvellous ability of all these bodhisattvas, from the first through to the tenth level, to manifest in impure beings' subjective realities. This verse focuses on the pure conduct of bodhisattvas of the second to seventh levels. It may remind many of the saying, 'In the world but not of the world'. Here we find at play the combined power of compassion and skilful means (wisdom), mentioned in the previous verse.

Through the power of their wisdom, they have transcended all worldly activity. Through the power of their compassion, they never abandon the worlds of various beings but act within them in order to bring the immature to maturity. Although this means interacting with other beings, the latter's defilements and pettiness never corrupt the pure mind, intention and action of these bodhisattvas. Although they bring the light of wisdom into our lives, the darkness of our confusion does not affect theirs.

72. *A lotus, born of water, by water remains unblemished.*
    Similarly, even though they are born in the world,
    by worldly beings they are unblemished.

An example to help us understand the above is that of the lotus. It grows in muddy ponds yet emerges in unblemished beauty, without a trace of dirt and slime on its petals, gracing the pool with its presence. The quality of these profoundly realised bodhisattvas is to remain totally unaffected by the confusion, neurosis and emotions of the beings they help. In practical terms, this leads to what is (for those being helped) a novel sort of intense relationship. In worldly situations, one usually expects a certain complicity from friends, relatives and lovers. The price of friendship is often a two-way sharing. In the process, people influence each other and personalities change accordingly. There is no relationship more intense than the trust and intimacy between a bodhisattva teacher and disciple. But because it is, in fact, the dialogue between truth and ignorance, it must remain a one-way relationship. This new sort of intimacy, in which one should never expect a worldly form of friendship, may take some getting used to.

In vajrayāna Buddhism, it takes the form of the guru–disciple bond. For it to work fully, the disciple must train in relating to the guru as the presence of enlightened wisdom and, by the same token, untrain the reflexes that want to relate to the teacher as just another human being. Thus it is said,

> *By relating to the teacher as a Buddha, one gains the Buddha's blessing. By relating to the teacher as a bodhisattva, one gains the bodhisattva's blessing and by relating to the teacher as a human being, one gains a wise human being's blessing. If you feel no devotion at all, you will receive no blessing.*[12]

73. *To accomplish their task, their brilliant intelligence*
    is like a fire blazing incessantly.
    They are at all times profoundly immersed
    in meditative union with peace.

This verse focuses upon the specific and irreversible qualities of bodhisattvas in the eighth and ninth levels. They are more advanced than those of the first seven levels because they no longer have distinct meditation and post-meditation experience, although there still persists a very subtle difference between relative and ultimate. They are constantly absorbed in deep meditation which itself is *peace*, because habitual concepts no longer disturb the profound absorption. The word used for their absorption in Tibetan is *snyoms 'jug* pronounced *nyomjook*. It is a technical term often found in Buddhist meditation texts under its Sanskrit form *samapatti*. Although the etymological sense is always the same – that of balance and deep penetration – its actual meaning will vary greatly depending upon the actual meditation practised. We find it used in the hinayāna descriptions of the eight dhyāna, in mahāyāna descriptions of buddha nature meditation, as here, and in vajrayāna descriptions of subtle body meditations. The experience and realisation of the meditator will be quite specific in each case.

These bodhisattvas' constant, deep absorption in mind's true nature, undisturbed by conceptual speculation, gives them an incessant and powerful radiance of activity to help beings. Before these levels, there is a slight on-off quality, due to the mind being more deeply absorbed at some moments than others, on account of superficial thought activity. This can be compared to having to tend to a fire of half-dry wood, in order to keep it burning brightly. From these extremely pure levels on, there is a mighty activity, compared to the roaring blaze of a fire of very dry wood, which cares for itself, growing brighter and brighter.

74. *Due to previous impetus and being concept-free,
    no effort need be made to bring beings to maturity.*

Bodhisattvas on the tenth level have all the qualities mentioned above. They have removed all but the most subtle of residual conditioning and, through the previous nine levels, gathered an enormous impetus of goodness. On the first level they could already emanate in one hundred worlds simultaneously to help other beings. By the tenth level, the number of their emanations is inconceivable and each is accomplishing virtue with consummate skill. They are on the threshold of perfect enlightenment. Thus the extent, profundity and quality of their altruistic activity surpasses even that of the previous levels. The innumerable times that they have developed the bodhisattva wish, coupled with the momentum of goodness they have been building up through the previous levels, makes their action quite spontaneous and effortless.

75. *They know precisely the ways and means*
to train anyone and whichever teaching,
physical form, mode of conduct or action
would be most appropriate.

One should not confuse these bodhisattvas' spontaneity with lack of precision. Their activity responds exactly to the requirements of the beings they are helping. Each of the latter has the feeling that the bodhisattva was tailor-made for himself or herself. Even to see them sitting, moving, resting or speaking becomes a teaching in itself. Just as one sees one's own perfect image in a pure mirror, one receives just the teachings one requires when in their presence. Thus some will see miracles, others will experience pure conduct and yet others will receive intellectual information. It is always timely, never a minute too early or a minute too late.

76. *In this way, those of unhindered intelligence*
excellently engage themselves in benefiting
beings as limitless as the sky,
continually and spontaneously.

Tenth-level bodhisattvas are called 'those of unhindered intelligence' on account of the unimpeded way in which the clarity of their buddha nature manifests. Their level is called the *cloud of dharma* since it showers down teachings like a great monsoon raincloud, ripening all sorts of plants and crops. Their activity reaches as far as there are sentient beings, i.e. to the limits of space itself. It is continuous both through its constancy and through the endless number of beings to be helped. It is spontaneous because of these bodhisattvas' transcendence of duality.

77. *The way in which these bodhisattvas act in the worlds,*
to help beings, during their post-meditation phase,
is the same as the tathāgatas' way of truly liberating beings.

Both tenth-level bodhisattvas and perfect buddhas act in an extremely pure way to help beings emerge from the ocean of worldly confusion. This aspect of their manifestation is called *rjes.thob* in Tibetan (pronounced *jay-top*) – a word which usually means 'post-meditation' and literally means 'subsequent' or 'ancillary'. To gain some understanding of its meaning in this context, one must consider the gulf which exists, initially, between everyday experience and the inner quiet of sitting meditation. With the development of meditation, this boundary blurs. The awareness of meditation is carried into everyday life and the compassionate experience of life gives loving warmth to meditation. When meditation is no longer a specific act but a non-stop activity, the term *rjes.thob* comes to refer to the aspect of it which concerns helping others, as is the case here.

Through such shared abilities as the six types of clear cognition, the ten powers[13] and so forth, and the fact that their minds rest in sameness, the altruistic activity of tenth-level bodhisattvas is considered to be similar to that of buddhas. This is in the area of *rjes.thob*.

78. *Although this is true, the differences
between these bodhisattvas and the buddhas
are like those between the Earth and an atom
or between an ox's hoof-print and the ocean.*

Although their activity to help others may be similar, there are enormous differences in their degree of spiritual development, as measured by their qualities of purification and realisation. Buddhas have total, perfect purity and have brought forth every possible quality. They have achieved all that can be achieved and, having completed their own path of purification, are no longer 'developing'. The blockages remaining in tenth-level bodhisattvas are far more subtle than the ordinary mind could ever imagine. They are the last, finest and most difficult-to-remove of all. Inasmuch as they still have this work to complete, these bodhisattvas are still evolving. For all their marvellous qualities, they are far from having the qualities of a Buddha.

To provide us with some idea of the difference between these two types of exalted being, the text gives the example of the difference in size between a mote of dust and a planet. The second example is that of the water that could gather in an ox's hoof-print and the water in the ocean. Note that in both examples the differences are not in the nature of the material – earth in the first example and water in the second – but in its extent.

Changelessness of buddha nature in the completely-pure phase

79. *Because it has inexhaustible qualities,*
    its nature is not to alter.
    It is the refuge of beings
    because it has no limits in the future.
    Right to the very end, it is always non-dual
    because it is non-conceptual.
    It is also of indestructible character
    because it is non-compounded, by nature.

This verse introduces us to the main points of changelessness in the completely pure phase: that of perfect buddhas. As has been made clear, buddha nature itself never changes throughout the three phases of ordinary beings, bodhisattvas and buddhas. When a tenth-level bodhisattva achieves perfect, total enlightenment, the buddha nature remains as it always was, i.e. dharmakāya. It is just that it is no longer veiled, even by the subtlest forms of ignorance. At such a time:

▸ Its permanence manifests as an inexhaustible wealth of qualities. These qualities never change, never deteriorate.
▸ Being beyond birth and death, it lasts for ever. As it will remain until saṃsāra's end, it is a true refuge for beings.
▸ Being non-conceptual, it has none of the duality which fractions things into temporal or spatial realities, into saṃsāra and nirvāṇa.
▸ Never having been created, it will never disintegrate.

80. *This has no birth because it is permanent,*
    no death because it is enduring,
    no ailment because it is peace and
    no ageing because it is unchanging.

Buddha nature manifests as dharmakāya, sambhogakāya and nirmāṇakāya, to buddhas, bodhisattvas and ordinary beings respectively. In these three instances, the syllable *kāya* means *body* or *embodiment*. The three kāya are not three separate bodies but simply three different ways of experiencing the same thing.

Buddha nature – dharmakāya, the essence of all three kāya – is not a 'body' which is born, ages and dies. It is beyond the birth, ageing, sickness and death which characterise all corporeal existences, from the gross bodies of beings in the six realms through to the bodies of light of bodhisattvas and arhats. Even though the latter are spiritual beings of great value and tremendous quality, they are still 'beings' which come and go, as opposed to buddha nature, which is the timeless, ultimate state, beyond coming and going, as is explained in the following verses.

81. *It has no birth in a mental form because it is permanent.*
    It has no inconceivable death and transmigration,
    because it is everlasting

▸ Being permanent and changeless, this true nature of mind is never born physically at one point or another, not even as the subtle mental bodies of arhats are born.
▸ As it lasts for ever, it will never die, not even the 'unimaginable death' of the arhat's light body or the subtle death associated with transmigrating to another state.

82. *It is unharmed by the disease of the finer imprints of karma,*
    because it is peace.
    It has no ageing produced by untainted karma
    because it is immutable.

- It has no ailment of ignorance, not even in the subtlest of latent forms of ignorance as found in arhats, because its peacefulness knows no subject and object, no saṃsāra and nirvāṇa.
- It is the immutable swastika,[14] being even without the mental creations of untainted karma that are the lot of arhats.

83. *This uncreated space has the attributes of permanence, etc.,*
    which should be known respectively
    through the first pair of verses, and likewise the next pair
    and the next pair and the last.

The term 'uncreated space' refers mainly to voidness, while 'buddha nature' refers to clarity. This verse associates the four attributes of voidness – permanence, eternity, peace and immutability – with their respective qualities of having no birth, death, sickness or ageing, thus pairing together the four points made in verse 79 with the four made in verses 81 and 82. Verse 84, which follows, has been added to the Tibetan version of the root text from Asaṅga's own commentary. It explains the reasons linking these sets of four points.

84. *Being endowed with inexhaustible qualities,*
    it has the attribute of permanence, the quality of not altering.
    Because it equals the furthest end,
    its attribute is everlastingness, the nature of a refuge.
    Because its very character is not to conceptualise,
    it has the attribute of peace: the non-dual true nature.
    As its qualities are not things fabricated,
    its attribute is immutability – the changeless nature.

The nirvāṇa represented by the purity of dharmakāya is not like that attained by arhats. Their nirvāṇa is simply the cessation of suffering and their state, although long-lasting, is not eternal. Its qualities are the product of their meditation. Dharmakāya is the ultimate 'nirvāṇa without remains'.[15] It will never alter into another state and its innate qualities are inexhaustible. It is permanent.

It co-exists with every instance of saṃsāra, whatever and

wherever it may seem to be. This co-existence is not inert but supportive, aiding beings continuously and unfailingly. Thus it truly possesses the quality of a refuge.

The very nature of its voidness is absence of concepts, peace. As its qualities are not fabrications due to causes, they will never end. Thus it is the Changeless Nature.

10. Inseparability of its Qualities

It is the dharmakāya. It is the tathāgata.
It is the highest truth. It is the ultimately-true nirvāṇa.
Like the sun and its rays, these aspects are inseparable:
thus there is no nirvāṇa apart from buddhahood itself.

These four lines are a continuation of verse 84 above. Buddha nature has many names, according to which of its facets one wishes to highlight. Here we find four key names being underlined as being one and the same thing. It is:

- *dharmakāya*, the 'embodiment of all things' because it is the true nature of all beings and phenomena. It is the one rope behind a myriad different snake illusions.
- *tathāgata*, 'become That', inasmuch as it is what one becomes at the fruition of one's path.
- *noble truth* or *truth of the realised*, since to understand it and experience it directly is to see anything and everything as it truly is, and in particular the natures of suffering and liberation.
- *ultimately true nirvāṇa*, being not simply the nirvāṇa of arhats, which amounts to undoing the conditioning of confusion, but total integration with true reality. The former is sometimes referred to as 'compounded nirvāṇa' whereas the latter is 'uncompounded nirvāṇa'.

Although the four meanings above each have their specific sense, they cannot be separated from buddha nature itself, nor from each other. Like the sun and its light, they are indissociable. In particular, there is no true nirvāṇa until one has attained this essence in its totality. All other 'nirvāṇa' are only true in the etymological sense of being 'conditions beyond suffering' but they are not *the* nirvāṇa as they do not possess the endless qualities of wisdom, love and power that are part of this buddha nature.

85. *In brief, since the meaning of this untainted domain*
    is classified into four aspects, dharmakāya and so forth,
    the latter should be known as four synonyms for it:

86. *that inseparable from the buddha qualities,*
    the achievement of the potential, just as it is,
    the true nature, neither false nor unreliable and
    that having, from time immemorial, the very nature of peace.

These four synonyms highlight different aspects of buddha nature, the untainted domain:

- *dharmakāya* shows the inseparability of its qualities, such as the ten powers, the four fearlessnesses, eighteen distinctive qualities, etc.
- *tathāgata* shows us that the causal basis for buddhahood has been in all beings since beginningless time.
- *highest truth* points out the unfailing and totally reliable nature of this essence. It contains no falsehood or expedient truth. It never fades into something else and is known by realised beings and buddhas, who recognise its presence in beings throughout the dreams of their illusions. When someone properly recognises this timeless nature, they attain highest truth and become a realised being, an *arya*.
- *nirvāṇa* indicates that this is the timeless state to be discovered when one has gone beyond suffering. It is free from all impurities, pain and ignorance.

87. *Buddhahood is every aspect of true, perfect enlightenment.*
    Nirvāṇa is total removal of impurities and conditioning.
    In the true sense, these are not different.

Nirvāṇa means many things. In itself, it simply denotes an absence of suffering: 'suffering transcended'. For hinayāna Buddhists, the Buddha transcended worldly suffering and its causes – karma and defilement. He removed these totally and radically, along with any trace of conditioning. Thus, he is defined primarily by what he is not. For Middle Way mahayanists, he is defined not only by what he is not, but also by what he is: the plenitude of dharmakāya's inseparable qualities, and in particular the two forms of primordial wisdom; thusness wisdom and all-encompassing wisdom.

These two are not different, since the qualities of wisdom are revealed by removing the impurities which veiled them. However, absolutely every trace of impurity, even the most subtle, needs to go before perfect buddhahood is manifest. This is where the nirvāṇa of the arhats falls short. Subtle forms of ignorance and latent conditioning still remain in it. Although arhats abide in a state of sublime peace, they are cut off from the vast magnificence of buddha nature. By removing their subtle veils of ignorance, great nirvāṇa is achieved and that is buddhahood. This is well shown by the two syllables of *sangs.rgyas*, the Tibetan word for Buddha. The first means totally purified and the second means totally blossomed.

88. *The characteristic of liberation*
    is to be inseparable from its qualities –
    replete, numberless, inconceivable and stainless.
    This liberation is the tathāgata.

Whereas the previous verse focused upon the inseparability, or non-duality, of nirvāṇa and buddhahood, this verse focuses upon the inseparability of four aspects within liberation. There are various degrees of liberation to be achieved on the dharma path. The ultimate liberation is to attain buddha nature, in which case the word *liberation* implies:

▸ the six pāramitā are complete, since every impurity has been removed. One should understand the development of each pāramitā not as being the construction of a quality, such as generosity, but the removal of its opposite (selfishness), thereby letting the natural generosity of the true nature manifest. Equally, one does not develop right conduct, but

removes wrong conduct – and so on and so forth. When the six pāramitā are completely unveiled, buddhahood is manifest, replete with all its qualities.
▸ these qualities are numberless. Although the scriptures may enumerate ten powers, four fearlessnesses, etc., one should be aware that these are not limiting.
▸ the extent, power and nature of these qualities are inconceivable.
▸ they are stainless, free from any trace of defilement or duality.

88. (Contd.) *Compare this to artists specialised in drawing,*
one part or another of the body.
However, whichever part one knew,
the others had not fully mastered.

This verse continues with an example. It is that of some hypothetical artists, each a master at drawing one or another part of the human body. One draws heads to perfection, another hands, and so on and so forth. However, each of their masteries does not extend to the special domain of the others.

89. *Their king and ruler gives them a canvas, with the order,*
'All of you must now away and paint my picture.'

The monarch of their land summons them so that a royal portrait can be painted. As each is such a specialist, the hands, face and so forth will each be accurately reproduced.

90. *Having received the command,*
they commence the painting as best they can.
However, one of them departs,
leaving for some far and foreign land.

The painting gets under way. It is probably a huge canvas, and each artist has his own part to paint, the parts to be assembled once complete. Unfortunately, all does not go well. One artist, for reasons of his own, leaves, never to return.

91. *Since the man was missing,*
    through having gone to another land,
    the portrait, in all its parts, could not be finished.
    This is the example.

Therefore the portrait could not be finished and the final canvas was never stitched together. The king's intended portrait could not be achieved. No matter how beautiful or complete each of the parts, they fail to serve their final purpose if they are not all present. Imagine how a giant, classical portrait (modern art weakens this example!) would look ridiculous and unsatisfying if the mouth or nose were missing.

92. *The artists are generosity, right conduct, patience and so on.*
    Voidness, endowed with every finest aspect,
    is said to be like the royal portrait.

Buddha nature is referred to here by another of its epithets: voidness endowed with every finest aspect. This term is very dear to vajrayāna Buddhism. It shows the essence of mind – buddha nature – to be the embodiment of the six pāramitā: those of generosity, right conduct, forbearance, diligence, meditation and wisdom. Pāramitā means 'highest and most perfect'. Thus buddha nature embodies the highest and most perfect generosity etc.

Only when each pāramitā is perfectly present is there perfect buddhahood, as denoted by the word Tathāgata in the previous verses. Just as the king's portrait cannot come into being until all the constituent parts are completed, each in an expert way, so neither will buddha nature be revealed in its fullness until each pāramitā has been brought to absolute perfection. This, indeed, is the work of the ten bodhisattva levels. Once attained, buddha nature reveals itself to be the inseparability of the pāramitā, just as the hands, face and so forth are all part of the one king.

93. *Prajñā, jñāna and perfect liberation are like*
    the sun's light beams and orb,
    being respectively bright, radiant and pure
    and being inseparable.

No examples for buddha nature are ever one hundred percent satisfactory. That of the king's portrait helps us to understand the multitude of qualities which constitute buddha nature. This present example, of the sun, highlights the inseparability of wisdom, in its two aspects of prajñā and jñāna, and liberation. Prajñā is profound wisdom related to the relative and ultimate characteristics of things. Jñāna is primordial wisdom of the absolute. Liberation is freedom from the veils of defilements, dualistic concepts and meditation-blockages. Whatever prajñā exists in the four inseparable qualities of dharmakāya, tathāgata, ultimate truth and nirvāṇa, is like the light of the sun. Whatever jñāna exists in those four is like the beams of sunlight. Whatever liberation is present is like the orb of the sun.

94. *Therefore, until the achievement of buddhahood,*
    Nirvāṇa is never achieved,
    just as without sunlight and sunbeams,
    the sun could never be seen.

Prajñā and jñāna are present as seeds or potentials in ordinary beings. As the various veils are removed, their light of truth can shine more and more. Wisdom develops and reveals the true nature of things. The total unveiling of this 'sun-orb' of full liberation will, in itself, allow the light and beams to shine and radiate to their fullest. In other words, prajñā and jñāna are needed for liberation to be achieved and, conversely, full prajñā and jñāna only come with perfect liberation. They are one and the same thing. Wisdom reveals wisdom. Wisdom liberates the veils of ignorance which block wisdom. But, in particular, the emphasis here is on the fact that the profoundest mahāyāna wisdom of voidness is needed to achieve true nirvāṇa. The partial wisdom of ego-voidness which brings arhats nirvāṇa is not at all the same thing. It cannot reveal buddha nature.

Notes

1 'Gems of Dharma, Jewels of Freedom'pps 6–13.

2 *Tirthika* is the Sanskrit term (Tib. mu *stegs pa*) used to describe followers of non-Buddhists faiths. This term is sometimes translated as 'heretics'. This is unfortunate, as it has been explained to us (by Khempo Tsultim) as being complimentary rather than derogatory. It means those 'on the edge', 'on the threshold' and gives a sense of being well on the way, perhaps almost there, but not quite. Khempo described it as someone with one foot on the ladder. He explained that the moral values and contemplative experience of other faiths takes people away from the world and in a spiritual direction. It is just that the spirituality is out-of-synch. with ultimate reality.

3 The absorption attained through concentration meditation. According to which dhyāna is being practised, there can be mental and/or physical bliss.

4 *Limitless, great compassionate love* is the term used in bodhisattva scriptures to indicate that love and compassion are fused as one, that this is not mere sentiment but great love, supported by all the qualities of the *pāramitā*, and finally that it is limitless, since its scope embraces all sentient beings, who are without limit.

5 The differences between the arhat state and buddhahood are dealth with on several occasions in this text (see index). For more details of the arhat's awakening, see 'Gems of Dharma, Jewels of Freedom' pps. 8–10.

6 Gampopa was a Buddhist teacher of the highest order. One of his epithets is Dvagspo Rinpoche, the 'Precious Master from Dvagspo' and the ensemble of Kagyu traditions, i.e. the four greater and eight minor schools, are known collectively as the Dvagspo Kagyu, in his honour. This is because they all stem from him and his disciples. His greatness lay in the fact that he embodied the qualities of every level of Buddhism. He was a perfect monk, a great scholar, an exemplar of the bodhisattva way and an enlightened yogin, inheriting the entire wealth of teachings transmitted by the Indian masters Tilopa, Naropa and Maitripa. His life was predicted by Buddha Sakyamuni, in the *samādhi-rajasūtra*. His book, translated by us as 'Gems of Dharma, Jewels of Freedom' and also in translation as 'Jewel Ornament of Liberation', is the principal mainstream Buddhist handbook of the Kagyu tradition.

7 Gems of Dharma, pps. 6–13

8 See 'Gems' pps.11–12 on activated or dormant mahāyāna potential.

9 See 'Gems', chapter on the levels pps. 268–289.

10 Skt: *ayonisomanasikara*, Tib: *tshul bzhin ma yin pa yid la byed pa*

11 See 'Gems', chapters on paths and levels.

12 Quoted from Jamgon Kongtrul the First's "Torch of Certainty", in which he attributes these words to the 'great Kagyu masters'.

13 See 'Gems', p. 284.

14 *Swastika* – an ancient Asian symbol of the unchanging. This sacred, and usually multicoloured, symbol, in use for many thousands of years, has nothing to do with the evil of Nazism, which took a black form of it as its emblem.

15 There are four categories of Arhat: those with and without 'adornment' (of meditation prowess) and those with and without 'remainder' (of suffering as a result of karma).

C. Nine examples showing how buddha nature is changeless while concealed

95. *Thus has the Victors' essence been described
through a tenfold presentation.
One should understand, from the following examples,
its presence within the confines of the defilements.*

After this appreciation of buddha nature from ten different angles, the text now gives nine examples to help us establish confidence in its changelessness. This is very helpful, since one may find it hard to believe that the perfection of Buddha exists within the evil or mediocre situations of daily life.

The Buddha, when he taught, often gave reasons proving the truth of what he was saying. Rather than preaching a take-it-or-leave-it dogma, he encouraged his listeners to confirm for themselves the validity of what he was pointing out. Some teachings are easy to verify. It suffices to observe life, and then reflect for a while, to appreciate their perspicacity. Other things, such as karma or the higher states of mind, cannot be verified directly by the senses and therefore require indirect proof. A watertight system of Buddhist logic evolved in India. It served both to investigate the more subtle points of existence and to defend the Buddhist conclusions in debate with other faiths.

Inferential proofs require two main things. The indicator, or 'sign', must be both valid and universally applicable. Take, for instance, the deduction of the existence of fire behind a hill, through seeing a plume of smoke. Smoke must be a valid sign of fire; it would be pointless to say that there must be fire behind the hill because one can see, say, a treetop. Treetops are not signs of fire whereas smoke is. But more than this, the sign has to be universally applicable. It would not be if, for instance, smoke were also produced by something other than fire. In the development of inferential proofs, examples can be very important. The nine examples given in this section are first used (in verses 96–129) to make it clear that something beautiful and precious can remain unchanged and unaffected while hidden by something unpleasant and changing. Then verses 130–155 show a deeper and more specific point brought out by each example.

96. *Similar to a buddha in a decaying lotus,*
    honey amidst bees, grains in their husks,
    gold in filth, a treasure under the ground,
    shoots and the like piercing through fruits,
    a buddha statue inside tattered rags,

97. *a monarch in a poor and wretched woman's womb,*
    or a precious image inside some clay,
    this nature is present within all beings
    but obscured by the impurity of passing defilement.

These two verses simply list the nine examples and say what they all exemplify – buddha nature.

98. *The impurities correspond to the lotus, the insects, the husks,*
    filth, the ground, the fruit, the tattered rags,
    the woman severely afflicted by burning sorrows, and clay.
    The buddha, honey, grains, gold, treasure,
    nyagrodha tree, precious statue,
    supreme ruler of the continents and precious image
    correspond to this supreme, immaculate nature.

In the nine examples, various sorts of blockage and defilement will be exemplified by nine impure coverings: a lotus, insects, husks of grains, filth, dirt, a rotting fruit, tattered rags, a pitiful pregnant pauper and clay. The various qualities of buddha nature will be exemplified by a buddha, honey, grains, gold, a treasure, a mighty tree, a precious statue, a universal ruler and a precious image.

Each example will now be given through three verses. The first gives the example, the second shows what is exemplified and the third relates the example and buddha nature.

first example: a Buddha in a decaying lotus

99. Someone endowed with pure divine vision, upon seeing
a tathāgata shining and adorned with a thousand signs,
within a rotting lotus, would remove him from the prison
formed by the petals of the 'water-born'.

100. Similarly the sugatas, with their buddha eyes,
see their own nature even in those in the worst of hells.
Their nature being compassion present until the very end,
they bring freedom from all those veils.

101. Once the sugata within the closed, decaying lotus
had been seen by one with divine vision,
the petals were sliced asunder.
Likewise, when the buddhas see
the essence of perfect buddhahood in beings,
yet obscured by an impure shell of desire, hatred and so on,
these victors, through compassion, destroy such obscuration.

In this story, a person or god possessing clairvoyance knows that a real Buddha, physically radiant with all the major and minor signs of perfect being, has somehow ended up inside a smelly, decaying lotus flower and is therefore invisible to other beings. 'Water-born' is one of many Indian names for lotuses. In order that this buddha's magnificence can be seen by all, the clairvoyant cuts away the rotting lotus petals.

As buddha nature is like nothing else, nothing other than a real Buddha can be used to exemplify it. In this rather strange example, the Buddha is peacefully residing within the lotus, which represents desire and all the aggression, jealousy and so forth which grow out of our desires and needs – in brief, all the defilements. The person with divine vision represents the Sugatas, i.e. the Buddhas. Their 'wisdom-eyes', i.e. their primordial wisdom, recognise buddha nature within each and every being – even those in the worst of hells. Although the buddha nature is already there, it is unrecognised and ineffective. Through their great compassion, which endures until each being's saṃsāra is finished, Buddhas teach them how to cut away the 'petals' of passions, desires, anger and so forth, and thus liberate the buddha within.

second example: honey amid bees

102. *A clever person trying to get the honey amid the swarm*
would, having spotted it, employ skilful means
to separate that honey from the host of bees
and then actually take hold of it.

103. *Likewise, the great sages with their omniscient vision,*
upon seeing the honey-like causal basis, the essence,
bring total radical relinquishment of bee-like obscurations.

104. *The person trying to get honey surrounded by myriad bees*
disperses them all and procures the honey just as planned.
The untainted intelligence in all beings is like the honey.
The Buddhas, skilful victors over bee-like defilements,
are like the person.

A clever person, seeing a swarm of bees, knows that there may be honey to be had, even though what he or she actually sees is something quite scaring and offputting. The person will use skilful means, such as smoke, in order to calm or disperse the bees and eventually get the honey without being stung. He or she ends up with a tasty treat.

Like this, the buddhas, with their eyes of primordial wisdom, recognise the untainted intelligence of sweet, nourishing buddha nature within sentient beings, even within their anger and violence. Like the bee-keeper, they find the skilful methods which allow the essence to be obtained and the harmful swarming defilements to be radically removed. The precious reward is obtained.

third example: grains in their husks

105. *Humans cannot use kernels of grain still in their husks.*
 Whoever wants them as food must first de-husk them.

106. *Similarly, while buddhahood, present in all beings*
 but combined with defilement impurities,
 has not been freed from the defilements,
 buddha activity in the three realms will not be accomplished.

107. *Incompletely-threshed kernels of rice, buckwheat and barley*
 that are not fully de-husked still have husks and beards.
 Just as these are not usable, tasty food for humans
 likewise the 'lord of all qualities', present in living beings,
 and whose form has not yet been freed from defilements,
 will not give the taste of dharma joy
 to beings afflicted by the hunger of defilements.

Grains are one of the most nourishing foods. Yet, to be eaten by humans, they must first be de-husked. Wheat, barley and so forth need to be threshed so that their inedible 'beards', husks and other chaff are discarded, leaving the edible grain.

Even a whole silo full of unthreshed grain is completely useless as food and will remain so for as long as the useful parts remain mixed up with the useless ones. While the seed of enlightenment – buddha nature – remains within beings yet mixed up, covered up, with the impurities of defilements, it cannot fulfil its function: that of nourishing the three realms of beings with enlightened activity. The three realms are the three domains of mind's activity: those of the senses, formal mental activity and formless mental activity. Once the chaff of defilements has been thrashed away, this wholesome grain will give the delicious taste of truth and dharma to beings.

fourth example: gold in filth

108. *The gold of a man on a journey fell
into a place containing much rotting filth.
Being itself of incorruptible nature
the gold remained there for many a century
in that same place yet quite unchanged.*

109. *A god with great divine vision, upon noticing it there,
told someone, 'There is gold here. Once you have cleansed
this most prized thing, do what can be done
with such a precious substance.'*

110. *In a similar way, the Victors see the quality of beings
which has sunken into the filth-like defilements
and shower upon them a rain of true dharma
that they may be purified of defilement's mire.*

111. *Just as the gold fallen into the place rotting with garbage
was seen there by a god who, with great insistence,
showed the man that most beautiful of things
so that it might be completely cleansed,
so also do the Victors perceive
that most precious perfect buddhahood
within all beings has fallen in defilement's great mire.
Therefore they teach them all the dharma
in order that they may be purified.*

The example itself is fairly obvious from the verses. Long ago, someone had lost some gold, which fell into a garbage-heap. For centuries it lay among the filth, with perhaps even more filth being added. A clairvoyant god or person noticed it there and told a passer-by of its existence, exhorting him to rescue the gold and turn it to good use. This the man does and becomes rich.

Likewise, the wisdom-eyes of Buddhas recognise buddha nature in sentient beings, even though it is hidden and obscured by the various defilements, compared here to all the different sorts of rubbish that can accumulate in a garbage-tip. Buddhas tell people about their buddha-nature and help them cleanse off the impurities by showering down a rain of teachings.

Note that it is precisely because there is rubbish that the Buddhas teach. Otherwise buddha-nature would be obvious and no path of purification would be needed. Also note that were there no 'gold', i.e. buddha nature, there would be no point in spending so much time understanding and working with rubbish. Although so much of what we have to do involves facing up to angers and desires, the whole point of the exercise transcends them and is concerned with the qualities that they have been disguising.

Gold is immutable by nature and can remain uncorrupted for centuries, even in the filthiest of rubbish. Once cleansed, it has all its qualities and value. Likewise buddha nature is hidden by defilements yet not affected by them. Once purification has been completed, all its value and qualities become evident.

Gold can be very useful. But while it is covered with rubbish, it remains useless. Just as the man needs a clairvoyant to tell him about the presence of gold in rubbish, so do we need the Buddhas to point out the power of wisdom lying latent within our instability and troubles. Just as the man became rich through the gold and then was able to do many things, individuals can discover their inner richness of thusness wisdom and all-encompassing wisdom. This will bring all sorts of benefits and eventually carry them to enlightenment.

fifth example: a treasure buried beneath the earth

112. *Were there an inexhaustible treasure underground,*
beneath a poor man's hovel,
neither would he know of its presence
nor could the treasure tell him, 'I am here.'

113. *Similarly, as they have not realised*
the very precious treasure contained within their mind,
the immaculate nature to which nothing need be added
and from which nothing need be taken, beings
continually experience many varied sufferings of deprivation.

114. *The jewel treasure contained in the poor man's house*
cannot tell him, 'I, the precious treasure, am here'
and the man would never know it to be there.

All beings, who possess the dharmakāya treasure
within the mansion of their mind, resemble the pauper.
Hence the Great Sages have taken worldly birth, perfectly,
so that those beings may obtain the treasure.

Buddha nature is represented here by a buried treasure so extensive that one could not spend it all in a lifetime. It is situated beneath the shabby hovel of a pauper. Although it could solve all his financial problems so easily, if unearthed, the treasure itself is mute and cannot call out to the man. The man, separated from the gold, jewels and diamonds by a few metres of soil, is totally ignorant of the presence of this unimaginable wealth. He continues in poverty. Years pass by.

Like this, the extensive and unimaginable treasure of dharmakāya exists in beings but is buried beneath all the latent habits of thought and behaviour each has acquired over the ages. Dharmakāya is perfect in itself, like all the pieces of jewellery and coins, already perfectly fashioned. Nothing needs to be added to it or removed from it. It simply needs to be acquired. Until that happens, individuals live in spiritual poverty and undergo all the miseries of worldly life. For all its qualities, dharmakāya cannot break through the 'earth' of our conditioning to tell us of its presence and so most beings ignore its presence. To acquire the treasure, we need to understand what it is, where it is and then remove the earth. This is why buddhas take on human form, most perfectly, and become guides in our lives.

sixth example: seeds within a fruit

115. *Just as, in the seeds of mangoes and other fruits,*
the imperishable quality of germinating
meeting the presence of prepared soil, water and so forth,
will gradually produce the body of a regal tree,

116. *so also, within the 'rind' confine of beings' ignorance*
and the like, is contained the pure dharma nature.
When this is sustained by virtue it will gradually attain
the very substance of a 'king of victors'.

117. *Just as a tree grows from within*
the skin of a banana or mango fruit,
due to conditions – humidity, sunlight, air, soil, space and time,
likewise is the seed and germ of perfect buddhahood contained
within the skin of that fruit: sentient beings' defilements.
Due to the condition, virtue, this true nature
will be seen and augment.

Tiny seeds contain all the power and genetic programming to produce mighty results – gigantic trees or shrubs, lush with hundreds of bananas or mangoes. For the end result to happen, the seed first needs to burst through the rotting rind of the fruit which contains it. It makes a germ, then a shoot and so on and so forth until the full plant is complete. Someone looking at the seed cannot see the fruit or tree that it could produce; it is just a tiny, uninteresting seed. But a horticulturist sees it with eyes that know its potential. Applying the appropriate knowledge, he or she understands just how to plant the seed, nurture and water it, give it just the right exposure to sunlight and so on, so that it produces a healthy and magnificent result.

Buddhas recognise the potential in ordinary beings, even though, to other eyes, their lives seem merely to be confused and destructive. They know how to place this potential in the nourishing soil of virtue so that, step by step, the 'rind' of defilements can be pierced and the full potential achieved.

seventh example: a Buddha image wrapped in tattered rags

118. *A deva, having discovered a precious image of a tathāgata*
by the road, yet wrapped in smelly, tattered rags,
would tell someone about it lying there, on the wayside,
in order that it be recovered.

119. *Similarly, when those of unhindered vision, the Buddhas,*
see the very substance of the tathāgatas (present even in beasts),
but wrapped within the envelope of defilement,
they also show the means by which it may be set free.

120. *A god with divine vision who had perceived the image*
of the tathāgata, precious by nature, yet wrapped
in smelly rags and lying by the roadside
would point it out to people, that it might be freed.
Just like that, the Victors see buddha nature (even in animals)
Lying by saṃsāra's road, wrapped in defilements' tatters,
and they teach the dharma in order that it be liberated.

This example may seem quite similar to the previous ones of the Buddha in the rotting lotus or the gold in filth. The specific significance of the Buddha statue and tattered rags becomes apparent in later verses. The intervention of the deva is necessary, otherwise the beautiful and precious statue would remain unnoticed and wasted. Remember that holy statues were treated with great veneration in India. They were kept in high places in clean temples, in quiet, sacred locations. The thought of an exceedingly beautiful holy image on the ground, in a place of worldly traffic and wrapped up in filthy rags, was a very shocking one. The natural reflex would be to retrieve it, clean it and place it where it ought to be.

Buddha nature is out of place amid the defilements. It needs to be appreciated in the temple of insight meditation, amid the cleanliness of a virtuous mind. Buddhas see this precious nature in each and every being – 'even in beasts'. They themselves cannot remove the tattered rags but they can tell beings about the precious thing they have inside them, so that they themselves remove the rags.

eighth example: a future king in the womb of a wretched woman

121. *A wretched woman, having no one to whom to turn*
and living in a pauper hostel, may hold the glory
of a future king within her womb
yet not know this ruler of men to be present within her.

122. *Worldly existence is like the pauper hostel*
and impure beings are like the pregnant woman.
Having this being within her, she has a protector
and the embryo is like the immaculate nature.

123. *The woman is dressed in dirty clothes,*
her form is unpleasant and she must endure,
in the pauper home, the worst of sorrows
even though a ruler dwells within her womb.
Similarly, even though a protector resides within,
beings believe themselves undefended and never find
peace of mind. By defilements overpowered,
they remain in the 'ground of suffering'.

This verse gives a touching insight into the compassionate vision of Buddhas. A woman, in pitiable circumstances, is destitute and pregnant. She finds refuge in a hostel in which the living conditions are terrible. Without husband, family, money or friends, she goes through the physical hardship of pregnancy feeling low and miserable. What she does not know, cannot know, is that the child she will bear will one day rule several worlds and be able to protect and care for her. To know this would give her hope and joy and may temper her bad character. Yet she lives in misery.

Buddha nature is like the future monarch. Its power and influence will be more widespread than we can imagine at present. It will protect us and thousands of other beings, bringing bountiful riches. Yet at present it is concealed by a covering that is unattractive, poor in quality and living in the hovel of saṃsāra, where one finds no true peace of mind.

ninth example: a golden statue in a clay mould

124. *Upon seeing a complete and peaceful statue*
cast in gold yet still within its mould, externally like clay,
those who know remove the outer covering
to expose the gold that lies within.

125. *The perfectly enlightened perfectly see that the nature of mind,*
clarity, is covered by transient impurities.
Hence, they cleanse beings, who are like mines
of precious gems, of their obscurations.

126. *Just as an expert removes all the clay, knowing the nature*
of the peaceful statue contained in the bright, stainless gold,
likewise the omniscient know mental peace, like cleansed gold.
Chipping away, by means of dharma explanations,
they clean off each and every obscuration.

Someone has cast a breathtakingly beautiful statue in gold. While in its clay mould, it looks merely like a lump of clay to the untrained eye. Yet an expert statue-maker would know it immediately to be a mould and remove the statue, first roughly removing the outer clay and then proceeding with more and more finesse as the gold itself is approached. In the later stages of the process, the beauty and value of the image will start to make itself apparent.

The clear light nature of mind is like the pure gold. The clay of impurities is just a passing shell, of no importance or relevance at all to the statue – buddha nature itself. It needs to be discarded using various skills, appropriate to the layer being removed. In the later stages of the process, many of buddha nature's qualities are already apparent and the cleansing process deals with quite subtle aspects of thought and needs to be highly refined and skilful.

recapitulation of the nine examples and their meaning

127. *Within the lotus, bees, husk, filth, ground, fruit skin,*
tattered rags, woman's womb and the clay mould are

In the above nine examples, the various types of veil (see below vvs. 130–143) obscuring buddha nature have been exemplified by the nine impure and transient 'shells' listed in this verse.

128. *the buddha, honey, kernel, gold, treasure, great tree,*
precious image, universal monarch and golden figure.

Likewise, nine facets of buddha nature (see below vvs. 144–152) are represented by the nine pure and lasting 'contents' listed here.

129. *Similarly it is said that the shell of defilement covering the nature of beings is beginningless and unconnected with it and that the stainlessness of that nature of mind is beginningless.*

All examples have their limits. These nine cannot properly represent buddha nature because nothing in our relative world is like it. They simply give us an appreciation of how something pure, useful and noble can be hidden within something impure and ignoble. They help us distinguish between natures which have no link with each other. Unlike the inseparable natures of roundness and whiteness of a conch shell, which are each aspects of the same thing, the rags and the statue, the earth and the buried treasure are separate things. Each has its own history. They just happen to co-habit, the one hiding the other.

The continuum of desires, frustrations, ignorance and so forth which obliterate awareness of buddha nature go back to time immemorial. They are beginningless in a 'chicken-and-egg' way: present effects had past causes, which were themselves effects of previous causes and so on *ad infinitum*. It is even more complicated than that. Even the chicken that laid the latest egg was fed on grains, looked after by a farmer and so forth. Each cause that contributed to its life has its own causes and history. As soon as one looks more than superficially into what caused the latest egg, one discovers not one but an enormous number of things. It is not possible simply to follow causal chains back in a one-makes-one basis. Anyone who has retraced their family tree will understand the complexity even in establishing direct ascendancy, let alone all the contributory factors involved in each ancestor's life.

The continuum of ignorance is also beginningless because the whole notion of linear time is merely a non-true, conceptual interpretation, based upon sequences of events which are themselves illusions. Time is much more complex than the popular consciousness believes it to be. Furthermore, from the Buddhist perspective, personal defilement is beginningless but not endless. Buddha nature is also beginningless, as it does not belong to relative realities which have beginnings, middles and ends. It is located in what Buddhism calls 'timeless time', primordial eternity.

130. *Desire, aversion and ignorance and these in active state*
or as latent imprints to be abandoned through insight,
or to be abandoned through cultivation (of insight) –
the impurities present in the impure
and the impurities present in the pure –

131. *are nine things illustrated by*
the example of the lotus 'shell' and so forth.
The 'shell' of subsidiary defilements
divides into infinite categories.

132. *Summarised briefly, the nine impurities, desire, etc.,*
have been well illustrated through nine examples,
the lotus 'shell' and so forth respectively.

The impurities present in the impure (ordinary individuals) and in the pure (arhats and bodhisattvas) are summarised in the table opposite and explained more fully in the verses which follow. One could make many categories of defilements, sub-defilements and the situations they precipitate. The nine shown here take the three main defilements – desire, aversion and ignorance – as representative of them all and show them in nine important situations.

133. *These impurities cause, respectively,*
the four impurities of ordinary beings,
one of arhats, two of beings training in dharma
and two impurities of the wise.

The first four examples show the defilements in beings of the six realms, still undergoing rebirth through the driving force of defilement and karma. These are known as 'ordinary beings', 'individuals' or 'the immature'. The treasure buried beneath the soil repre-

example	represents defilement as
lotus	desire and attachment in individuals
bees	anger, hatred, frustration in individuals
husk	ignorance in individuals
filth	the above in an active state
dirt	latent traces of the above in arhats
fruit skin	obscurations as creations that are to be removed by bodhisattvas in the stage of insight
rags	conceptual traces of the above, to be removed by bodhisattvas in the stage of cultivation
womb	impurities in bodhisattvas of levels 1–7
clay	impurities in bodhisattvas of levels 8–10

sents latent karmic traces in arhats. The fruit skin and the tattered rags represent the more subtle defilements that are removed by bodhisattvas in the stages of *insight* and *cultivation*, referred to here as 'those training in dharma' (as opposed to the Buddhas, who have no more training to accomplish). The last two examples approach these same bodhisattvas – the 'wise' – from a slightly different point of view.

134. *The mind is delighted by the 'mud-born', the lotus,*
     but later becomes disappointed: such is desire's happiness.

The lotus is a most exquisite flower which grows out of muddy pools. The 'mud-born' is one of its many Sanskrit epithets. A beautiful flower is used here to represent desire and attachment. When one sees a beautiful flower, the heart is gladdened. Later, as it withers and smells bad, the pleasure disappears. The beings of saṃsāra are each attracted to their particular objects: men to women, women to men, birds to eating worms, hippopotami to bathing in mud. Desire makes things seem more attractive than they are. At first things bring pleasure, but with time comes suffering and disappointment.

135. *When irritated, bees sting. Likewise, anger arises*
and brings but suffering to the heart.

Bees are attached to their honey. When someone tries to take it, they can get irritated and give pain to others by stinging. This is chosen as an example of anger. It is rooted in losing, or not having, what one wants; in dissatisfaction. Often, one type of frustration triggers another, like bees buzzing and swarming together and working each other into a frenzy. Anger makes one irritable and capable of hurting others by words or actions. It also pains the angry person or being by the discomfort it brings.

136. *Just as kernels of rice and other grains are covered*
outwardly by husks and skins,
so is the vision of the very essence
obscured by the 'shell' of ignorance.

Ignorance is, by its very definition, not knowing. The grossness and busyness of the mind – wrapped up in its thoughts, feelings and emotions – is like a thick shell enveloping the true nature of mind just as a husk envelops its grain.

137. *Filth is something unpleasant. Akin to it is the active state,*
causing those who are involved to indulge in gratification

One might be helped in considering this example by thinking of the terrible sights and smells found today in third-world slums, or by considering accounts of Europe in the Middle Ages. Disgusting to see and naturally sickening, such is the heap of filth used here to portray the defilements when they are active. People driven by desire, maddened by hatred and possessed by all the other defilements cause their own undoing and bring suffering to others. To a peaceful, enlightened mind, it is nothing but a revolting heap of unnecessary rubbish.

Those under the sway of the defilements are not revolted by them but hypnotised by them. Desire leads to greater desire. As the scriptures say, 'it is like drinking salt water to quench a thirst'. Anger leads to more anger. Pride to greater pride. Life in the six realms is a constant striving to satisfy these manifestations of ego's needs and dislikes.

138. *When the wealth was covered over, they did not know*
and could not obtain its treasures.
In a similar way, the spontaneously-arising
is concealed by ignorance's latent traces.

This example specifically relates to arhats. Through magnificent purification and excellent concentration meditation, they have taken their minds beyond suffering, for ever. They abide in profound peace with many insights. Yet they ignore the true nature of mind – buddha nature with all its qualities. This is because of the continued presence of a very subtle level of ignorance. The great treasure of enlightened qualities lies beneath this, yet the arhats remain in the relative poverty of mere peace.

139. *Just as the germ and so forth split*
the husk of their grain, through a gradual growth,
likewise insight into thatness dispels
the obscurations to be abandoned through insight.

While one is a worldly being, one is unable to have direct realisation of the true nature of one's own mind. Whatever remains of karma and defilements in one's existence will act as a barrier to that insight. They are like the rind of the fruit. Buddhist practices that worldly beings engage in are like the heat of the soil and its humidity, enabling the seed to germinate and break through its rind. But the power to grow is in the seed itself.

The wisdom innate to buddha nature has the power to pierce through the illusions and habits of worldliness. Through the stages of 'accumulation' and 'integration',[1] one nurtures the buddha nature seed through virtue, meditation and intellectual wisdom. At the stage of insight,[2] which corresponds to the first of the ten bodhisattva levels, the fabric of saṃsāra is shattered and insight into the truth of mind attained irreversibly. One sees the rope as a rope and primordial wisdom starts its refinement towards perfection.

140. *Those who, by following the path of the realised,*
have overcome the very pith, beliefs
that the destructible and multiple is a self
still have obscurations to be abandoned,
through the primordial wisdom of the path of cultivation.
These have been illustrated as being like tattered rags.

Although first level bodhisattvas have attained insight into the truth about mind, they are far from being Buddhas. They still have a long process of purification to accomplish, through cultivating their insight. The path of cultivation is the fourth stage, covering bodhisattva levels two through to ten and carrying the bodhisattva all the way to the fifth stage, buddhahood itself.

Insight removes the biggest mistakes – the ones that keep saṃsāra alive. These mistakes, of intricate complexity, all involve some delusion of lasting identity. The illusion of permanence and uniqueness is projected onto things which are impermanent and multiple, namely the five aggregates. The cultivation of bodhisattva insight is particularly concerned with removing whatever remains, through habit, of such illusions. These are somewhat like mental echoes of the past, still occurring as brief flashes and reactions within the peace of their meditations. Although powerless, this fall-out from the past is nevertheless present, forming a subtle veil of obscuration.

Just as tattered rags used to be real clothes, these passing thoughts and reflexes of the mind used to be one's ideology. Like tattered rags around a statue, they are relatively easy to remove.

141. *The impurities which remain in the seven profound levels*
are compared to the impurities in the confines of a womb.
Release from them is like freedom from that womb
whereas non-conceptual jñāna is like finally maturing.

A baby develops progressively in the womb. Each day brings it closer to birth. Its senses and strength increase. Bodhisattvas in the first seven levels are also progressing steadily. They systematically work through the remnants of duality which still arise in their mind yet no longer cause loss of awareness of true reality. First the grosser thoughts and, step by step, finer and finer levels of discrete thoughts are purified. The various qualities of buddha nature can shine more and more with each veiling layer removed.

142. *The impurities in the three profound levels*
should be known as similar to the traces of clay.
These are the ones to be eliminated by
the vajra-like samādhi of the 'great self'.

Because of their immaculate purity, absence of duality and presence of qualities, the last three bodhisattva levels, i.e. eight, nine and ten, are called the *three pure levels*. Whatever impurity remains to be removed is now very subtle, hence compared to the final traces of clay clinging to a gold statue. It takes the skilled hand of a craftsman and a sharp, hard tool to remove them successfully, without scratching the gold. The purification work in these levels is accomplished by remaining perfectly absorbed in the 'vajra-like' samādhi. A vajra is an invincible weapon, victorious over all.

Although most Buddhist reasoning and philosophy denies the existence of self, it is, in fact, only refuting *deluded notions* of self, based upon the aggregates. Buddha nature is the true self, inasmuch as it is the universal identity which we all share. By remaining absorbed in buddha nature, one is resting in the vajra-like samādhi of the great self.

143. *Thus nine impurities, desire and so forth,*
correspond to the lotus and other (examples).
Buddha nature corresponds to the buddha and so on,
being the union of three natures.

The previous verses explored the various impurities covering buddha nature. The following verses will explore the significance of the various pure things being covered in each example. They will be shown to express three natures, inseparable within buddha nature.

144. *Its three natures are dharmakāya, tathatā and gotra,*
     to be understood respectively
     through three, one and five examples.

These three Sanskrit words have caused much ink to flow. As their meanings are both subtle and complex, the original terms have been kept in this verse, although elsewhere in this book they are in English translation. Buddha nature is not, in itself, divided; a point made earlier in this text. However, from our point of view, it is useful to differentiate various aspects of it. As we have seen, the colour, heat and shape of a flame are just three things that the observer can single out and make use of intellectually, even though they are not distinct entities in themselves but aspects of the one flame. The colour is produced by the burning heat and the area of combustion determines the shape of the flame.

Dharmakāya is the clarity (wisdom) aspect of buddha nature. Tathatā, or thatness, is the voidness aspect. Gotra, or potential,[3] is the aspect of full manifestation. The first three examples were about dharmakāya, the fourth was about tathatā and the remaining five were about gotra.

145. *The dharmakāya should be known as two:*
     the perfectly immaculate dharmadhātu
     and the favourable conditions for it –
     the teachings in their profound and manifold aspects.

There is ultimate dharmakāya and relative dharmakāya. The former is truly dharmakāya: the luminous clarity which is the domain of self-cognisant, primordial wisdom. It is sometimes known as *dharmadhātu*. From a relative point of view, there is dharmakāya as the body of dharma, which we saw in the Second Vajra Abode to be the dharma as realisation and dharma as teachings. In Buddhism in general, and particularly in mahāyāna, the more profound aspects of dharma, dealing with voidness, are known as the *deep* teachings. The manifold teachings relevant to the various mentalities and needs of beings on the dharma path are known as the *vast* teachings.

146. *As it transcends the world, there is no example for it
manifest within the world, thus it has been represented
by representing the essence by the form of a Tathāgata.*

The Buddha inside a fading lotus in the first example represents the ultimate dharmakāya. This is a real Buddha, not a Buddha statue. Nothing in this world is at all like dharmakāya and so no example, other than the Tathāgata himself, can represent it. We use examples to evoke similar qualities. For instance, someone may never have seen a sapphire and could get some notion of it by being told that it was a bit like a diamond, but blue. Blue like what? Like the Mediterranean sky. Thus, someone who had previously seen a diamond and visited the Mediterranean shores could imagine a sapphire. Examples employ past experiences to bring unexperienced things to the imagination. The problem is that no one ever experienced anything remotely like dharmakāya, for the simple reason that it is quite unique. Only the self-cognisant primordial wisdom of buddha properly knows it.

147. *The teachings in their subtle and profound aspect
Should be known to be like the unique taste of honey.
The teachings in their manifold aspect
Are like the various grains in their husks.*

The taste of honey is quite subtle and unique. Even though lavender honey, clover honey and chestnut honey have quite different flavours, they all share the unique, indescribable 'honey' taste. The relative dharmakāya, as the deep teachings on voidness, is represented by honey in this example, precisely because of the subtlety of these teachings and the one taste of voidness shared by all the various phenomena.

The relative dharmakāya, as the vast teachings of the paths and levels, is represented by the various grains in their husks. Rice, wheat, barley and so forth are quite different in taste but are all very nourishing.

148. *Thatness is said to be similar to the substance of gold because this essence is immutable, perfectly pure and noble.*

The gold (in the rubbish heap) represents thatness, the voidness aspect of buddha nature. Thatness – we could call it suchness – is the true nature of things, devoid of all illusions and anything which is not the perfection of buddha wisdom. It never changes, never has changed, never will change. It is pure inasmuch as it is free of innate or transient impurities and its nature is noble, as to be it is to be buddha.

149. *One should know the potential as having two aspects, similar to the treasure and the tree grown from the fruit: that naturally present since beginningless time and that perfected through proper cultivation.*

The remaining five examples deal with buddha nature as *gotra* – a potential, a quasi-genetic heritage, a seed of buddhahood. This potential also has ultimate and relative aspects. The ultimate truth of potential is what it really is, represented in the example by the treasure buried beneath the ground. For centuries, millennia, cosmic aeons, buddha nature has been the ever-present underground force. Whenever given a chance, it has started to manifest its qualities, bringing peace and spirituality in one's life. At other times it has been completely ignored and has had even more earth piled onto it. The potential has not only always been there but has always possessed the totality of the result. Beyond our delusions, we are already enlightened. This is the *potential as it innately exists*, naturally present since beginningless time.

From our relative point of view, the unearthing of this potential is a progressive spiritual development. We go through the long evolution from an ordinary being, through bodhisattvahood, to becoming what we always were: a buddha. This is like the seed, which already holds all its genetic programming, slowly breaking out through the rotting fruit and eventually growing into a king of trees, every characteristic of which was already written into its genes. This gradual unlocking of buddha nature's potential is known as the *potential perfected through proper cultivation*.

150. *From this twofold potential comes achievement*
of the three buddhakāya: the first through the former
and the other two through the latter.

This verse introduces the last three examples of buddha nature as potential. Here we discover the outcome of the potential, i.e. the kāya, or embodiments, of perfect buddhahood. Yet again it must be stressed that buddhahood is not divided into separate kāya. The different kāya are distinctions we make intellectually, in order to discern various facets of buddha. Here the analysis is threefold:

▸ the embodiment of the essence (*svabhavikakāya*),
▸ the embodiment of perfect expression (*sambhogakāya*) and
▸ the embodiment as emanations (*nirmāṇakāya*).

The first is seen as being the outcome of the innate potential. The latter two are the outcome of the potential perfected through cultivation.

Although the way these verses are expressed could lead one to think that the innate and cultivated potentials are causes, creating the three kāya as their result, this is not quite the case. We are not considering causes and effects wherein one thing creates another over a period of time and in which the cause must necessarily disappear in order to give way to the result, as is the case with a seed and its resulting plant. The three kāya are the three ways in which buddha nature is experienced. The presence of the two potentials (innately existing and properly cultivated) is the basis for that experience. The kāya are never created afresh by causes and conditions.

151. *The embodiment of the magnificent essence*
should be known as being similar to the statue
made of precious substances, being natural and non-created
and a treasure of jewel-like qualities

The innate potential manifests as the embodiment of the essence, svabhavikakāya. This is represented by the buddha statue made of precious substances (wrapped in tattered rags). The gold and gems of which the statue is made have natural qualities of colour, resilience and so forth. Many natural, precious things have been combined in a beautiful whole. Like natural gems, the specific qualities innate to buddha nature as a whole are not fabrications; not results of dharma activities done previously. They are natural and timeless.

152. *The perfect expression is like the chakravartin,*
being endowed with the greater dharma's majesty.
Like the golden image are the emanations,
having the very nature of a representation.

The embodiment of perfect expression (sambhogakāya) is the way in which buddha nature is experienced by bodhisattvas in the ten levels. It manifests to them as sights, sounds and so forth – visions which convey the magnificence and majesty of dharma, itself beyond colour, shape, sound and so forth. The pure lands, inhabited by buddhas and their unimaginable wonders, experienced by bodhisattvas, are therefore representations, natural symbols which well forth from the pure nature of mind. These are expressions of the *potential to be perfectly developed*.

The embryo in the poor woman's womb will one day rule many continents in great majesty and dignity. He will have palaces, a retinue of intelligent and beautiful people, and everything befitting a mighty king. As the relative potential of buddha nature is developed in the ten bodhisattva levels, the mind comes home to its innate splendour and its birthright of primordial majesty.

The embodiment as emanations (nirmāṇakāya) is buddha nature as it is experienced by ordinary beings, through their virtue. The grossness of their minds does not permit experience of the pure lands but does enable various types of emanation to be encountered. As these tangibly represent the real, intangible buddha in these beings' lives, they are represented in the examples by the golden statue (in the clay mould). These emanations are the other outcome of the potential to be cultivated.

153. *This ultimate truth of the spontaneously born*
is to be understood by faith alone:
the orb of the sun may shine
but it cannot be seen by the blind.

The nine examples, developed at length in the preceding verses, may help give some idea of buddha nature, the ultimate truth of existence; that which arises naturally. However, deduction, imagery and examples can only take one so far. They cannot bring unflinching certainty about the absolute. They cannot bring realisation of the absolute. One needs faith, in the sense of needing to trust the teachings of Maitreya and the Buddha, who *do* have direct experience of buddha nature. Furthermore, faith is a necessity inasmuch as it becomes one's greatest ally in the practical meditation work of unveiling buddha nature.

As far as the sun itself is concerned, it has never been obscured but is always in the presence of its own light. However, although it may be shining away, the blind cannot see its brilliant orb. Buddha nature has always been there, with all its qualities. Beings blinded by the thick darkness of ignorance cannot appreciate it, even though it is their very essence. Faith, in all its aspects, will help them to dispel, swiftly and efficiently, the shadows of not-knowing. Faith takes on a crucial importance in the practice of vajrayāna and the mahāmudrā teachings of the Kagyu lineage.

This verse and the two which follow are important statements of this text. They echo verses found in the Śrīmālādevīsūtra and in the Mahāparinirvāṇasūtra.

154. *There is nothing whatever to remove from this*
nor the slightest thing thereon to add.
Truly beholding the true nature,
when truly[1] seen, complete liberation.

This beautiful and haiku-like verse is worth committing to memory. It sums up some of the profoundest Buddhist philosophy and can be an invaluable guide in meditation, the whole object of which is to bring one to recognition of buddha nature.

Let us continue the example of the previous verse. In order for the blind to see the sun's orb, it is not the sun which needs to be changed but whatever stops the eyes from seeing. Buddha nature itself has always been untouched by impurity. There are no veils to be removed from *it*, but from the way of seeing it. Nothing whatsoever need be removed from *it*. In meditation, one needs to learn, when the time is right, how not to 'interfere negatively', i.e. how not to suppress the play of the mind or try to purify it.

There is nothing to be added to it. Being already endowed with every enlightened quality, no thing that anyone can do could ever improve it. Our Buddhist path is not meant to generate buddha-nature enhancers. In meditation, when the time is right, one needs also to learn how not to 'interfere positively', i.e. not try to create qualities or maintain them.

The art is in learning how to 'see' perfectly. This is not a question of visual awareness or anything to do with the play of consciousnesses. It is one of seeing truth directly with the 'eyes' of wisdom, i.e. *seeing through* delusions and recognising buddha nature. The wisdom which 'sees' has nothing to do with thinking or mental commentary. It is stark, direct recognition of truth. When the eyes of primordial wisdom see the truth perfectly, all concepts of *is* or *is not* and so forth are unimportant. Liberated from conceptual delusions and from the defilements they create, one is the peaceful freedom of dharmakāya wisdom. Allowing this wisdom to come to its completion by resting within primordial wisdom itself will bring the total liberation of buddhahood.

155. *This element is devoid of transient things to be purified,*
that have a character separable from it.
It is not devoid of the ultimate qualities
of character indifferentiable from it.

Whereas the previous verse highlighted the natural perfection which is the very character of buddha nature, this verse clearly defines what it is, or is not, devoid of. This is the key statement of voidness in this text.

Buddha nature – referred to here as the ultimate element – is totally devoid of the ignorance, dualistic thoughts and defilements which come and go in the mind. Being untrue and delusory, they have no own reality. However, buddha nature is not devoid of the ultimate qualities, such as the ten powers, which are an indissociable part of its nature. This gives us a good definition of voidness, thereby avoiding any confusion with mere emptiness or nihilism. We can define voidness succinctly as meaning *devoid of transient impurities yet not devoid of enlightened qualities*.

Some Buddhists believe that the ultimate goal – voidness – is merely emptiness and that any qualities, such as the ten powers or any other expression of compassion, only occur on a relative level, transiently, due to circumstances. Maitreya makes it clear that this is not the case and that all the enlightened qualities are an integral part of the ultimate nature.

D. The purpose of the buddha nature teachings

156. *He had taught in various places that every knowable thing is ever void, like a cloud, dream or illusion.*
Why therefore did the Buddha declare the essence of buddhahood to be present in every sentient being?

In the Deer Forest[5] and other places, the Enlightened One turned the Wheel of Dharma. This is the Buddhist way of saying that he taught, giving the basic teachings, such as the Four Truths, which are common to all forms of Buddhism and which are based on voidness as meaning devoid of ego.

On the Vulture Peak and in other places of this world and also in non-material dimensions, he turned the Wheel of Dharma for a second time, teaching the Greater Vehicle message of compassion and voidness of all things. This revealed not only the voidness of ego, of suffering and of the defilements of saṃsāra but also the voidness of the dharmas he had so perfectly taught, such as the aggregates, elements and entrances. The prajñāpāramitā gives eighteen types of voidness, including the voidness of voidness itself. In these teachings, he compared knowable things to clouds, dreams and illusions.

Why, having taught voidness as a negation of accepted realities, did the Buddha, towards the end of his life on Earth, turn the Wheel a third time and teach voidness as the *presence* of limitless enlightened qualities?

157. *There are five mistakes: faint-heartedness,*
contempt for those of lesser ability, belief in the false,
slandering the true meaning and self-cherishing.
So that those in whom the above exist may rid themselves
of these, thus was it declared.

Not understanding the presence of buddha nature in all beings, one could make one or more of the mistakes mentioned in this verse and treated more fully in the verses below. We have already learnt that ordinary beings and arhats do not have any awareness at all of this perfect buddhahood within themselves and other beings. Even great bodhisattvas have a limited, if true, realisation of it. Thus it was very necessary to define precisely its nature, its qualities and so forth – as we are doing in this text, which summarises the Third Turning teachings – so as to avoid the five main mistakes. This is also why these teachings form a necessary basis for meditation, in which one is face to face with the likelihood of these mistakes.

It is important not to consider the three Turnings as contradictory. They represent the unfolding of the story of truth, step by step. Thus, the various Buddhist traditions which base themselves particularly on one or another of these teachings are not in conflict with each other but emphasise one or another part of the whole teaching.

158. *The ultimate and true nature is always devoid*
of any compounded thing.
Therefore it is taught that defilements, actions
and their full maturation are like clouds and so forth.

The Second Turning is embodied in the scriptures of the prajñā-pāramitā. This exists in very long, long, medium, short and ultra-condensed forms.[6] It uses the imagery of clouds, dreams and conjurations to discern the apparently true from the really true. These three images were originally taught together in the *saddharmapundarikasūtra*.

159. *The defilements are taught to be like clouds,*
     karma is likened to the experience in dreams
     and the full ripening of karma and defilements,
     the aggregates, are likened to conjurations.

Clouds are used to portray the defilements, because clouds are intangible and unpredictable, coming and going unexpectedly. Their presence seems to darken the sky yet the sky itself remains unaffected by them. Defilements lead to action (karma), compared to the deeds of dreams. Although dream sights, sounds and so forth seem so real at the time, they have no substance whatsoever in reality. Actions give rise to many short and long-term consequences. 'Full maturations' are the rebirths they create, i.e. the various sorts of wordly existence that are the subjective experience of beings. Magical illusion is used to portray the voidness of these. The conjurations or illusions referred to here are a sort of hypnosis, under the influence of which one imagines oneself spending many years living another life in a certain land, even though one may be under the spell only for minutes.

160. *Thus was it presented previously and then*
     'the element exists' was taught ultimately
     as this continuum in this way
     so that these five faults could be abandoned.

The Second Turning presented the ultimate voidness of all relative things and concentrated on their absence of real entity. In particular, it showed the ultimate non-existence of the relative elements, be they the eighteen elements of consciousness or the six prime elements. This precise elimination of possible delusions about the mind, as the play of *consciousness*, paved the way for the Third Turning, in which the ultimate truth of voidness itself was explored more profoundly, to reveal the 'existence' of the ultimate element: buddha nature, as primordial *wisdom*.

There is no conflict between the two Turnings. In fact, many vajrayāna texts explore this difference between the relative nature of consciousness and the ultimate nature of primordial wisdom, which has nothing to do with sensorial or mental consciousness.

161. *Not learning this, some people are disheartened,*
through mistaken self-contempt;
bodhicitta will not develop in them.

Someone who does not know, or is not convinced, of the existence of perfect buddha wisdom within their mind, may well feel inadequate for the task of enlightenment. The wonderful things accomplished by bodhisattvas may seem like fairy-stories or something to which only a few, privileged, beings might aspire. They may feel unable to overcome their own weaknesses and defilements. They may feel unable to help others or to practise dharma. But they are wrong. Every being has the capacity to do these things, as we have seen at length in this text.

Without the self-confidence that comes from knowing that one is really buddha, it will be hard to develop the compassion and wisdom that are the two motor forces of bodhicitta. To help us strengthen confidence, many mahāyāna and vajrayāna practices help us transmute our habits of identification. We shift from mechanical processes of self-identifying, due to past tendencies, in which we relate to the conditioned human persona we have grown up with, to identifying ourselves as bodhisattvas with bodies of light. Understanding the meaning of this verse alone throws great light on the visualisations of vajrayāna Buddhism, in which one identifies totally with one or another form of enlightenment.

162. *Some people, through pride, think, 'I am better,'*
because bodhicitta has dawned in them.
They dwell insistently in the notion that
those in whom it has not dawned are inferior.

This Buddhist self-confidence should in no way be confused with pride. To be convinced that one is oneself truly Buddha should be also to be convinced that each 'other' being is equally Buddha. We are all truly Buddhas: the only differences are in the varying thicknesses of personal veils of hypnosis, due to ignorance, which keep us unaware of that fact. Not knowing this, people who practice Buddhist meditation and the other five pāramitā may change, quite quickly, for the better and note the immense difference between the quality of their lives and the destructive, pointless quality of many other beings' lives. This could give rise to pride, which is a poison capable of destroying the value of all one's dharma work.

163. *Right understanding cannot arise*
in those who think like this.
Thus, since they misinterpret the true,
they will not understand the truth.

Deluded are those who take the impermanent mental images of their moment-by-moment perception to be true reality. The strength of their delusion acts as a blockage preventing direct realisation of the truth: voidness as buddha nature. They misinterpret the universal buddha nature identity and mistake it for a personal self or a personal God. Ego and various religious beliefs distort the truth and close the mind to its recognition. Furthermore, through ignoring this true identity, one will relate to other beings in terms of their faults rather than their buddha nature.

164. *Beings' defects are not truly real,*
as they are but a fabrication and incidental.
In reality, these faults are not entities
whereas the qualities are naturally pure.

The previous verse was concerned with believing in the untrue. This one, very similar but slightly different, deals with speaking or thinking wrongly about what is true, i.e. the lasting and perfect presence of all the enlightened qualities in every being. What ostensibly seems to be their lives, their faults and so forth is really only the momentary coming-together of circumstances to produce a certain perception. Many causes and conditions combine, in any given moment, to make an image of the world, or of another person. It is a hollow fabrication of circumstances, not a true reality. Thus it is like an hallucination, a delusion of fever or the apparent play of light on rippling water. Having no substance of its own, it is incidental to true lasting reality, the changeless essence of mind portrayed in this text.

To overcome the habit of relating to habitual projections of other people, bodhisattvas train in not speaking ill of the true nature, i.e. in recognising buddhajñāna in everyone and everything that they perceive.

165. *If one clings to the faults, the untrue,*
and disparages the qualities, the true,
one will not have the loving kindness of the wise
which sees the similarity of oneself and others.

Clinging to habitual, false projections and not recognising the truth of buddha qualities in others will stop the development of a bodhisattva's loving kindness. The basis for the latter is a sincere recognition of the similarity of oneself and others, through the common identity of buddha nature. This mature love is not a pity, which looks down on lesser beings in suffering, but a profound empathy rooted in truth.

166. *Through learning in such a fashion, there arises*
enthusiastic diligence, respect (as for a Buddha),
prajñā, jñāna and great love.

By understanding buddha nature through this text and the scriptures of the Third Turning, one will avoid the five mistakes explained above. Five qualities will emerge in their stead:
- enthusiastic diligence instead of faint-heartedness,
- not pride but respect for others, as though they were Buddhas,
- prajñā instead of belief in the non-true,
- jñāna instead of denial of what is true and
- mature love instead of self-cherishing.

167. *Due to the growth of these five qualities,*
unhealthy aspects will be absent and similarity will be seen.
Through faultlessness, innate qualities and loving kindness
which recognises the similarity of self and other,
buddhahood will be swiftly achieved.

In conclusion, by cleansing the five habitual faults from one's mind and allowing its innate perfection to manifest and through the mature loving kindness which recognises the sameness of all beings, one will swiftly achieve buddhahood. One could use this verse as a checklist for one's own progress. It also closes this chapter and leads into the next, enlightenment.

Notes

1 The first two of the five stages of the path to enlightenment. See 'Gems', chapter on the paths.
2 The third stage, see note 1 above.
3 Potential made fully manifest/full potential. The reason for the use of this term, which may confuse the reader in this verse (a seeming dissonance between the words *potential* and *full manifestation*) will become clear in verses 149 onwards.
4 The many 'truly's in this verse translate the repeated Tibetan term *yang dag*, which translates the Sankrit *upsarga*. These are adverbs which carry a superlative meaning giving the action of a verb its highest or noblest value. The different *yang dag* could have been translated as *perfectly* or *properly* or *excellently* etc. 'Truly' fits most of the meanings and, furthermore, echoes the notion of truth. However, such a translation could be contentious.
5 I have a lingering suspicion that many people hearing the more familiar translation of Deer Park imagine some sort of civic gardens or tended place. The lineage explanation is that the original term alluding to deer, as a token of wildlife in general, showed that it was a wilderness, and hence far from human influence and suitable for meditation.
6 The prajñāpāramitā exists in many forms, from very large to highly-condensed. The number of verses can be 100,000, 25,000, 18,000, 10,000, 8,000, 2,500 and so forth down to 500 lines, 300 lines, 25 lines or the few words of the GATE mantra.

The Fifth Vajra Abode
– enlightenment –

168. *Purity, achievement, freedom, benefit for oneself and others,*
basis, depth, vastness, greatness of nature,
their enduring nature and suchness itself

169. *present the state of buddhahood according to*
its nature, cause, fruit, function, endowments,
manifestation, permanence and inconceivability

This chapter has the eight sections – nature, cause, fruit, function, endowments, manifestation, permanence and inconceivability. Each of these topics represents a particular facet of enlightenment listed, respectively, in the first verse:
- the *nature* of enlightenment is **purity**. All transient obscurations, confusing and blinding the mind, have been removed.
- enlightenment is *caused* by the Buddhist path of practice. This **achievement** of total primordial wisdom is accomplished through bringing the wisdoms of study, reflection and meditation to their full conclusion. There is no more to be known and

188   Maitreya on Buddha Nature

- no more ignorance to be eliminated.
- as a *fruition*, it is total **freedom** from impurity.
- the *function* of enlightenment is to bring the **highest fulfilment to both oneself and others**. One is free from even the subtlest aspects of saṃsāra and can therefore illuminate the way for many other beings to be likewise.
- the *basis* from which these benefits manifest is the presence of the **qualities** of buddhahood.
- enlightenment *manifests* these qualities as its three embodiments (*kāya*), known by the keywords **depth** (dharmakāya), **vastness** (sambhogakāya) and **greatness of nature** (nirmanakāya).
- the *permanence* of enlightenment reflects its **enduring nature**.
- the *inconceivability* of enlightenment shows it to be the **suchness** of mind: a wisdom beyond concepts.

The first two of these points are closely linked. Enlightenment's *nature* is total purity, since its *cause* is a thorough and radical process of purification. Therefore Maitreya's text first considers both points, in brief, and then in more detail, one by one.

A. The Nature and Cause of Enlightenment

Treated together in brief

170.   *That which has been described as 'its nature is lucid clarity'*
       is like the sun and space, obscured by the thick veils
       of those multitudes of 'clouds' which are merely incidental;
       the defilements and the cognitive obscuration.
       Buddhahood has no stain, is endowed with buddha-qualities
       and is permanent, everlasting and without change.
       Its achievement depends upon non-conceptual jñāna
       and analytical jñāna regarding all phenomena

The very nature of enlightenment is lucid clarity, often referred to figuratively as 'clear light'. This conveys two notions: *clarity* points to the purity of enlightenment and *lucidity* to its primordial wisdom. In this verse, the brilliant wisdom, which is the essential character (*garbha*) of enlightenment, is compared to the sun. The purity of being – enlightenment's nature (*svabhāva*) – in which this wisdom shines is compared to space.

Two things happen simultaneously when perfect enlightenment is attained: the last remaining impurities disappear and total wisdom emerges. The impurities are the 'obscuring clouds' of defilement and dualistic thought. Their disappearance reveals the 'infinite space' of purity and the 'powerful sunlight' of wisdom, illuminating all things in its compassionate light. Purity, the very nature of enlightenment, has three main particularities:

- It does not have any 'stain'.
- It does have all the 64 main and innumerable other qualities.
- This absence of stain and presence of qualities is permanent, everlasting and unchanging.

There is also a fourth particularity. The cause for all of this is the complete activity of two types of primordial wisdom. *Non-conceptual primordial wisdom* manifests from the first bodhisattva level onwards. Because of its presence, the ten levels are already considered to be a form of enlightenment. It becomes perfectly complete with the total enlightenment of a Buddha. Non-conceptual jñāna first manifests in the 'meditation' phase, i.e. when mind is focused on the nature of mind itself (*dharmata*), as in formal meditation. It is the aspect of primordial wisdom which recognises the sameness of nature of all things.

The second form of primordial wisdom is *analytical primordial wisdom*. This develops in the 'post-meditation' phase, i.e. when the mind is focused on the various details (*dharma*) of existence. It is the aspect of primordial wisdom which recognises the specificity of all that manifests, within the sameness recognised by non-conceptual wisdom. It would be easy for simple Buddhists to understand these two forms of primordial wisdom through the simile of their own practice, by comparing them to the wisdom which emerges from the introspective quiet of formal sitting meditation and that which emerges between sitting sessions, when one is relating to life as an illusion. However, this comparison would not be very accurate.

In both cases we are discussing primordial wisdom, which is like unto nothing we have ever experienced. Furthermore, although some mahāyāna texts describe these two as the long-term outcomes of the processes we set into motion by proper sitting meditation and proper practice in between sessions, it is worthwhile bearing in mind the fact that there is much less of a rigid distinction between these two in the trainings of mahāmudrā and vajrayāna. These encourage an understanding, from the outset, that these are but two facets of one and the same wisdom; not two different ones.

The nature of enlightenment (in detail)

171. *Buddhahood is indivisible yet one can categorise it*
 according to its qualities of purity –
 the two qualities of jñāna and freedom,
 comparable to the sun and to space.

actual nature: What, essentially and ultimately, was the enlightenment that the Buddha attained – not the relative story of a bodhisattva's many lives of purification, ending under the *ficus* tree in Bodh Gaya, but whatever it was that he attained, on that extraordinary dawn in May, that made Sakyamuni a Buddha? It was purity. Enlightenment is purity in two senses: one an absence and the other a presence. The first is freedom from transient impurity – the Buddha's total liberation. The second concerns the quality of the primordial wisdom (jñāna) attained at enlightenment, which has a perfection like that of the purest gold, a flawless diamond or a perfectly developed flower.

These qualities of wisdom and liberation have already been compared to the sun and space. It is important at this stage for us to go beyond the limits of the two examples and recognise that these two aspects of purity are in fact one and the same thing. The wisdom is perfect because no transient impurity obstructs or limits it. The wisdom itself is a recognition of primordial purity, untainted by transient impurity, in oneself and every detail of existence. Despite their limitations, the two examples are very useful, showing the infinite extent (space) of existence and the brilliant power (sun) of the wisdom which knows it. These are sometimes called, respectively, dharmadhātu and dharmakāya.

172. *This lucid clarity is uncreated.*
It is that which pervades without any differentiation,
possessing all buddhahood's qualities, far greater in number
than the sand grains in the river Ganges.

The way in which it possesses its qualities: the various qualities of buddhahood are sometimes summarised as the famous three – wisdom, compassion and power. In the following chapter we will discover 64 enlightened qualities, i.e. the 4 fearlessnesses, 18 unique qualities, 10 powers and 32 signs. But in fact the number of qualities is limitless, since the primordial purity of enlightenment can manifest anything and everything, according to the circumstances. Just as a mirror assumes the form of the person standing before it, or a gem assumes the hue of the cloth upon which it is placed, enlightenment manifests many things without actually being them. Its qualities are, in fact, as limitless as the number of sand-grains on the banks of the river Ganges. They are inseparable inasmuch as, like each image in a mirror, they are of the same quality, even though the details vary. As Jampal Bengar Zangpo says:[1]

nothing whatsoever, it manifests as anything whatsoever

With enlightenment comes total recognition of this fact. Limitless flexibility is lucid clarity, that was always innate to buddha nature, now made fully manifest. Although the way it is manifest, i.e. experienced, depends upon the circumstances of the experiencer, enlightenment itself does not rely upon any causes or conditions for its innate wisdom. It is non-created and unlimited, temporally or spatially. It pervades each and every being.

173. *The defilement and cognitive obscurations are said to be*
like covering clouds, since they are, by nature, non-existent,
they spread everywhere and are but incidental.

The way in which it is obscured: In the example of the rope and the snake, the snake never had any real existence. In that respect it is very different from the rope, which truly existed. The snake was but the temporary product of a confused mind. It caused the mind to be blind to the real thing (the rope) and to experience a completely false one (the snake).

The brilliant sun-like wisdom and space-like liberation are the real, innately-existing, purities. Yet, in immature beings, they remain unrecognised. The latter are blind to them and only see their own confused delusions, compared here to dense clouds obscuring the sun and space. Just as there is a difference between the real rope and the imaginary snake, there is a fundamental difference of nature between the primordial purity of wisdom and the temporary delusions of relative existence. Clouds appear in space but are not in themselves of the nature of space. Like clouds, the impurities of defilements and dualistic perception have no lasting substance, spread everywhere, filling one's vision, and have no effect on the space in which they come and go. Being incidental, they can be removed.

Enlightenment's cause (in detail)

174. The two jñāna, considered as non-conceptual and ensuing, cause freedom from these two veils.

The causes for obscurations being removed: the defilements 'obscure' liberation and dualistic thinking obscures lucid clarity. Desire and other impulses are the outcome of a dark, self-centred confusion which disappears in the light of the non-conceptual wisdom developed during meditation. The latter is perfected through the various stages of the path to become suchness jñāna. Dualistic thoughts are transcended through the 'ensuing' wisdom which develops in between meditation sessions, as one relates to all the various details of life and to other people. Inter-session, or ensuing, wisdom allows one to distinguish between all the phenomena of relative truth (the 'vast') and their ultimate voidness (the 'deep'). It eventually will become all-encompassing jñāna.

C. Enlightenment's fruition

In brief, as a summary of the examples of stainlessness

175. *Like a lake of purest water gradually overspread by lotuses,*
like the full moon set free from Rahu's mouth
and like the sun liberated from the banked defilement clouds,
this is radiantly manifest; stainless and bearing all qualities.

176. *Such buddhahood is like the Victor, the best of all,*
like the honey, the kernels, the gold, so valuable,
the treasure, the great tree, the image of the Sugata,
made of what is precious and pure,
like the king of the worlds and like the statue of gold.

If enlightenment is a fruition, there are, logically, only two ways in which it could occur. Either it is created as something, from things other than itself, or else it already exists and is a 'fruition', once whatever formerly obscured it has been removed. Maitreya's *uttara tantra*, as we have seen, firmly declares it to be the latter. Some Buddhists disagree with this, and consider enlightenment to be the product of one's actions on the path. However, were enlightenment a created product, acquired afresh, it would be subject to impermanence. As an innately-existing nature that is non-created, it is eternal.

Enlightenment is a 'result by removal'. The first set of examples describe the removal of the defilements. The removal of desire is compared to lotuses that have grown out of the filthy mud at the bottom of a pond. Removal of anger is compared to the moon 'freed from Rahu's mouth', i.e. emerged from an eclipse. Freedom from ignorance is compared to the sun free from clouds. The remaining nine examples, found previously in the *buddha nature* chapter, refer, in this instance, to the removal of the cognitive obscuration.

More detailed explanation

177. *Purity, as absence of incidental defilements, desire and so on,
is like the waters of the lake and so forth.
In brief, it is described as being the fruit of non-conceptual jñāna.*

The fruition achieved through meditation jñāna: The primordial wisdom developed through non-conceptual jñāna brings purity, by removing the impurity of the defilements. The latter hide buddha nature, just as thick, slimy mud conceals the lotus seed under the waters of a lake or just as an eclipse hides the moon and clouds hide the sun. Although the lotus seed, moon and sun remain where they have always been, one can perceive nothing of them. All one sees is, respectively, murky water, a dark shadow and clouds. Likewise, all that beings perceive – and are often obsessed with – are the needs, dislikes, opinions and so forth which constitute the superficial stuff of ordinary life. Rarely do they glimpse the great clarity and beauty which this superficial busyness conceals.

Skilful meditation, under the guidance of a teacher carrying the power of a true lineage, enables one to pierce through the hypnotic play of mind's superficialities and discover its true nature. This is a little like someone who had been fascinated by films all his life turning away from the fascinating screen for the first time, to discover the clear light of the projector, before it hits the cellulose. Non-conceptual jñāna, as its name implies, knows things directly for what they are, without thinking about them in any way. Just as all movies are the play of shapes and colours originating from a white light passing through a film, so are all experiences but the play of the clear light of the mind, coloured and shaped by the conditioning of thousands of lifetimes.

178. *Authentic attainment of the buddhakāya,
endowed with the finest of all qualities,
is taught as being the fruit of ensuing jñāna.*

The fruition achieved through ensuing jñāna: As one becomes aware of the true nature of one's own mind's experiences, through the profound truth revealed in meditation, one tries to extend this awareness and maintain its meditative clarity while encountering the many details of life, in between meditation sessions. What was recognised as being true for one's own mind, during meditation, is then seen to be equally true for all other experiences: for each and every thing. This extension of truth into every domain of life may take considerable time, even under powerful guidance. In Milarépa's 'Hundred Thousand Dohas', in the story called 'Later Stay at Ragma' or 'The Shepherd's Search for Mind',[2] Milarépa counsels the young shepherd:

Understanding the voidness of self is relatively simple. If you want to realise the truth of all things, you should meditate intensely, as I have done, for twelve years.

179. *This is like the lake of pure waters and so on because the silt of desire has been removed and because it causes the waters of meditative stability to sustain the 'lotus' beings who are to be trained.*

180. *It is like the unblemished full moon since, freed from hatred's 'Rahu', it embraces all beings with its light of great compassion and loving kindness.*

181. *Buddhahood is like the immaculate sun because, completely free of ignorance's clouds, it dispels beings' darkness with the radiance of its primordial wisdom.*

The fruition's freedom from the three poisons: It helps to have visited India and seen some of its muddy pools to appreciate this example. Imagine the wonder of people who saw one of the most beautiful things on Earth – a lotus flower – develop in the slimy ponds of their villages, the immaculate, delicate shades of its petals showing no trace of filth or impurity. Like the lotus seed germinating in the silt at the bottom of the pool, our lives can evolve and start to express the potential of buddha nature. In the pond, the growth is made possible by water. In us, it is made possible by meditation, which first elevates us beyond the 'silt' of desire and then carries us to a dimension of clarity, like the lotus which reaches the water's surface. The buoyancy of the water maintains it there.

The moon is bright, cooling and soothing, especially in India where the sun can be so aggressive. Yet the moon's beautiful presence can suddenly be taken away by an eclipse. Likewise, the many qualities that we can develop as human beings may all, one day, be 'eclipsed' by anger, which can, in seconds, turn an otherwise loving person into an unkind one whose only wish is to hurt another. To overcome anger, definitively, is as beautiful and magnificent as the moon emerging from an eclipse.

Ignorance does not take quite the same form as the other defilements. It is not a powerful impulse, as are desires, angers, jealousies and so forth. It is more like a constant undertone or backdrop, or perhaps like walls which limit and obscure. Here it is compared to dense banks of clouds, obscuring the sun. When the sky is clear, the sun can make flowers grow and crops ripen. Clouds impede and slow down this process. When a being is obscured by ignorance, the sun of primordial wisdom cannot do its work of bringing one to maturity and bringing forth the splendid qualities that are a true birthright. To shed worldly ignorance is to be like the sun emerging from clouds.

The various main obscurations are listed in the teachings of abhidharma. There are ten basic ones[3] and twenty-one subsidiary ones.[4] Obscurations can also be considered in terms of their relevance to various stages of the path. The milestones of the path to liberation are set by the falling away of successive layers of obscuration which, in each case, gives access to a new world of purity and understanding. Of particular note are:

▸ the obscurations which need to be removed in order to gain the Stage of Insight and thereby become a first level bodhisattva
▸ thereafter, the obscurations which fall away during the other nine bodhisattva levels. These are known as 'the obscurations to be removed for cultivation of insight'.[5]

Sometimes the defilements are explained mainly as the *five poisons* (desire, hostility, ignorance, jealousy, pride). Here, all of these various defilements are comprised in the three root poisons: desire, hostility and ignorance.

182. *Because it has peerless qualities, gives the taste of true dharma and is free from the shell of ignorance,*
it is likened unto the Sugata, the honey and the kernel.

183. *Because it is naturally pure,*
because it dispels beings' poverty by its own wealth of qualities and because it gives the fruit of total liberation,
it is likened unto gold, a treasure and the great tree.

184. *Because it is the 'embodiment of jewel qualities',*
because it is the 'supreme lord of bipeds'
and because its form is an image precious in its composition,
it is likened to the bejewelled object, the king and what is golden.

Its meaning related to the nine examples: Although employed a little differently in the previous chapter, the nine examples are used here to portray freedom from dualistic concepts, otherwise known as 'the cognitive obscurations'. The first example is that of the body of a real Buddha, showing that nothing else is comparable to enlightenment, the qualities of which are peerless. Once free from the habit of duality, one experiences the true taste of dharma, exemplified here by the taste of honey. Dualistic ignorance is like a confining shell. When this rough confine is cast aside, the non-dual truth can bring nourishment to many beings, and this is compared to the various grains freed from their husks.

The following three examples show the great power and richness of non-dual enlightenment. Like gold, an inexhaustible treasure or a great tree, it removes the poverty of those stuck in worldliness and suffering from lack of wisdom, lack of faith and lack of happiness. By teaching the universal truths of mind, enlightenment brings a long-term help which remedies the very root of existential problems. The purity of this help is compared to gold, its power to dispel spiritual poverty is compared to a great treasure and the way it brings one being after another to great fruition is compared to a mighty tree growing from a small fruit.

The remaining three examples show how the falling-away of dualistic ignorance reveals the three buddhakāya. The *dharmakāya* is compared to an image made solely of precious substances, showing that its primordial wisdom has nothing whatsoever to do with normal dualistic perception. The image has no fake glass gems; it is totally authentic. The *sambhogakāya* is the aspect of enlightenment that cares for and protects all beings in the worlds. Thus it is compared to a benevolent universal monarch. The *nirmanakāya* has the special quality of bringing happiness into the world. The inspiring presence of the Buddha is like a wish-fulfilling gem, bringing undreamed-of goodness to those in its proximity. This is portrayed here by the exquisite form of the statue.

These nine examples are in three groups of three. The first three are indicative of the difference between Buddhas and arhats. Although both are free from the coarse defilements, only Buddhas are free from the cognitive obscuration. The Buddhas' extra freedom unveils the qualities of enlightened body, speech and mind, represented respectively by the Buddha, the one taste of honey and the grain freed from its husk. The next three examples portray the naturalness of enlightenment. Gold is naturally pure, a treasure is naturally rich and a tree is the natural full manifestation of its seed's potential. The last three examples are those of the three kāya.

D. Enlightenment's function

in brief

185. *Enlightenment, untainted and all-pervading,*
     is of an indestructible nature
     because it is everlasting, at peace, permanent and undying.
     It is the ground for benefiting beings.
     The tathāgata are like space, the basis
     for the objects of the six sense faculties
     to be experienced by those who are excellent.

The way in which it achieves two-fold benefit: Having considered what enlightenment *is*, what *causes* it and how it is the *fruition* of all the work of the bodhisattva path, we now go on to consider what it *does*, i.e. its function. With enlightenment comes the zenith of attainment for oneself and the greatest possible benefit for others. This two-fold benefit is presented through four points:

▸ it reveals the state tainted by neither action (karma), defilements (kleśa) nor any psychological conditioning (*vasana*) due to action and defilement. This is the liberation aspect.
▸ it reveals that which is all-embracing. This is the wisdom aspect.
▸ it brings indestructibility, since it is liberated from ageing, sickness, birth and death. Being free from ageing, it is eternal; free from sickness, it is peace; free from birth, it is permanent and free from death, it is immortal.
▸ it is the universal basis, i.e. the ground for everything and in particular for benefiting other beings.

186. *It is the condition for form beyond the four elements to be seen,*
 for the good and pure sound to be heard,
 for the pure fragrance of the Sugatas' perfect conduct to be smelled,
 for the taste of the dharma of the great
 and of the deeply-realised to be savoured,

187. *for the bliss felt in samādhi to be experienced*
 and for the very essence, the profound nature, to be realised.
 Therefore, when considered in a very fine way,
 the tathāgata, who give birth to true bliss,
 are like space, devoid of reasons.

The function when all is pure: Enlightenment is the truth of primordial wisdom (jñāna) and not the play of deluded consciousness (vijñāna). The deluded consciousnesses of the six types of being fabricate all sorts of experiences, which manifest as seeming objects of the five senses and as mental images. The removal of these illusions makes way for a completely new sort of experience. The total purity of buddha nature, as experienced by the partially-enlightened bodhisattvas of the ten levels, manifests as the very special sense experiences of the 'pure lands', which are not a physical perception of worlds which are 'other' but the radiant manifestation of the innate world of perfection. In these experiences, the myriad qualities of formless ultimate truth, which is not a creation based on the four elements, are expressed as forms.

Bodhisattvas 'see' Buddhas, with their eyes of wisdom. They 'hear' the constant sweet music of mahāyāna teachings. The moral purity of perfection is experienced as the most wonderful perfume, and the one sweet taste of the voidness of all things is savoured. The sense of physical sensation, as ordinary beings know it, becomes, for them, the profound bliss of deep meditative absorption.

Besides the five sense consciousnesses, there is mental consciousness. The pure version of this,[6] as experienced by bodhisattvas, is a direct recognition of the true nature. Although all these bodhisattva experiences stem from their contact with enlightenment's purity, and are expressions of it, they are not it. Total enlightenment is therefore like space, inasmuch as it is the primordially pure expanse of mind in which all the pure lands take place, just as all the play of worldly experiences happens in ordinary space. Like space, Buddhas are non-created and spontaneously present. Extraordinarily, this timeless space is not just the inert substratum of existence – like a blank video tape – but the source of great benefit, and nothing but benefit, for endless beings.

in greater detail

188. *The function of the two jñāna, put concisely, is to be known
as the perfect fulfilment of the vimuktikāya and
the accomplishment of dharmakāya.*

189. *Since they are untainted, all-embracing
and the uncreated ground,
the vimuktikāya and the dharmakāya should be known
as having two attributes and one attribute.*

The aspects of buddha nature through which the two-fold benefit is accomplished: The function of enlightenment is to fulfil the two-fold benefit. These two verses and the following four verses will now develop the four main points of the fulfilment mentioned above.

At this point in the text, we are introduced to a new pair of terms: *vimuktikāya* and *dharmakāya*. The perfect fulfilment for oneself comes through the total liberation mentioned briefly above as being untainted, all-embracing and indestructible. *Vimukti* is simply the Sanskrit for total liberation. *Kāya*, as previously, means embodiment. *Vimuktikāya* results from non-conceptual wisdom developed during meditation. It is limitless, as opposed to the limited liberation attained by arhats. *Dharmakāya* is the embodiment of the all-encompassing wisdom, developed through inter-sessions practice. In fact, vimuktikāya and dharmakāya are both facets of what is more generally called dharmakāya. Here they are singled out in order to show clearly which aspect fulfils which function of enlightenment and to show the value of deep meditation and the value of inter-session practice.

Vimuktikāya and dharmakāya have respectively the qualities of untaintedness and all-pervasiveness. Both of these facets of enlightenment share the quality of not being creations and of being, therefore, beyond birth, ageing, sickness and death, i.e. indestructible. Furthermore, dharmakāya has the special quality of being the ground from which springs every benefit for others. It is the wisdom of enlightenment: a lucid, non-created, true awareness which is the lamp guiding everyone to its primordial truth.

190.   *It is untainted because the defilements,*
       along with their accompanying conditioning, have ceased.
       Jñāna is considered as all-embracing
       since it is unattached and unimpeded.

191.   *They are uncreated since their nature*
       is at all times indestructible,
       mentioned and explained as everlastingness and so on.

*192. Destructibility is to be known through the following four aspects,
since they are the counterparts of everlastingness and so forth:
decay, drastic change, interruption and
the inconceivable change of death.*

*193. Since enlightenment is free of change, it should be known as
everlasting, at peace, permanent and deathless.*

How it is the best possible benefit for oneself: It should be clear by now that purity means freedom from defilements. Here we are considering the particular difference between arhats and Buddhas in this respect. Arhats have rid themselves from suffering (*dukha*) and its causes (karma and kleśa) and will never return to worldliness. However, fine traces of psychological conditioning (*vasana*), imprinted by karma and kleśa, remain. It takes the finest meditative work of the ten bodhisattva levels to remove these. Their total, radical, removal is an extraordinary accomplishment of purity. That is what the Buddha Sakyamuni finally achieved two thousand, five hundred years ago.

The primordial wisdom that manifests at enlightenment knows neither limitation nor obstacle. It is not attached to any conceptual basis: not even that of a body made of light, as is the case with arhats. It is not the partial view or understanding of a particular being but the universal true nature of all things, endowed with its own wisdom.

Whereas all specific things come to an end and are either destroyed or disintegrate of their own accord, enlightenment lasts for ever. The four main blows dealt to ordinary things by impermanence are described in the above verses, as follows:

decay	refers to the process of ageing,
drastic change	refers to sickness,
interruption	refers to birth and
inconceivable change	refers to death, even the arhat's subtle death.

Itself free from these four, enlightenment is known as being their counterparts, respectively, *everlasting, at peace, permanent* and *deathless*.

This intelligence, so stainless, is 'the ground'
Because it is the foundation for all virtuous qualities.

194. *Just as space, which is without cause, is the cause*
for the seeing, hearing and so forth of
forms, sounds, odours, sensations and mental data

195. *Likewise, this is the condition for the untainted qualities*
to arise as objects of stable beings' sense faculties,
through their unimpeded connection with the two kāya.

How it is the best possible benefit for others: Just as the presence of one rope forms the basis for resolving all the various snake illusions projected onto it, so does the true nature of mind serve as the basis for resolving all the mental deformations of ordinary deluded consciousness. But more than this, the true nature of mind is the most lucid and far-reaching intelligence, crystal clear on account of its utter purity. Its very nature is compassionate goodness and, within it, all the pāramitā are complete. It is the true, ultimate bodhicitta – a purity so profound and awe-inspiring that it gives rise to all the virtuous actions of relative bodhicitta and naturally inspires the ethical values of the ten virtuous actions[7] which form the natural morality of good people everywhere.

Space is not the direct cause of visual forms, sounds, odours and the like, but it is the condition for the visual, auditive and other faculties to operate. Shapes, sounds, odours and flavours manifest within space but are not produced by it. Similarly, the ultimate space of enlightenment is not the prime cause but the condition through which beings on the path of integration and the paths of insight and cultivation[8] can experience the pure forms of the Buddhas and their pure lands. These visions convey a direct, rather than a merely theoretical, appreciation of the ultimate nature of all things, as the vimuktikāya and dharmakāya.

E. Endowments

196. *Buddhahood is inconceivable, permanent, everlasting, at peace, immutable, perfectly at peace, all-embracing and concept-free. Like space, it is uninvolved, completely unhindered, free of coarse sensation, invisible, imperceptible, wholesome and immaculate.*

Enlightenment is endowed with fifteen principal qualities. It is:

1. *inconceivable* because it can only be understood by auto-cognisant jñāna,
2. *permanent* because it has no birth,
3. *everlasting* because it has no ageing,
4. *at peace* because it has no change through sickness,
5. *immutable* because it has no death,
6. *perfectly at peace* because it is free from suffering due to karma,
7. *all-embracing* through its all-encompassing primordial wisdom,
8. *concept-free* through its suchness primordial wisdom,
9. *uninvolved* since it is free from defilements,
10. *completely unhindered,* being free from the cognitive obscuration,
11. *free of coarse sensations* since it is the true sphere of meditation,
12. *invisible* because it is formless,
13. *imperceptible* since it has no characteristics,
14. *wholesome* through the utter purity of its nature and
15. *immaculate* as it is free from all incidental impurities.

197. *One's own fulfilment and benefit for beings are made manifest through the vimuktikāya and the dharmakāya.*
These two foundations, of own-benefit and benefit for others, have the above qualities of inconceivability and so forth.

The single root *budh* in Sanskrit gives rise to several well-known terms such as Buddha, bodhi, bodhi-sattva and bodhi-citta. It has two main meanings, reflected in this verse: liberation ('free from the sleep of ignorance') and plenitude ('all qualities perfect'). Its translations, in English, are usually variants of the terms *enlightenment* and *buddhahood*. The fifteen endowments of enlightenment (*bodhi*) listed in the previous verse are those of the vimuktikāya and dharmakāya. The former is the manifestation of buddhahood's highest fulfilment for oneself and the latter serves as the foundation from which emerges great benefit for other beings. The following verses will develop these fifteen qualities in more detail.

198. *Buddhahood is the domain of omniscient jñāna
and not within the scope of the three forms of prajñā.
Therefore the jñānakāya should be understood
as being inconceivable for beings.*

1. The first endowment is inconceivability. This has prime mention because it applies not only to buddhahood itself but to each of the remaining fourteen endowments. The auto-cognisant clarity of enlightenment itself – 'omniscient jñāna' as it is called here – is the one and only wisdom that can know enlightenment for what it really is. This wisdom-of-itself is so important that it is expressed as a kāya, an embodiment of enlightenment. However, one would be mistaken if one thought of this jñānakāya as being something other than vimuktikāya or dharmakāya. It is just as way of highlighting their self-wisdom.

Buddhists cultivate wisdom (*prajñā*) in three ways. The first is **study**, formerly through listening to discourses and memorising them and – more recently due to the advent of printing – through studying texts. Study is the first step: the phase of acquiring information and discovering ideas. It opens doorways of knowledge that one never even knew existed.

The second degree of wisdom is **deep reflection**. One could also say contemplation but this word means meditation in some languages and cultures and has led to some confusion. Through deep reflection, one 'gets to the bottom' of the ideas one has studied. To do this, doubts must be resolved and a meaning needs to fit properly into place with other meanings one has discovered, through study or personal experience. There is a characteristic 'eureka' feeling and one prayer[9] describes it as emerging from darkness into light.

The third stage of wisdom is that of **direct experience** or meditation. Through the calm, precision and clarity of meditation, the subject matter becomes totally familiar and, most importantly, experienced directly rather than intellectually. Although this verse says that none of these three forms of prajñā can know enlightenment, it is referring to them as they occur in most Buddhists. The meditation-wisdom of bodhisattvas is an exception. It does bring some limited, but nevertheless direct, experience of enlightenment. However, this is more a linguistic problem than anything else, since, when prajñā becomes that good, it is no longer called prajñā but jñāna.

199. *Being so subtle, it is not an object of study.*
Being the ultimate truth, it is not contemplation's domain.
Being the profound universal essence, it falls outwith the scope of mundane sorts of meditation and their like.

Considering the three sorts of prajñā described above, it becomes clear why enlightenment falls outwith their scope. The wisdom of study operates through abstract thought which is a relatively gross instrument of understanding. It can only ever think abstractly *about* enlightenment but never know it directly, as only fine and subtle meditation can. Deep reflection may be much less gross, but it is primarily a cross-referencing of the ideas and experiences of relative reality. As we have seen in earlier chapters, enlightenment is like nothing one has ever experienced and therefore no relative points of reference can even approach it. Finally, none of the direct experiences of immature beings' meditations have anything to do with it (although many people mistake mundane experiences of deep peace or bliss for it).

200. *This is because the immature have never seen this before,*
just like those born blind confronted with visible form.
Even the deeply realised are like the newly born
seeing sunlight from within their room.

The Fifth Vajra Abode – enlightenment 207

This verse develops the certainty that no relative points of reference have any relevance to enlightenment. Every word, label, idea and image that the mind can conjure up has its roots in the past: in former experience. It is impossible to have a mental image of something one has never experienced. Of course, one could imagine a purple, pin-striped dog with horns, even though one has never met one. But that is only because one *has* already experienced purple as a colour, pin-stripes as a design, a dog as an animal and horns as an attribute. Just as those blind from birth have no memory-bank of visual images and can neither see forms before them nor even imagine them from past data, likewise 'immature beings', i.e. those who have not attained the first bodhisattva level, are incapable of either perceiving enlightenment directly or reconstituting it from previously-experienced phenomena.

Furthermore, even those who attain the first bodhisattva level have a very limited, if direct, awareness of enlightenment. They are compared, as in the *Śrīmālādevīsūtra*, to a newly born baby. After spending all its life in the dark confines of the womb, it is born to see daylight for the very first time. Although it has seen the light, and light is simply light wherever it may be, it has yet to experience all the nuances of light that the adult knows or has experienced. One needs to travel to the hinterland of Aix-en-Provence really to understand the play of light which Cézanne and his contemporaries painted so exquisitely. Could our newly born baby even imagine such hues from its neon-lit hospital crib?

The clear light of enlightenment remains the same lucid clarity throughout. Like the growing child, the bodhisattva grows to realise the unimaginable extent of this clarity as progress is made through levels two, three, four and so forth. A first level bodhisattva could not even imagine the lot of a second level one and the extraordinary joys and qualities of a clarity yet to be unfolded.

201. *It is permanent, as it has no origination,*
everlasting, as it has no cessation,
at peace, being free from both,
immutable, since it abides in the true nature,

The next four endowments are those mentioned above in verse 193. Together, they show enlightenment to be endowed with changelessness, in contrast to the impermanence which is characteristic of worldliness and even true, in a subtle way, of the arhat's achievement.

2. No birth. Enlightenment is permanent because it is not a temporary delusion which comes into being through causes and conditions. It is not a product of interdependent origination.
3. No death. It is everlasting (one could use the heavier term eternal), as it never ceases, for the same reasons.
4. No sickness. It is at peace, i.e. undisturbed by the comings-and-goings, impermanence and suffering typical of all mental creations.
5. No ageing. It is immutable, being none other than the changeless, timeless true nature of mind, as opposed to the ephemeral creations of a deluded mind.

202. *perfectly at peace, since it is the truth of cessation,*
all-embracing, since all has been understood,
concept-free, since it does not dwell,
non-clinging, since all defilements have been dispelled,

203. *always unhindered, since obscurations to knowledge are purified,*
free from coarse sensations, being without two and highly-suited,

The next six endowments express the purity of its realisation:

6. It is perfectly at peace because it is the Truth of Cessation, i.e. every suffering and its cause has been eradicated for ever.
7. Its wisdom is all-embracing, since the cognitive obscuration has been eradicated. As conceptual labels which determine ordinary knowledge no longer confine and limit awareness, everything is known as clearly as though it were in the palm of the hand and as part of an infinite inter-connectivity.
8. It is concept-free, as enlightenment does not depend upon thoughts.
9. It is uninvolved. Unlike ordinary personality projections or even some meditations, its realisation does not depend upon any

identification with this or that mental formulation.
10. It is unhindered. Its awareness reaches all things. This and the following example are particularly relevant to meditation, showing enlightenment as being the total perfection of meditation. Meditations, as they are known on other levels, are restricted.
11. It is free from coarse sensations. This refers to the total absence of all the meditation obstacles defined under the two headings of hyper-activity and hypo-awareness (often called agitation and drowsiness for simplicity). Being the essence of all things, it is a highly suitable basis for awareness of things.

204. *invisible, since it is formless,*
imperceptible, because it has no characteristic,
wholesome since its nature is pure and
immaculate, as all impurities have been removed,

The remaining four endowments express further purity:

12. It is invisible, since it is formless.
13. It is imperceptible because it has no concrete characteristics.
14. It is wholesome as not one thing in it is impure.
15. It is immaculate since there is no impediment to meditation.

F. Actualisation

in brief

This section deals with the interpenetration of enlightenment and unenlightened illusion. The title could have been translated as 'manifestation' or as 'penetration', for the following reasons. From the angle of enlightenment, this section shows the various ways in which enlightenment's one nature *manifests* as the three *kāya*, to the pure, the partially pure and the impure, respectively. From the angle of the non-enlightened, it shows how non-enlightened minds can *penetrate* enlightenment's mysteries. This is a fairly long section of the chapter. First the main subject matter is introduced in verses

205 through to 208. Then greater detail is given in verses 209 through to 228.

205. *Beginningless, centreless and endless, completely indivisible, free from the two, free from the three, stainless and concept-free, such is dharmadhātu. Understanding of its nature is the vision of the yogin who abides in meditation.*

Who understands this dharmadhātu nature? This verse is about the voidness aspect of enlightenment, dharmadhātu, which is explained through five characteristics.

- ▸ it is not a creation and is therefore beginningless, centreless and endless, with all the significance that these words had in the first chapter, on buddha.
- ▸ the voidness of dharmadhātu cannot be separated in any way from its primordial wisdom. Voidness and wisdom are not like black and white strands of thread, woven into a rope in which each colour is still visible, despite the mixing of the threads. This might have been the case, were voidness a mere absence, such as the absence of horns on a rabbit. But here voidness *is* the wisdom that recognises the absence of limited entity within the limitlessness of interdependence. The absence of illusion *is* the presence of wisdom, and not mere blankness.
- ▸ it is free from the two intellectual extremes of overstatement and understatement. The former would tend to attribute a lasting self or God to buddha nature and the latter would deny or underestimate it and its relation with interdependence.
- ▸ it is free from the three obscurations: defilements, the cognitive obscuration and obstacles to spontaneous, perfect meditation.
- ▸ it cannot be the object of thoughts or of any dualistic perception. Hence it is the 'vision' of the buddha eyes of primordial wisdom: those of the supreme Yogin, the Buddha.

206. *Unfathomable, greater in number than sand grains in the Ganges, inconceivable and unequalled are the qualities of the immaculate space of the tathāgata, purged of every defect and related conditioning.*

The five characteristics of dharmakāya: whereas dharmadhātu represents the voidness aspect of enlightenment, dharmakāya represents its primordial wisdom. It is:

- unfathomable, inasmuch as it has so many qualities and these are not located in any precise place or within any particular concrete reality. Normal wisdom is wise about something, somewhere and is fairly specific. Enlightenment is the innate wisdom of each and every thing and hence is present everywhere, in everything, as an unimaginably vast and deep pleiad of qualities.
- these qualities of wisdom are truly incalculable, greater in number than the grains of sand on the banks and bed of the river Ganges.
- inconceivable, since this wisdom is so profound and unique.
- unequalled by anything, be it in the world and tainted by defilement or be it comprised within the fruition of the hinayāna path, which is merely peace.
- immaculate. The previous four qualities referred directly to the primordial wisdom of dharmakāya and this last point highlights the purity of that wisdom, free from every obscuration and associated mental conditioning.

The reader will recognise many of these points from previous sections and chapters and may be wondering why they are repeated here. In this section, until now, we have been considering enlightenment as Buddhas know it, as dharmadhātu and dharmakāya. This is necessarily very similar to the teachings on buddha nature. The repitition is extremely useful: it reminds us of this absolute nature of enlightenment before we consider how it is perceived relatively. In the remainder of this section, we will be considering enlightenment as it is experienced by beings other than Buddhas.

207. *By various facets of the true dharma,*
through its radiant embodiments and diligence
in accomplishing the aim of liberating beings,
its deeds are like those of a king of wishing-gems.
Although it takes different 'substantial' forms,
it is not really of such a character.

The five characteristics of sambhogakāya:
- the various facets are the *deep* teachings of dharma, expressing voidness, and the *vast* ones, expressing all the manifold details of the various paths to enlightenment. Whereas dharmakāya is the mind of enlightenment, sambhogakāya is its uninterrupted speech. Within sambhogakāya, one finds further subdivision into body, speech and mind qualities. These are those of its speech.
- the deep and vast teachings are experienced by bodhisattvas as being given by radiant forms of Buddhas, in their respective pure lands. These forms exhibit the 32 major and 80 other signs of a fully enlightened being. This is the body aspect.
- the mind of sambhogakāya is continuously and diligently engaged in its natural activity of liberating beings.
- the sambhogakāya accomplishes its various tasks with complete naturalness and spontaneity, and without prior thought or intention. In this respect, it is like a wish-fulfilling gem.
- its deeds take the myriad forms of the pure lands, which in turn constitute the basis from which not only the bodhisattvas in the ten levels, but also other beings, are benefited. Although these manifestations *appear* to be substantial, they are not.

208. *The form aspects are the cause, establishing worldlings*
on the path to peace, bringing them to maturity and predicting.
Moreover, their presence always graces these worlds
just as space is the constant abode of the element of form.

The nirmanakāya: This is the embodiment of enlightenment perceptible by beings still under the sway of saṃsāra's delusions, but with relatively little obscuration. One can recognise three main stages of the development of such beings in which the nirmanakāya plays a special role. The first is that of leading them away from worldliness and into the Buddhist path. The second is that of helping those already on the path to gain realisation and purify their defilements. The third is that of predicting, to those who are already very pure, the time and place of their future enlightenment.

The nirmanakāya is permanent in the sense that it is always active somewhere. As the activity can take the form of appearing in a world, teaching and passing away, as did Buddha Sakyamuni, one might think of nirmanakāya as being quite impermanent. Yet, on further reflection, when one considers all the other nirmanakāya activity in this world and other worlds, it becomes apparent that there is uninterrupted activity. Just as the various animal, human and other dimensions of the 'form realms' have a constant location in space, despite the comings and goings of individual beings and geographical features, so is the radiance of nirmanakāya (*sprul.sku* in Tibetan, pronounced *tulku*) – mind's truth and wisdom – constantly active in the worlds of confusion.

One can consider the above from a slightly different angle. The permanent presence of nirmanakāya gives a constant potential for 'spiritual' experience. Once a being's mind opens to this potential through faith and good karma, he or she will find the guidance needed at that point, whether the world around the person is spiritual or not. This is very vividly exemplified in the life stories of Naropa and Gampopa and it is very encouraging: no matter where or when one happens to be, faith will open up the doorways to enlightenment in a way which is perfectly tailored to one's own mind. In practice, one needs to continually deepen ones conviction of the power of faith. At one and the same time, either alone or with the help of one's teachers, one must learn how to distinguish genuine contact between mind and its true nature from the deceptive contact between mind and its illusions. In this respect, it may help to be aware of the sway that a powerful – but not necessarily good – being can exercise over a weaker one and the pseudo-spiritual experiences that this can produce.

in more detail

209. *That called 'the self-existent', 'omniscience', 'buddhahood', 'supreme nirvāṇa', 'inconceivability', 'victory over the enemy' and the 'self-nature'*

210. *is categorised according to its qualities*
of profundity, vastness and magnanimity,
through the essence-kāya and so forth

General classification: The three kāya described briefly above together constitute enlightenment. The text now gives us seven significant synonyms for it:
- the 'self-existent', as it depends upon nothing other than itself, i.e. buddha nature.
- 'omniscience', through its perfect wisdom.
- 'buddhahood' because of its simultaneous purity and wisdom, as evoked by the etymological root *budh*.
- 'supreme nirvāṇa', being the most perfect of the various sorts of nirvāṇa, i.e. states beyond suffering.
- 'inconceivability' because no ordinary prajñā can cope with it.
- 'victory over the enemy', the enemy being saṃsāra and
- the 'self-cognisant nature', through its apperceptive jñāna.

There follows now a description of each of the kāya, in which the dharmakāya, which has been presented so far in this section under its aspects of dharmakāya, dharmadhātu and vimuktikāya, will now appear under the name of *svābhāvikakāya*. This is not another, separate, embodiment of buddha. *Svābhāvika* means quintessence. Svābhāvikakāya shows enlightenment's quintessential qualities, which enable it to manifest severally as all the other kāya. It is almost identical in definition to dharmakāya and is indistinguishable from it in reality.

PRESENTATION OF EACH KĀYA: A. THE SVABHAVIKAKĀYA

211. *Of these, the buddhas' essence-kāya should be known as having five intrinsic characteristics and, in brief, five qualities.*

The essence *kāya* has five intrinsic qualities and five qualities in terms of its presentation to the unenlightened.

212. *It is uncreated and indivisible,*
utterly purged, purified of the two extremes,

*definitively liberated from the three obscurations –
defilements, ideas and hindrances to mastery in meditation –*

213. *it is stainless, completely beyond concepts and
it is clarity, through being the domain of the yogin
and through the dharmadhātu being quintessentially pure.*

Five intrinsic qualities of the essence kāya:
- it is not a creation, having neither beginning, middle nor end. Within it, voidness (dharmadhātu) and primordial wisdom (dharmakāya) are indistinguishable and indivisible. Of these two:
  1. the voidness of dharmadhātu can be understood through the teachings of the second turning of the wheel of dharma, as the absence of absolute entity in any relative *dharma*. This is because each phenomenon is but a manifestation of interdependence and therefore naturally void (*rang stong*) of a unique, independent being.
  2. the primordial wisdom of dharmakāya can be understood through the buddha nature teachings of the third turning, which show the ultimate truth, buddha nature, to be universally present and devoid of anything other (*gzhan stong*) than itself.
- in the wisdom of svābhāvikakāya, there is not one iota of the 'two extreme notions' which:
  1. either overcharge it with divinity, and would wish to add something to it, or
  2. underrate its universality, and would wish to remove something from it.

This absence of extreme ideas is the final outcome of the wisdom that one tries to cultivate in meditation, as one learns to leave the mind to itself. One trains in this by first receiving clear instruction that mind's true nature *is* voidness and clarity. With time, one comes to a first-hand conviction of this fact and eventually learns how to remain comfortably within the primordial nature, overcoming habitual tendencies to want to 'improve the meditation' or to remove and deny thoughts.
- it is liberated for ever from the three obscurations: defilements,

- the cognitive obscuration and obstacles to meditation.
- ▸ it is stainless, in the particular sense of being absolutely, totally free of any of the dualistic concepts which are the real source of the three obscurations mentioned above.
- ▸ it is total clarity. Any worldly knowledge of the ultimate is merely intellectual speculation. The supramundane knowledge of arhats and bodhisattvas is restricted by the limits of their own condition. This, however, is the unique and complete vision of the supreme yogin, the Buddha, who alone enjoys the full extent of dharmadhātu's purity and who at all times is the union of wisdom and skilful means.

214. *The svabhavikakāya is truly endowed with the qualities
of inestimability, incalculability, inconceivability,
incomparability and ultimate purity.*

215. *It is respectively immeasurable and so forth
because it is vast, unquantifiable, beyond the scope
of intellectual speculation, unique and rid of even conditioning.*

Five principal qualities of the essence-kāya: besides the above-mentioned characteristics intrinsic to the essence-kāya, there are five general ones more relevant to other beings' quest for knowledge about it:
- ▸ it is inestimable, being without colour, form or any specific attribute that would limit it, temporally or spatially.
- ▸ it is incalculable, as its qualities are unlimited.
- ▸ it is inconceivable, being beyond the four extremes and the eight conceptual fabrications explained in the prajñāpāramitā.
- ▸ it is incomparable, being the unique domain of the supreme yogin and unlike anything in the world. The yogin understands this essence kāya not to be a mere blank or absence but the extraordinary clarity and infinite possibility of pure mind, adorned with the beautiful, compassionate qualities of a Buddha.
- ▸ it is utterly, totally pure, being free from even the finest echo-like traces of conditioning due to past delusions.

PRESENTATION OF EACH KĀYA: B. THE SAMBHOGAKĀYA

Enlightenment is known by Buddhas as the formless essence kāya explained above. From this manifest two sorts of form kāya. The pure bodhisattvas of the ten levels experience enlightenment as the sambhogakāya and very fortunate worldly individuals experience it as the nirmanakāya. The manifestation of these two form kāya is often compared to the reflection of the moon in water. The rocks, soil, leaves and bushes of the Earth are too rough to reflect the moon, which is nevertheless in the sky. Water, however, is smooth enough to capture an image of the real moon. Pure, completely calm water will give a faithful reproduction of the moon. The bodhisattva mind is like this. Dirty, slightly ruffled water with maybe a small plant or two growing on it, will give some sort of image of the moon. Ordinary beings' minds are like that.

Bodhisattvas and fortunate beings both experience 'Buddhas'. The former, through their realisation of voidness, have a very direct and inspiring experience, which translates the qualities of enlightenment into the powerful imagery of the Buddhas' pure lands, in which every thing is an expression of the profound and meaningful truths of the universe. The latter receive a less direct guidance. Due to their own confusion and weak motivation, they need gradual guidance through the maze of purification of their thoughts and feelings. They need to undergo a complete apprenticeship in love, compassion and bodhicitta.

216. *It takes the form of perfect expression because*
it perfectly uses the various dharmas, it manifests real attributes,
it has uninterrupted activity which benefits beings,
as it is the natural outflow of pure compassion,

217. *it fulfils aspirations, completely, exactly,*
spontaneously and without conceptual agitation,
and because it has miraculous abilities,
like those of a wish-fulfilling gem.

Five principal aspects of the sambhogakāya: Sambhoga means perfect access or appreciation. Bodhisattvas have a relatively direct access to, or appreciation of, enlightenment, even if all the latter's qualities are not experienced directly but interpreted through sense messages. If we view the expression sambhogakāya from the perspective of enlightenment rather than from the bodhisattva's experience, it becomes the kāya of perfect expression. Its own five principal aspects are:

- to employ perfectly the dharma, expressing every aspect of mahāyāna dharma constantly. This is the speech aspect.
- to manifest the forms of Buddhas, their entourages and pure lands. These forms are authentic, inasmuch as they are a just representation of dharmakāya's qualities, just as the reflection of the moon in perfectly calm, clear water is a faithful one. This is the body aspect.
- it is the pure compassion of the Buddha. This is the mind aspect, through which there is incessant benefit for other beings. From the dharmakāya's compassion springs this sambhogakāya and from the compassionate love which is sambhogakāya springs the activity of the nirmanakāya.
- its acts are spontaneous, fulfilling beings' aspirations completely, exactly, spontaneously and without conceptual agitation.
- it manifests what is not its real nature, even though its forms and speech are a faithful interpretation of the formless qualities of dharmakāya. This is compared to a perfectly clear gem, which takes on the colour of the cloth against which it is set, appearing blue on blue velvet, red on red velvet and so forth. Although it looks red, it is not, in itself, red. The true nature, 'coloured' by the relative but very pure mind of the bodhisattva, is experienced as sambhogakāya with great sensual fulfilment, in a world of inspirational forms expressing the formless.

218. *It is shown here in five facets, those of uninterrupted speech,*
     emanations and deeds, and through the fact that
     these are not at all contrived
     and do not manifest its true identity.

Five principal qualities of the sambhogakāya: The text now considers the five principal aspects explained above in terms of their permanence.

▸ the interaction between the bodhisattva and enlightenment is a constant and uninterrupted one. Each bodhisattva is continually experiencing sambhogakāya's pure speech. One should bear in mind the fact that a first-level bodhisattva can receive one hundred different teachings simultaneously and be in one hundred pure lands simultaneously. This number increases almost exponentially as progress is made from level to level.
▸ likewise, the bodhisattva is constantly in the presence of the forms of hundreds, or thousands, of Buddhas, each bearing the 32 and 80 signs of perfection.
▸ the compassionate mind of sambhogakāya is constant.
▸ its spontaneous, non-conceptual activity of body, speech and mind is happening continuously.
▸ it can manifest that which it is not, in order to help and guide beings. It shows changing forms and actions, teaches with sounds and so forth, yet is, in truth, the formless, changeless dharmakāya.

219. *Just as a gem is not really the various hues it can assume, so likewise is the all-embracing not as it appears to be through the circumstances of various beings.*

How sambhogakāya manifests according to circumstances: This verse underlines the point that all the various Buddha forms etc. are not real entities but the joint product of the almost-pure awareness of bodhisattvas and the real qualities of dharmakāya. As Kalu Rinpoché used to say, Buddhists should not believe that, somewhere in space, there are Buddhas sitting with their arms in awkward positions, holding various attributes, for century upon century, like cosmic automatons. Only buddha nature truly exists. All formal experiences of it are the result of the relative mind having some sort of interface with the ultimate.

The simile used to explain this is that of a clear jewel, as explained above. The important point here is that, like the jewel, the dharmakāya remains changeless throughout. Different people see varying colours, highlights and patterns in a gem, according to where they are positioned. The mental 'position' of the bodhisattva or another being will determine how he or she actually experiences the enlightenment of buddha nature.

PRESENTATION OF EACH KĀYA: C. THE NIRMANAKĀYA

The nirmanakāya referred to here is a 'supreme nirmanakāya', such as the historical Buddha Sakyamuni or the future Buddha, Maitreya. These emanations manifest, even to worldly beings, as having the thirty-two major marks and eighty signs of perfection of an Enlightened Being, teaching dharma in order to set the world into a cycle of wisdom and goodness. According to the Good Aeon Sūtra, 1,002 such Buddhas come during the lifetime of this world, to awaken it over and over again to the timeless universal truths. Sakyamuni was but the fourth of these. Maitreya, the 'Loving One', will be the fifth, and the being who is known in these times as the Gyalwa Karmapa will be the sixth, the 'Lion Buddha'.

The various major events of Sakyamuni's life, such as his family background, his asceticism, etc., were not simple accidents but the meaningful and perfect conclusion to a very long and special story. In Mahāyāna Buddhism, it is considered that, from the time he first uttered the bodhisattva vow, the bodhisattva who was to become Sakyamuni Buddha took many hundreds of lifetimes to reach ultimate perfection. Altogether, these incarnations of systematic purification and steady development along the bodhisattva path spanned three cosmic aeons (a cosmic aeon, in this case, is the time from the inception of a solar system, such as our own, until its final destruction). After this extraordinary length of time, in which three universes had come and gone, he had purified absolutely everything in his being that there was to purify and he had attained every quality that a human being can attain.

He achieved his final enlightenment in the 'Highest' deva realm, called *aknstha*, in Sanskrit, and *og.min*[10] in Tibetan. From there, he emanated into all the human realms of the thousand million cosmic systems with which he was associated. His 'lives' in those realms, such as the one he led in India some 2,500 years ago, were a very meaningful yet spontaneous drama, enacted to make the dharma teachings he imparted have the finest and most enduring effect on the world. Such a vision of the purposefulness of the Buddha's life gives a very different image of him than that of a simple prince, at first influenced by Hinduism, who gradually became disillusioned with the royal life and one day set out into the unknown on a spiritual quest. His wisdom and perfection were there from the start, as bore witness the special signs on his body and the golden aura which shone for almost a kilometre around him as a child. The twelve major activities of his life, and their significance, are given in the following verses.

220. *Through greatest compassion knowing all worlds,*
having seen all worlds, while never leaving the dharmakāya,
through various forms, apparitional by nature,
the one excellently born into the highest birth

Manifestation of the twelve deeds of a supreme nirmanakāya: The great master Jamgon Kongtrul underlines the wonder of these deeds. They are amazing, inasmuch as the enlightened mind, without ever leaving its pure domain of formless dharmakāya, manifests awe-inspiringly beautiful and meaningful forms in many worlds, such as our own, through the deepest of compassion. These emanations are the best thing that ever happened in our universe. The presence of the Buddha in each world, playing out the story of the most meaningful of lives, is even more wonderful since it takes place like an apparition, i.e. it is vividly apparent but totally insubstantial, like a rainbow.

In the particular case of Sakyamuni, he first emanated as 'Summit of Goodness'[11] to the deva paradise called Realm of Great Joy' (Tuṣita) and taught many gods there the paths to liberation and maturity. Then he had a fivefold vision, indicating that our world was ready for the dharma and that the many beings with whom he had established a dharma link in previous incarnations were now born or being reborn on Earth. The fivefold vision was:

- the *place* was right: our world was ready for the dharma and Northern India was an advanced society in which the dharma could become established and spread through the civilised world.
- the *time* was right. Sakyamuni was due to come when the maximum lifespan here was about one hundred (lunar) years. The significance of this becomes clear in the Kalachakra teachings which show various epochs during the life of this world, some with beings of very subtle bodies having extraordinarily long lifespans and others with degenerate beings, having very brief lifespans (two decades) in times of great darkness and pollution.
- the *entourage* of all his former disciples was gathering in India. These would be beings capable of receiving and perpetuating his teaching.
- there was a suitable *mother*, Queen Mahāmāya, capable of bearing such an extraordinary child.
- her *caste* (royal caste) would be the best one for a great teacher to be born into at that time. The previous Buddha, Kaśyapa, for example, had found it more advantageous to be born into the priestly caste, as it was more prestigious in that age.

Although the above details form the prelude to the Buddha's life on Earth, they are not included in the twelve deeds, properly speaking, as they did not take place in our world. The twelve are:

1. Knowing, through this vision, that the time had come, he *left Tusita and came to our world, Jambudvipa*. This is the dharmakāya's compassionate response to the hopes and prayers of good beings in the world. It is the arrival of the great light which illuminates the path to happiness and liberation, which shows the value of virtue and which accomplishes its work with a limitless love and totally fearless resolution.

> 221. *descends from the 'Realm of Great Joy',*
> *enters the royal womb and is nobly born in Jambudvipa.*
> *Perfectly skilled in each science and art,*

2. His teachings of dharma would later point out the limitations of worldly wealth, status and achievement. It would be very necessary that these worldly goals be removed from their pedestal and given their proper place by someone who had known them to the full. The words of a social failure, denouncing gain and fame, may just be dismissed as 'sour grapes', as personal rancour. His future father, King Suddhodhana, was a respected and wealthy monarch. His mother, Mahāmāya, was a beautiful queen, capable of bearing him. Therefore, he *entered the royal womb*. His mother dreamed of a white, six-tusked elephant entering her womb, as though it were a beautiful palace. There was celestial music and many other miraculous signs.

3. He was *born* painlessly from her right side in a grove in Lumbini, presently near the Indo-Nepalese frontier. To those present, he was seen simply to emerge on a beam of light. When his feet touched the ground, lotus flowers of light sprung up. He took seven steps in each of the cardinal directions and 'was heard to declare' (i.e. everyone knew spontaneously) himself to be the Enlightened One, Lord of the World. The major gods of the planet came and prostrated before him.

However, of equal importance with these miracles was the fact that, to most other people, he was later thought of as having been born 'ordinarily' as a human being. This was crucial for his teaching. People would think that an ordinary human being like themselves, and not a celestial one, had achieved enlightenment and that they could therefore do likewise.

4. As he grew up, he *exhibited matchless prowess in every field of learning*. His beautiful athletic body surpassed all others in sports such as wrestling, archery and so on. He mastered sixty different dialects and soon outclassed his teachers in the various domains of academic study and artistic expression. As we see so clearly these days, people can value highly – perhaps overvalue – scientific understanding, art or physical prowess. In order for the Buddha's teaching to show the transience and limitations of such worldly prowess, compared with the true science of mind and existence itself, it was indeed helpful that he had known them and excelled in each of them more than anyone of his day. It is said that his

fame as an athlete and scholar spread far beyond his own kingdom. He was a legend long before his enlightenment: the wisest, most gifted youth that humankind had ever seen.

222. *Delighting in his royal consorts' company, then renouncing,*
 practising the path of hardship and difficulty,
 going to the place called 'Enlightenment's Very Heart',
 he vanquishes the hosts of evil,

5. In order to fulfil his duty to his parents and provide an heir to the throne (he was their only child), he *married and enjoyed the company of his royal consorts*. The quest for a happy marriage, sexual satisfaction, parenthood and companionship is something which dominates peoples' lives in societies everywhere. Given the strength of human beings' illusions, their hopes and their biological drives, it would not be easy, later on, for the Buddha to point out the futility of the time and energy spent in this quest, and its high price. There would be more chance of his audience heeding someone who, as was his case, had married and satisfied three of the most beautiful brides in the land and who had enjoyed the company of the many young consorts in his royal harem. Of these, the beautiful Yasodhara, a princess in her own right, was his main bride and the mother to his only official child, Rahula.

6. Having established his excellence in all these domains in the eyes of the world and fulfilled his duty to his parents by providing an heir, at the age of twenty-nine he *renounced worldliness*. The details of his fourfold vision of ageing, sickness, death and a renunciate, and the story of the feast on his last day at the palace, when Rahula was born, are poignant indeed. One common version of the renunciation is that he had his servant, whom he had sworn to secrecy, bring him his horse, Katanka, late that same evening. He rode far into the jungle. Cutting off his long hair – the symbol of his royalty – with his own sword, he entered the religious life.

The mahāyāna version is that the Buddhas of the past, present and future emanated a crystal stupa, which gave him the vows of monastic ordination, his robes and hair-cutting, and that he set off on the eternal way of the monk. To teach others renunciation, he had himself to show the courage and ability to leave behind all the wonders and joys of his temporal life, in order to seek ageless wisdom.

7. It would be necessary for him to teach effectively not only the inadequacies of worldly life but also those of self-mortification. Who could do this better than one who had been the most rigid of ascetics? For six years, much of it spent in the company of five other ascetics, he *practised meditation and asceticism*. He trained under the finest meditation teachers of his day, but soon exhausted what they had to teach him. He then devoted himself to austerities. He ate less, endured the burning sun more and practised hardships more stringently than anyone had ever done. Much of this occurred in the area of the river Neranjara.

Often, he meditated for many days, without eating or moving, beneath the tall trees on its banks, with a rock for a cushion. At the end, he was such a skeletal bag of bones that his spine could be seen protruding through the skin of his abdomen. His brilliant aura and special marks had disappeared. This severe self-denial would not only serve as a proper basis for dismissing asceticism as the main way to truth, but would also demonstrate his own mastery of diligence and show his teaching to be not just an intellectual conclusion but the fruit of powerful personal experience.

His ascetic period ended with him receiving the offering of a special bowl of rice gruel. Someone who had made a deep commitment to Sakyamuni, in a previous life when he was a bodhisattva, was reborn as a young milkmaid. She fed ten of her best cows with the milk of a hundred cows. Then she milked the ten cows and fed that milk to the best cow of all. Its milk she mixed with honey and the finest rice. Taking this in a golden bowl, she approached Sakyamuni and offered it to him. As he drank it, his special marks and halo returned in an instant and he cast the bowl into the river saying, "If I am to find enlightenment, may this bowl float upstream." It did.

8. He then *set out for Vajrāsana*, the place we now call Bodh Gaya. It is said to be the spiritual 'centre of gravity' of this world and the place where each of the 1,002 Buddhas manifests enlightenment. On the way there, he met another person with a

special dharma connection: a young man who offered him a bundle of *kusha* grass as a meditation cushion. Arriving beneath the great tree, a *ficus religiosus*, he arranged the grass and sat in meditation.

9. From an absolute point of view, Sakyamuni was already completely purified and realised. He had already become the perfection of dharmakāya. But to instil, on a relative level, an understanding of the need to attain total virtue and wisdom, he had himself to show attainment of this utter purity. Having taken up his seat under the bodhi tree, he entered into the absorption in dharmakāya known as the 'vajra-like samādhi'. With his manifestation of enlightenment imminent, the hosts of negative energies and beings of this world came to distract him. They produced phantasms of sensuality, hordes of frightening demon armies and other illusions, in a vain attempt to hinder his achievement. By his remaining unperturbed in the natural loving compassion and voidness of the vajra-like samādhi, the *hosts of negative forces (māra) were defeated*. The weapons they threw turned into flowers, adorning the Buddha's presence. It is said, in certain scriptures, that these evil entities were unable to affect India for many centuries following this: it seemed to them as though it were protected by a great wall of impenetrable fire. Thus the golden age of enlightened teachings could establish itself.

The outer 'evil forces' are the external mirror image of the internal ones. One could also consider the Buddha's total enlightenment as being the final elimination of every trace of the 'four evils' (four *māra*): those of death, the defilements, the aggregates and pride.

223. *Then, perfect enlightenment, the turning of the wheel of dharma and passing into supreme nirvāṇa.*
In all these places, so impure,
the nirmanakāya shows these deeds as long as worlds endure.

10. At dawn the next morning, the day of the full moon in the Vaiśākha[12] month, he *manifested total enlightenment*. He was thirty-five. After three cosmic aeons of association with this world, he at

last appeared in it as a fully purified being, a flawless expression of the absolute truth and the presence of omniscience. Thus he became a peerless guide for all living beings for thousands of years to come.

11. He did not start teaching the buddhadharma immediately but remained in silence for some weeks, in order to show the profundity of what he had realised and to give the *deva* of the planet the chance to gather virtue by requesting him to teach. They eventually came to him, prostrated and supplicated him to *turn the wheel of universal truth* for the welfare of beings on Earth. Something similar to this was happening in all the other planets that fell within the scope of his activity. In the deer forests near Benares and other places, he taught the Four Truths and 84,000 dharmas common to all Buddhism. At the Vulture Peak and other lesser-known places, he taught the special path of mahāyāna. To King Indrabhuti and others, he taught the secret teachings of vajrayāna. Over a forty-five year period, and through the three turnings of the wheel of dharma, he transmitted all that needed to be known: the profound path to peace and everlasting happiness.

12. Throughout all this time, the Buddha had been an expression of dharmakāya, which is beyond any coming or going. Yet, in order to instil diligence and a sense of urgency in his disciples, and in order to dispel the wrong notions of his having eternal, concrete divinity or the wrong notions of nihilism, he *passed into parinirvāṇa*. If even the physical presence of buddha must seem to die, how much more so the likes of ordinary beings! His passing also highlighted the need for all Buddhists to assume personal responsibility for their own welfare, and not to be over-dependent upon the spiritual radiance of others.

Buddha Sakyamuni's life, chosen here to exemplify the meaning of the term 'supreme nirmanakāya', is not unique. The twelve deeds are typical of the activity of such supreme nirmanakāya throughout the universe. Whenever worlds are ready to receive them, those already enlightened in sublime spheres demonstrate these twelve deeds, which establish the universal truths of dharma in the very best and most lasting way. It is the supreme dialogue between truth and ignorance, between the pure and the impure, that will continue for as long as worlds exist.

224. *Knowing the means (through such terms as*
'impermanence', 'suffering', 'no-self' and 'peace'),
the nirmanakāya instils weariness with the world
in beings of the three dimensions, thus causing them
to apply themselves to the transcendence of suffering.

The function of these manifestations: This and the following two verses highlight the main functions of the nirmanakāya:
- to lead beings into, and then along, the Buddhist path,
- to lead experienced hinayāna Buddhists into the mahāyāna path when they are ready and,
- to predict the future enlightenment of bodhisattvas.

Buddhas help beings to enter the Buddhist path by teaching them the relative truths, since they would be unable to grasp absolute truth at that stage. Using ideas and terminology which make sense to such beings, Buddhas point out the *impermanence* of all created things. They show that every situation tainted by emotional defilement must involve some *suffering*. Furthermore, they can start to introduce the truth of voidness by explaining the *absence of self-entity* within either beings or things, and by describing how illusions of personality dictate the way beings' lives are led. As they start to recognise the vivid relevance of these ideas, new Buddhists awaken to the truth of the human condition. This leads to a dissatisfaction with saṃsāra and a genuine longing for inner *peace* and lasting, spiritual happiness, rather than an impermanent, worldly one. The Buddhas then guide them to skill and maturity in the practice of meditation, wholesome conduct and wisdom.

225. *To those excellently established on the path of peace,*
who believe that they have already attained nirvāṇa,
it teaches the thatness of all phenomena,
in the 'White Lotus' and other (sūtra).

Those who have liberated themselves for ever from worldliness and worldly rebirth, by following the hinayāna path, attain the state of the arhat. Although this is nirvāṇa, in its strict sense of transcendence of suffering, it is not the nirvāṇa of the Buddha. It is, nevertheless, a wonderful achievement. At a certain point, arhats have a profound experience of the Buddha's body, speech and mind. Through hearing such teachings as those of the Lotus Sūtra,[13] they are guided into the way of mahāyāna. This will take them to the enlightenment of a Perfect Buddha.

226. *Through this, they turn away from their former belief
and are inspired to properly adopt wisdom and skilful means.
It brings them to maturity within the highest yāna
and predicts their enlightenment supreme.*

These arhats-become-bodhisattvas will need, as do all bodhisattvas, to develop the two qualities of wisdom and compassion in perfect harmony. Prajñā will take them beyond the voidness of ego to a recognition of the voidness of all things, as taught in the prajñā-pāramita This liberates them definitively from even the subtlest aspects of saṃsāra. Limitless, great compassion, referred to here as 'skilful means', relates to the first five of the six pāramitā. It is limitless in its scope and great by nature. Such compassion will impress upon them the need to care for all beings, not only for the beings' sake but also for their own attainment of enlightenment. This will free them from attachment both to their own welfare and to the limited absorptions of concentration meditation. The combining of wisdom and compassion will lead arhats to the non-abiding nirvāṇa of the Buddhas.

One very special task of the form kāya is to predict the future enlightenment of bodhisattvas. This usually happens to bodhisattvas of the three 'extremely pure' levels, i.e. the eighth, ninth and tenth. They experience the Buddha declaring publicly, "Later, in such and such an age, you will become the Buddha known as .... , whose main disciples will be such and such. Your teachings will endure for such a length of time and your buddhafield will be known as ...."

Actualisation [grouping]

*227. Being profound, the very best of all powers and
the most clever guidance for the immature,
according to their individual needs, these are known, respectively,
as 'deep', 'vast' and 'great by nature'.*

Grouped by reason: Although some five or six kāya have been evoked in this chapter, they all fall within the three main ones: dharmakāya, sambhogakāya and nirmanakāya. Dharmakāya is termed the 'profound kāya', as it cannot be known properly by any but the enlightened. This is because it is the deep, true nature which transcends all projections of the relative mind and particularly the four philosophical extremes (existence, non-existence, both, neither) and the eight mental fabrications (production, extinction, annihilation, permanence, unity, diversity, coming, departure). It is also deep in terms of meditation. To be aware of it is like being aware of the depths of the ocean, as opposed to being fascinated with the lapping of the ocean's waves: the superficial play of deluded consciousness.

Sambhogakāya has the quality of great power, since it expresses truth in a way which is vividly representative of its real nature. Thus it manifests many thousands of vast buddhafields, each evoking specific combinations of enlightened qualities and serving as the basis for guiding beings on all levels. The knowledgeable reader may wish to reflect on the teachings of Avalokitesvara and the Sukhavati (Déwachen in Tibetan) pure land as just one example of this. Many people practise these teachings and there is a reasonable body of published information on Sukhavati and the OM MANI PADME HUNG mantra. One needs to consider that all of it represents a drop in the ocean of sambhogakāya's pure lands. Sambhogakāya is known as the 'vast kāya'. Its teachings cover the immense spiritual journey from first recognition of buddha nature through to total enlightenment.

Nirmanakāya is known as the 'kāya of great nature', as it demonstrates the life of the Buddha, supreme of all beings, and teaches the world that which is noble and virtuous. It does this in ways accessible to each individual, and in forms that seem very real to those experiencing them.

228. *The first of the above is dharmakāya and the latter the form kāya. Just as forms abide in space, the latter abide in the former.*

Grouped by nature: Dharmakāya is the depth of dharmadhātu. Sambhogakāya expresses the vastness of enlightened activity. Nirmanakāya expresses enlightenment's great nature of compassion. These last two kāya are known collectively as the 'form' kāya. Once again, the text points out these two kāya are not something other than dharmakāya, and that they are located in it, just as forms are located in space. This example is used because the form kāya are something seen, heard and so forth by the consciousnesses of unenlightened beings. Just as we see and touch form, and at the same time know that it exists in space, likewise we can sometimes see and hear the Buddhas but also know that they are really the primordial space of dharmadhātu, experienced in a way to which our mind can relate.

G. Permanence

in brief

229. *Through infinite causes, an inexhaustible number of beings, compassionate love, miraculous powers, perfect knowledge, having the 'best possible' and mastery over all qualities, through having vanquished the evil of death, insubstantiality and being the protector of the worlds, they are permanent.*

Enlightenment is the presence of the three kāya. These are all permanent but in three different ways: by nature, through continuity and through incessant activity. Their permanence will be explained through ten points, three relevant to the dharmakāya and seven relevant to the form kāya:

1. Enlightenment is achieved through the combination of various causes. One of these is the accumulation of incalculable virtue through the skilful and long-term practice of the six pāramitā, throughout the stages of the path and the bodhisattva levels. Another cause is the accumulation of insight, again and again over great periods of time, during meditation. The perfect completion of these two accumulations of virtue and wisdom will bring manifestation of the two form kāya at enlightenment. Infinite causes produce the infinite results of a continuous manifestation of sambhogakāya and the uninterrupted activity of nirmanakāya.

2. The form kāya work spontaneously to help all beings. As the number of beings to be liberated is infinite, the work of these kāya will be permanent.

3. Unlike the on-off compassion of ordinary beings or the limited compassion of the bodhisattvas, the natural compassion of buddha nature is infinite in its vastness and depth. As it is non-referential, its duration is not limited by this or that circumstance.

4. The clear cognition and miraculous powers of the enlightened mind render it capable of helping these infinite beings in all sorts of unimaginable ways. Other beings may feel compassion and wish to help, but may not have the necessary skill to do so under all circumstances.

5. Since enlightened wisdom knows the sameness of saṃsāra and nirvāṇa, its altruistic activity bears no risk of being corrupted by worldly defilement, just as an awakened person will not be deluded by the confused rambling of a sleeper.

6. Enlightenment possesses the best possible happiness, i.e. the untainted, natural happiness of the true nature of mind. Its attainment is the end of a beginningless quest for well-being and the final substitution of a timeless, natural happiness for a limited, contrived one. As it needs nothing more for itself, it is fearless of suffering and thus totally dedicated to bringing this happiness to others.

7. In a similar vein, enlightenment brings mastery over all qualities. The limitless qualities of the true nature are natural, spontaneous and magnificent.
8. The three final reasons for permanence concern the dharmakāya. It is permanent because it never ends, the 'evil' (*māra*) of death having been definitively vanquished.
9. It has none of the impermanence of creations as it is not a compounded phenomenon. It has no material essence.
10. It is the all-pervading refuge of the world.

further explanation

The first seven reasons above explain the permanence of the form kāya. Of these, the first four are particularly relevant to their permanent presence in saṃsāra, and the final three explain why it never forsakes saṃsāra. The following verses develop these notions.

230. *They are permanent because they uphold the true dharma,*
     having devoted their body, life and resources to it,
     because they completely fulfil their promise to benefit beings,

1. Enlightenment as the form kāya is the fruition of endless causes. These all emerge from the bodhisattvas' repeated commitment to attain enlightenment in order to bring benefit to all beings, a purpose to which they devote lifetime after lifetime to that end. In each of these existences, their body, life and resources are sincerely dedicated hour after hour, day after day, to perfecting the pāramitā. Each good action is done with bodhicitta intention and dedicated to all beings. It is also performed within the context of true dharma, i.e. the wisdom of voidness. Just one such action, performed with impeccable love and devotion, can produce unimaginable fruits. The sum total of the bodhisattva's actions over cosmic aeons produces the incalculable result of both his form kāya, which finally completely fulfil the altruistic wish to help beings. Although this activity will effectively be

limited to those who have established a connection with the bodhisattva during his evolution to enlightenment, the fact that the number of bodhisattvas becoming enlightened is limitless means that their form kāya are limitless also.

231. *because the stainless and pure compassion of the buddhas permeates each and every being,*
because they manifest through the bases of miraculous powers, by which they display abiding,

2. We now consider the same idea, but this time in terms of those to be helped, rather than that which is helping. The welfare of any individual being will be achieved when he or she is brought to enlightenment. At that point, the form kāya's work to help that particular being will be over. But since the number of beings to be helped is infinite, the form kāya are permanent.

3. Even though beings to be helped are infinite in number, enlightenment will only help them all if it cares for them all. The basis for the 'four infinite contemplations',[14] which are the motive force of bodhicitta, is impartiality. The end result of all the bodhisattva's training in impartiality is the infinite love and compassion of enlightenment, which embraces each and every being equally, without any bias of sex, race or family. One interesting anecdote emerging from this can be seen in some people who have the good fortune to meet an enlightened emanation. They feel a very special relationship, as though the emanation *(tulku)* had an extraordinarily powerful and unique bond with them; a special facility of communication. Yet the same 'uniqueness' is happening for person after person, due to the impartial yet powerful love and clear mind of their teacher.

4. On the bodhisattva path, various miraculous powers emerge as meditation achieves great stability. What is really happening is that the mind is drawing closer to its real nature. With enlightenment and the total unveiling of the true nature, all 'miraculous' abilities are present, and in particular the power to appear in any world, as any being, for any duration of time. Although the form kāya appear as living beings, they are not interde-

pendent creations like other beings and do not have the latters' temporal and spacial limitations.

232. *because, having perfect knowledge, they are freed from believing in a saṃsāra-and-nirvāṇa duality, because they have the very best of bliss, of constant and unimaginable samādhi,*

5. We now turn to the three reasons why enlightened beings never forsake those still in saṃsāra. Buddhas' perfect primordial wisdom reveals the sameness of nature of saṃsāra and nirvāṇa, as discussed in earlier chapters. They no longer have any notion of a saṃsāra as something to be avoided, and nirvāṇa as something to be obtained. Were this not the case, the saṃsāra of other beings would be off-putting and present an obstacle to Buddhas' enlightened activity. Although individual beings experience the form kāya as something external to themselves and experience Buddhas as other beings, the vivid intelligence of buddhajñāna recognises all to be the play of mind: the interaction between clarity and confusion, without inner and outer, self and other. It cannot forsake beings because the latter are nothing other than itself.

6. Saṃsāra and nirvāṇa may be of the same nature, but would there still not be some pain and hardship involved in helping beings under the sway of its delusions? Enlightenment knows no such pain, as it is, by its very nature, constant, total bliss and compassion. The bliss comes from the profound absorption (samādhi) of enlightenment, the qualities of which are unimaginable, even for the bodhisattvas.

233. *because even though they act in the world, by worldly qualities they are unblemished,*

7. Just as the bliss of the form kāya cannot be tainted by worldly suffering and happiness, neither can skilful actions, which are the very expression of purity, be tainted by worldly 'qualities'. Were such corruption a possibility, their activity would be interrupted and weaker at some times than at others.

> because, being immortal and having attained the state of peace,
> there is no opportunity for the evil of death,

234. *because the Victors, whose nature is uncreated,*
have been for ever perfectly at peace
and because they are most suited as a refuge and so forth
for those without a source of refuge.

235. *The first seven reasons show the permanence of the form kāya*
and the last three show the permanence of dharmakāya.

8. The text now considers the permanence of the dharmakāya. Enlightenment is definitively rid of defilements, action (karma) and suffering. The heavy presence of these, in samsaric existences, is the cause for one worldly life after another to be generated. Each of these lives is impermanent, ending in death. Dharmakāya is not in the least like these forms of existence. The very definition of its peace is a total absence of defilement, karma and suffering. It is the natural, immortal state, never interrupted by the māra of death.

9. It is truly permanent because, as we saw at length in the first chapter, it is not a creation, with inception, existence and end. It is free from birth, ageing, sickness and death.

10. This primordial freedom and purity which is the permanent, true, non-dual condition of mind, is the natural refuge for all other conditions, which are impermanent, false, dual, limited and unnatural. Whereas the unnatural illusions come and go, with great impermanence, dharmakāya always remains as the constant refuge for all beings.

Thus the first seven points show the permanence of the form kāya and the last three that of the dharmakāya. The permanence of nirmanakāya is one of uninterruptedness, through its incessant activity. The permanence of sambhogakāya is one of continuity, of its five principal characteristics. The permanence of dharmakāya is one of a truly permanent nature.

H. Inconceivability

in brief

236. *Since it is ineffable, consists of the ultimately true,*
is not the object of intellectual investigation,
is beyond simile, is peerless and is comprised of
neither compounded existence nor 'peace',
it is the domain of the buddhas,
inconceivable for even the deeply realised.

Enlightenment is inconceivable, even for deeply-realised bodhisattvas, for six main reasons:
1. It is ineffable.
2. It is the ultimate truth.
3. It cannot be an object of intellectual investigation
4. It is beyond simile.
5. It is peerless.
6. It is comprised within neither the creations of worldly existence nor the 'mere peace' nirvāṇa of the arhat.

more detail

237. *Inconceivable because it is ineffable,*
ineffable because it is ultimately true,
ultimately true because it cannot be investigated intellectually,
unable to be investigated by the intellect
because it cannot be deduced,

1. It is ineffable. The ordinary phenomena of the relative world can be expressed through words, such as 'cup' or 'smile', which are no more than sounds conventionally associated with an object which is known through conscious perception. If something can be represented by words, it can be conceived of. However,

buddhahood is not an object of the five sense consciousnesses, nor of ordinary mental consciousness. It is unlike anything previously experienced. Thus, there are no adequate words to describe it and it remains in the realm of the inconceivable.

2. Concepts are all related to relative truth, which is tellingly called 'the truth of the totally false' (*kun rdzob bden pa*) in Tibetan. Relative truth, the play of deluded consciousness, cannot grasp ultimate truth, the sole domain of primordial wisdom. Buddhahood is ineffable because it is ultimate truth.

3. Not only is buddhahood not the object of the six consciousnesses; it is also beyond the scope of intellectual investigation. The intellect manipulates words which, as we have seen, are merely cyphers evoking past, relative experiences. None of the names, symbols, descriptions and so forth which form the arsenal of the intellect can even approach it. It is particularly beyond the simplistic conclusions of the four extremes (discussed in the second chapter) and the eight conceptual fabrications.

4. It cannot be investigated intellectually because there is no simile for it. Intellectual investigation takes place through either direct observation or deductive reasoning, or through a combination of the two. Ordinary consciousness cannot directly observe enlightenment. Neither can it be known through deductive reason, since the latter relies upon comparisons as a basis for inference. Something unknown can often be made familiar to the intellect by comparing it with similar, known, things. Someone who has never drunk Tibetan tea can gain a good mental image of it by combining ideas of milky tea, salt and rancid butter. Someone who has seen ponies and striped patterns can gain some notion of a zebra. But since there is nothing similar to enlightenment, the intellect has no way of approaching it.

238. *non-deducible because it is peerless,*
peerless because it does not comprise, and
non-comprising because it does not abide,
since qualities and faults are not contemplated.

5. There is nothing similar to it because it is peerless. None of the myriad phenomena within either worldly existence or the arhats' peace resembles it in any way. Enlightenment is unique.
6. Not only this, but enlightenment, which is a limitless mind of wisdom, comprises neither worldly existence nor the arhat's peace, which are limited states of consciousness.

Enlightenment is therefore inconceivable, through the above six reasons. The text goes on to make two further points in relation to its inconceivability:
- one of enlightenment's chief characteristics is not to comprise either saṃsāra or arhats' nirvāṇa, as it abides in neither.
- the reason for this is that enlightenment has no thoughts. Therefore it cannot entertain thoughts of either a 'bad' saṃsāra, to be relinquished, or a 'good' nirvāṇa, to be attained.

239. *For five reasons is the dharmakāya inconceivable,*
and through them it is extremely subtle.
Through the sixth reason are the form kāya inconceivable,
as they are non-substantial.

Through the first five reasons, explained above, the dharmakāya is taught as being inconceivable, through being extremely subtle and, therefore, outwith the scope of a gross mind. The sixth reason explains the inconceivability of the form kāya, since they are the manifestation of enlightenment in the world, but are neither of the world nor of the arhats' nirvāṇa.

240. *Through their attributes of insurpassable jñāna,*
great compassion and the like,
the Victors have perfected every quality and are inconceivable.
Therefore, this final point, the spontaneously present,
is not even understood by great sages
who have received empowerment.

Enlightenment *is* wisdom, compassion and power to help others. Within it is to be found the perfection of every quality. However, as this last section has made clear through its six points, what this really means is something completely inconceivable for ordinary beings. It is still extremely difficult for realised bodhisattvas to appreciate. Even the bodhisattvas of the tenth and last level, on the threshold of enlightenment, who are empowered to act in the world on the Buddhas' behalf, do not understand enlightenment fully.

Notes

1   In the short prayer to Vajradhara.

2   The reader will find this on pages 122–129 of Volume One if Garma Chang's two-volume translation.

3   Ignorance, desire, animosity, pride, doubt, ego-projections on the aggregates, extreme views, perverse attitudes, conviction of the rectitude and superiority of religious illusions and conviction of the rectitude and superiority of mistaken religious moral codes and rituals.

4   Wrath, resent, rage, irritation, jealousy, discontent, deceit, hypocrisy, absence of self-respect, ansence of shame, dissimulation, avarice, narcissism, absence of faith, time-wasting, negligence, unmindfulness, unawareness, torpor, agitation and total distraction.

5   Some people translate *sgoms lam* a little too literally, as *stage of meditation* rather than *stage of cultivation of insight*. This would be appropriate in the hinayāna way of interpreting the five stages, but much less so in the mahāyāna way.

6   Here we are following a sixfold model of consciousness, and can consider the sixth consciousness, i.e. mental consicousness, as including the universal basis consciousness and the deforming consciousness which combine with the six to make the eight consciousnesses of mahāyāna.

7   1. Not to kill but to preserve life. 2. Not to steal but to be generous. 3. Not to commit sexual misconduct but to observe purity. 4. Not to lie but to tell the truth. 5. Not to create emnity through calumny but to speak in a way which promotes peace and friendship. 6. Not to speak aggressively or woundingly but lovingly and positively. 7. Not to indulge in useless speech but to use speech mindfully and intelligently. 8. Not to covet but to be unattached and generous of spirit. 9. Not to harbour emnity but to cultivate loving compassion. 10. Not to foster ignorance but to cultivate wisdom.

8   These are respectively the second, third and fourth of the five stages of the path to enlightenment.

9   The IIIrd Karmapa, Rangjung Dorjé's 'Mahāmudra Prayer'.

10   It might be worth mentioning that most Westerners mispronounce this Tibetan word by pronouncing its transliteration, as *og min*. The actual sound is *o-min,* the suffix g being silent and clipping the sound of the vowel to the 'o' of clock.

11   Tib: *dam pa tog dkar*

12   usually in May, and known popularly among Buddhists in the West as *Wesak*.

13   *Saddharmapundarikasūtra*

14   Infinite love, compassion, sympathetic joy and impartiality.

The Sixth Vajra Abode
The Qualities of Buddhahood

Synopsis of the Number of Main Qualities and their Relation to the Kāya

241. *Fulfilment for oneself and benefit for others are*
     the ultimately true kāya and its dependent relative kāya.
     The fruits of freedom and perfect maturity
     are their sixty-four qualities.

Although the qualities of buddhahood are innumerable, there are sixty-four particular ones to which Maitreya draws our attention. They fall into two areas:
- the qualities of freedom, which bring perfect fulfilment for oneself and which are those of the ultimate truth kāya (*paramarthakāya*).
- the qualities of maturity, which bring great benefit to others and which are those of the relatively true kāya: the form kāya.

The Sixth Vajra Abode – qualities of buddhahood

The qualities of freedom are the qualities of wisdom, which we can resume as suchness jñāna and all-embracing jñāna. These are the true nature of mind, unrecognised by the unenlightened due to the presence of obscurations. They only appear fully, and as perfect personal fulfilment, when there is total freedom from obscuring defilements, dualistic thoughts and limitations in meditation. The wisdom then present is infinite. Its thirty-two main qualities stem from the ultimately true, which is revealed by this wisdom and which *is* this wisdom. We could consider these qualities to be like the illuminating power of the sun, which always possessed its fiery light but only now emerges from behind dense clouds.

The process of removing the obstacles, listed above, is a relative one. It takes place on the bodhisattva path, through continual refinement of the 'two accumulations', i.e. by developing virtue and wisdom. During this long period, the bodhisattva makes dharma connections and karma connections with many other beings. These personal links form the basis for later form-kāya activity, when one becomes a Buddha.

It is interesting to note that any link, be it positive or negative, with a bodhisattva, is a potent seed for the future. This is perhaps most remarkably seen in the link Sakyamuni, as a bodhisattva a long time ago, made with five flesh-eating demons, by offering them his own body and thereby satiating them and saving a village from any more of their ravages. These five beings crop up again and again, in different stories of Sakyamuni's evolution, each time strengthening their link with him. In the end, they became the five ascetic companions of Siddhartha and counted among his very first disciples. The thirty-two qualities of the form kāya, experienced by disciples as a Buddha's qualities, are the end result of a process of bringing the two accumulations to perfect maturity. They represent the zenith of teaching ability.

242. *The ground for acquiring fulfilment for oneself*
is the embodiment of the ultimate truth.
The symbolic embodiments of the great sages
are the ground for the greatest possible altruism.

243. *The first kāya is endowed with the qualities of freedom, powers and so forth, and the second with those of maturity, the marks of a perfect being.*

The basis from which one acquires the qualities of self-fulfilment is the embodiment (kāya) of ultimate truth. Being a total clarity of wisdom that depends in no way whatsoever upon impermanent thoughts or transient phenomena, it is a natural and permanent basis for the thirty-two qualities of freedom, which are:
- four qualities of fearlessness,
- the ten powers of wisdom and
- the eighteen qualities unique to enlightenment.

These qualities combine to make one be – and know oneself to be – at the very summit of existence. At the heart of all these thirty-two qualities lies primordial wisdom, made manifest through bringing to perfection the 'accumulation of wisdom'.

The form kāya manifest in two main ways: as the myriad Buddhas and pure lands of sambhogakāya and as the ultimate nirmānakāya, who brings truth to the worlds through the twelve deeds. These forms of Buddha bear the 32 major marks and 80 signs of an enlightened being. Their nature is to represent the formless qualities of true enlightenment through symbolic forms, perhaps nowhere so richly and well presented as in the iconography of Tibetan Buddhism. These help other beings through the confidence-inspiring presence of their perfect bodies. The form kāya are made manifest through bringing to perfection the 'accumulation of virtue'.

Others special beings, such as universal emperors (*chakravartin*) and some highly developed non-Buddhist sages (*rishi*), may have some or many of the 32 major signs. However, these signs are the same in name only. The actual details and context of each one is different from that of a Buddha, which is far and away superior.[1] The word *rishi* , which in other contexts may mean a non-Buddhist or an arhat, is used here to mean Buddha. It could be translated as *sage* or, using the Tibetan definition, as someone totally direct and truthful.

More Detailed Explanation of Each Category of Qualities

Introduction to the examples and their significance

244. *Counteracting ignorance's veils, the powers are like a vajra
and fearlessness in any situation is like a lion.
The tathāgata's distinctive qualities are like space
and the two aspects which Victors manifest
are like the moon in water.*

This verse gives us three similes for the qualities of freedom and one for the qualities of maturity. First, the ten powers of buddha wisdom are likened to a vajra, which can destroy anything but which itself is destroyed by nothing. Being innate to buddha nature, the ten powers of wisdom are indestructible. They have power to pierce through the deepest and subtlest forms of ignorance.

The four fearlessnesses are compared to the natural intrepidity of a lion. The lion knows that no other animal would even consider attacking him and that he is the king of beasts. The self-wisdom of buddhahood knows itself clearly to be the supreme state, the ultimate state, and has no fear of mistake, as would be the case of a wisdom based on value-judgements rooted in relative thoughts and experiences. It is said that even great bodhisattvas cannot imagine the clarity of bodhisattvas on higher levels than themselves. Needless to say, ordinary beings can always be wrong in their evaluation of things. In fact, any being, other than Buddha, lives with some degree of uncertainty and fear of being proven wrong in their assertions and beliefs.

The eighteen distinctive qualities of a Buddha are compared to space. Unlike earth, water, fire or wind, space does not exist in dependence upon the other elements. Space does not vary as do the other elements. It has different characteristics from them. Likewise Buddhahood has different characteristics from those of other beings and its character does not depend upon them.

The two form kāya are compared to the reflection of the moon in water. The moon has no intention to be reflected in this or that pool. The reflection does not think, "I am here because the moon is shining." The fact of the moon existing in space and the water lying on the ground is sufficient to produce a reflection for an observer. Likewise, dharmakāya has no intention to produce emanations as the form kāya. The form kāya are not separate entities, considering themselves different from dharmakkāya. As with the moon, various circumstances simply combine to produce a result, in this case the experience of nirmānakāya and sambhogakāya in beings' minds. The combination here is an interaction between two natures: the ultimate nature of mind and the openness in a being's relative mind, through good karma. The simile of the moon in water merits deep and long consideration: to grasp its meaning can dispel many delusions about Buddha emanations and the religious experience.

The qualities of freedom – the ultimately true kaya

1. TEN POWERS

245. *To know the possible and the impossible,*
 the full maturation of action, faculties, temperaments,
 wishes, the paths which determine each and every state,
246. *meditative stability and so on –*
 that unblemished by defilement,
 memory of former states, divine vision and peace:
 these are the ten powers of perfect awareness.

The ten powers of perfect awareness are:

1. Perfect awareness of the possible and the impossible (or the appropriate and the inappropriate). This awareness of action (karma), cause and effect, understands which causes can bring about a certain result and which ones cannot. Enlightened beings' perfect awareness of this is the end result of the growth of understanding of causality developed throughout the Buddhist path, but in particular that which emerges during the ten bodhisattva levels.

This is special inasmuch as it is supported by continuous, unwaning commitment to the welfare of all beings. This loving care of others obliges one to understand many aspects of karma – both positive and negative – which might never even be imagined when one's mind is solely concerned with one's own existence and its particular details. There is much to be learnt in observing great masters helping people to overcome their particular problems, caused by unremembered actions in past lives, and, on the positive side, helping them discover in themselves qualities that few would ever imagine they possessed.

Although the perfection of such awareness embraces all causality, it has the special clarity which knows directly and vividly that virtue is the long-term cause of happiness for the person who enacts it, and that non-virtue is the cause of suffering. It understands the great benefit which can come from taking Refuge or the Bodhisattva Vow or from other Buddhist acts, even though these may not be appreciated fully by those who perform them. This perfect awareness forms the basis for the fundamental teachings on the Four Noble Truths.

2. Perfect awareness of the full maturation of karma. Whereas the first awareness expresses the Buddha's clarity focused upon causes, this second one expresses it when focused upon results, and in particular those of 'full maturation'. There are several levels of consequence which emerge from actions.[2] Some of them influence the environment in which one lives and others affect the circumstances of life itself: the people one meets, the events which happen and so forth. 'Full maturation' however refers to rebirth itself – as a human or other being – as a consequence of action(s). Sometimes a single, powerful, action can produce a whole series of different rebirths. Sometimes the result of many repeated actions is a single rebirth.

Buddhas understand all of this spontaneously and perfectly. Their understanding is the culmination of all their work, as bodhisattvas, in understanding karma and helping others to understand it. An arhat may have great insight into karma, but could never know, for example, directly and without effort, the specific causes for the vivid blue colour in a peacock's tail-feather. A Buddha does.

3. Perfect awareness of the various faculties of beings. The word *faculty* (Skt. *indriya*) can have various meanings. In *abhidharma*,[3] twenty-two main faculties, such as the five senses, masculinity, femininity and so forth, are mentioned. Various beings throughout the vast cosmos possess differing combinations of these twenty-two as well as other faculties. Buddhas understand them all, knowing life-forms and places of which we could never dream, even with the imagination of modern science-fiction. More importantly, they know which teachings can be understood, and put into application, by each being. Some beings are very diligent and disciplined. Others are very relaxed or lazy. Some are very intelligent. Others are slow to understand.

This perfect awareness of each individual's capacity is the culmination of all the previous bodhisattva activity to help others. Through exposure to thousands of different people and through working patiently with each one to bring about some progress in his or her life, in an interaction devoid of any personal interest on the bodhisattva's part, a lucidity emerges which knows how to handle each unique mentality.

4. Perfect awareness of the different temperaments of beings. This understands the predominant psychological and karmic factors at play in an individual's existence. Some are dominated by anger, resentment or frustration. Some are driven by desires, ambitions and needs. Others are lonely, over-introspective or locked up in their thoughts. Not everyone is negative in these obvious ways. Some people exude positivity and strength, yet may need to erect rigid internal psychological structures to maintain it. In brief, each being is a complex mixture of drives, impulses, habits and karmic conditioning. The teachings a Buddhist master gives need to be able to tackle these effectively and in the appropriate order. As with the previous power, the Buddha's awareness is the culmination of a clarity and perspicacity which emerges through the long bodhisattva path.

5. Perfect awareness of beings' wishes. This aspect of enlightened awareness is focused upon the wishes and aspirations of beings. It is the culmination of the bodhisattva's awareness of the various aspirations at play in each individual psyche. Some are attracted to the hinayāna path, with its emphasis on the saṃgha and the Four Truths. Others are natural bodhisattvas. Some are keen on physical activities, like prostrations, making religious artefacts or helping the poor, sick and needy. Others prefer the pursuit of intellectual clarity. Yet others only want to meditate in simplicity, without any religious paraphernalia. Since a person will have natural enthusiasm and diligence for doing the things which he or she wants to do, it can be very helpful, with some people, to start them on a path of practice which harmonises with their character.

In relation to this question of the bodhisattva's awareness of people's temperaments, it may be the case that those who find their teacher's advice hard to implement are very fortunate Buddhists. Whereas they may have a sneaking feeling that their teacher does not understand them all that well, it could be that the teacher understands them a sight better than they could ever imagine. Rather than treating them 'with kid gloves', as a Buddhist master has to do with those of lesser good karma who are still hovering uncertainly on the brink of Buddhism, the master may be acknowledging the fact that there is enough powerful karma from former lives for the disciple to be given, from the very outset, an opportunity to confront his or her own weaknesses, without wasting precious time on niceties.

6. Perfect awareness of the paths that determine each and every state. This is the culmination of the bodhisattva's awareness of the various courses of action, and in particular the spiritual paths, which different beings take according to their various aspirations, faculties and so forth mentioned above. The Buddha's perfect awareness is totally familiar, on the one hand, with the paths of action which drag beings down into lower and lower states and, on the other hand, with both the hinayāna paths which bring liberation and happiness and the mahāyāna path which leads to perfect buddhahood.

7. Perfect awareness of meditative absorptions and penetrations. This is the culmination of the bodhisattva's awareness of the various qualities which meditation can bring forth. Not all meditation leads to liberation. When it is alloyed with defilements, such as pride, desire for existence, etc., it becomes solely a motor force for samsaric rebirth. Unchannelled, meditation can bring rebirth as a god, or as a human being with great powers of concentration and willpower, with all the dangers that such strength of personality can entail. Bodhisattvas take great care to sustain their meditation with the wholesomeness of loving kindness and the other three limitless contemplations.[4] They are aware of the various traps and dangers that await the meditator. They know where each meditation leads and how long each path of meditation may take for individuals with sharp faculties, or dull ones.

8. Total recall of former states. Most beings cannot remember past lives. Those who have mastered the *dhyāna* (meditative absorptions) can remember a certain number of existences. Arhats can remember something like a hundred former existences. Buddhas can recall every single previous existence in saṃsāra. This is the culmination of their meditative prowess as bodhisattvas and, in particular, of developing the spontaneous reflex of practising every virtue, no matter how small.

9. Perfect divine vision. The actual term for this,[5] literally 'vision like the gods', means clairvoyance, but since the latter term has lost its etymological meaning, of seeing perfectly clearly, and has come to mean any sort of intuition or subjective feeling, it is perhaps wiser to call it insight, to avoid any 'crystal ball' associations.[6] It is a quality clearly defined in the *abhidharma* scriptures as the ability to see things normally concealed, be it by their distance, by objects in between them and the seer, by their own minuteness or, on the contrary, by their magnitude, as well as seeing things concealed by time. This quality develops throughout the bodhisattva levels and is one of the five super-perceptions enabling bodhisattvas to help others, through a lucid understanding of things rather than mere intuition. They know what will happen in the future, which sort of rebirth a being will have, the particular circumstances each will encounter, and so on and so forth. This power of insight becomes perfect at Buddhahood.

10. Perfect awareness of peace. This is an auto-awareness of the total purity of Buddhahood. It is aware of the various mixtures of purity and impurity which constitute the lives of ordinary beings, arhats and bodhisattvas. It is the culmination of the bodhisattva's activity in teaching beings how to recognise and eliminate their own impurities, and also the bodhisattva's own path of purification through meditation.

247. *Such powers – the appropriate and inappropriate,*
full maturation, temperaments, beings' aspirations,
their various paths, the defiled and the perfectly pure,
the groupings of faculties, remembrance of former states,
divine vision and the way to exhaust impurity –
are like a vajra because they penetrate the armour of ignorance,
shatter its walls and fell its tree.

These ten aspects of the perfectly clear awareness of Buddhas are called 'powers' because they are truly powerful, as expressed through the vajra analogy in this verse. As each power is an aspect of the unique buddhajñāna, all are compared to one thing: a vajra. As the power exerts itself severally, according to the various types and degrees of obscurations to be removed, three main analogies are evoked. Ignorance itself is compared to armour, which cloaks true reality and makes it difficult to penetrate. The resilience and thickness of the obscurations is compared to a wall and the various developments (defilements, karma, etc.) that grow out of basic ignorance are compared to a mature tree. Enlightened wisdom overcomes all of these, in a way which no other being's understanding can.

2. FOUR FEARLESSNESSES

248. *In everything being perfectly enlightened,*
in bringing a definitive end to obstacles,
in teaching the path and in stating cessation,
they have four kinds of fearlessness.

An introduction to the four fearlessnesses. These four are Buddhas' absences of fear, such as fear that their enlightenment may not be *the* enlightenment, or that what they teach may, one day, be proven wrong, etc. In other words, these are four aspects of the certainty and confidence which comes with enlightenment. The latter is not an intellectual conclusion, but a total fusion with truth itself. Therefore it is relaxedly clear about what is true and beyond unenlightened beings' subjective opinons about what they *believe must be* true.

1. The first fearlessness is related to enlightenment's self-fulfilment. Buddhas know that their buddhajñāna, which embraces every thing (and which is everything) is perfect, with nothing more to be removed and nothing more to be obtained. They can state their own attainment of perfection and removal of all impurity, knowing that not even an iota of pride or jealousy remains in them and that their teaching emanates spontaneously from the ultimate universal truth. It is therefore unbiased and impartial, full of the same compassionate love for each and every being. This is the culmination of the bodhisattva's diligent work, through thorough meditation, in removing every trace of defilement and thereby revealing every natural quality.

2. The second fearlessness is related to enlightenment's benefit for others, through teaching. One of the main functions of buddhadharma is to make people aware of obscurations, obstacles and hindrances – all of which cause suffering. No one could ever prove the Buddhas wrong when they point out these things, because they are speaking the truth, which they know perfectly through their own achievement of putting an end to all personal suffering and its causes.

3. The third fearlessness is also related to benefit for others. Buddhas are fearless in proclaiming the path of dharma and in asserting that it *is* the way to liberation and enlightenment. They know this is the case because they have proven it through their own path of practice and attained the twofold buddhajñāna which reveals the same potential for enlighten-

ment to exist in all beings. This certainty is the culmination of their perfection of the five stages of the path and the thirty-seven factors of enlightenment.[7] These second and third aspects of fearlessness are in fact acquired long before total enlightenment, while the being is still a bodhisattva, but come to their perfection at enlightenment.

4. The fourth fearlessness, concerned with self-fulfilment, is in stating their own achievement of cessation. They know that no one could one day discover an impurity which they had ignored or forgotten to remove. They can also state their own cessation without being proud but simply as a matter of fact, since all pride has been removed on the bodhisattva path.

249. *Because they themselves know and help others know*
every aspect of that which is to be known,
because they have eliminated and help others eliminate
those things which must be eliminated,
because they teach and aid others to teach and
because they have attained and help others to attain
the utterly stainless highest attainment,
they truthfully tell others of their own realisation
and, in so doing, are unhindered in any way.

The function of the four fearlessnesses. The four aspects of enlightened confidence, described above, enable the Buddhas to state their realisation to other beings, truthfully and authoritatively. They do so without any pride, doubt, jealousy or the like:

1. They are omniscient, and this enables them to help all other beings raise themselves to the same level of total awareness.
2. They have removed every impurity, and this enables them to help others remove their own specific impurities.
3. They teach the path to total, perfect enlightenment, and help others to reveal it.
4. They have attained perfect cessation, and help others to attain it: the highest of all achievements.

250. *Just as, in every part of the jungle,*
the king of wild animals is ever fearless,
moving intrepidly among all other beasts,
so likewise is the 'lion', the king of Victors,
ever completely fearless, in any gathering:
independent, stable and highly skilful.

A simile for the fearlessnesses. The lion, the metaphorical king of the jungle, has a natural self-confidence and fearlessness, which manifests wherever the lion may be. This is unlike other beasts, which may show themselves strong and confident in the face of some animals, yet become fearful in the presence of others. Be they ordinary people, meditators or scholars, most unenlightened beings are strong and confident in some circumstances but have their confidence sabotaged by their own limitations and ignorance when in the company of those who know more, or who have deeper experience. Unlike this, Buddhas are ever fearless, because they are always proclaiming an uncompromising truth. There is no self-doubt in their ability to present it, and they are completely without expectation or paranoia in relation to their audience. Their skill and compassion remain constant throughout.

3. EIGHTEEN UNIQUE AND DISTINCTIVE QUALITIES

251. *Buddhas are never mistaken and do not chatter noisily.*
Their mindfulness is impeccable and their mind
is never not in meditative equipoise.
They do not harbour ideas of various kinds.

252. *Never is their indifference something unaware and*
their mighty aspiration is never subject to degradation;
nor is their diligence, their memory, their prajñā,
their perfect liberation and perception: the jñāna of liberation.

253. *Their activities are preceded by jñāna and this jñāna*
is not prone to any deterioration with time.
These eighteen qualities and others
are those teachers' attributes alone.

The eighteen unique qualities of a Buddha can be considered as falling into four categories:

- six unique qualities of conduct (1–6),
- six unique qualities of realisation (7–12),
- three unique qualities of enlightened activity (13–15) and
- three unique qualities of jñāna (16–18).

Six qualities related to Buddha conduct:

1. Buddhas never make mistakes in their physical behaviour. In this respect they are unique, since even an arhat can make mistakes sometimes, even though the arhat's behaviour is excellent, undefiled and supported by clear cognition.

2. Buddhas never speak in a meaningless, noisy or useless way. The corollary of this is very important in vajrayāna Buddhism, as one learns to relate to the guru's speech as being that of the Buddha and to interpret every word as being meaningful, whether it is given ostensibly as a teaching or not.

3. Buddhas' recollectedness never deteriorates. The Tibetan term for this (*dren pa*) means both mindfulness and memory. Mindfulness is defined as never losing pure intention through forgetting. Ordinary beings and arhats will always be subject to some forgetfulness, absent-mindedness or unmindfulness, but never Buddhas.

4. Their mind is always in meditation. This is expressed more accurately through a double negative in the verse above. Other beings may either be entirely without a mind steeped in profound meditation when they act, or else may experience variations in the degree of meditation which lies behind and sustains actions. Buddhas' actions always emanate from the profoundest of states, the vajra-meditation of buddha nature.

5. Buddhas do not think. They do not entertain any sort of notions of saṃsāra or nirvāṇa. Besides its general statement, this point has the very specific meaning that Buddhas never have an iota of intention to deceive other beings or have any other sort of what these days would probably be called 'personal agenda'. Their attitude towards others is at all times one of constant total truthfulness and total love, which is unbiased and equal towards all beings.

Above all, it is non-dual. The relation between a Buddha and a disciple is inconceivable, because it is not in any way a dialogue or a symbiosis.

6. They never act frivolously, always having a natural awareness of the short and long-term consequences of their actions. It may happen sometimes that they show indifference towards someone. This is not negligence of that person's welfare or accidental ignorance of the person's condition. It is an important and often very necessary way of teaching: one that can help overcome such faults as pride, attention-seeking, over-familiarity and so forth, either in the person or in his or her relation with the Buddha.

Six qualities related to the Buddha's attitude:

The following qualities are, in name, those found also in bodhisattvas and in other great beings. Even as early as in the second of the five stages of the path to enlightenment, one finds aspiration, diligence, mindfulness, prajñā and jñāna being cited as the keys to progress. Here we find them in their unique perfection at buddhahood.

7. A Buddha's altruistic aspiration never deteriorates, since it is the pure, natural and perfect bodhicitta of buddha nature.

8. Likewise their diligence in helping other beings never wanes.

9. Neither does their mindfulness of helping others wane.

10. Their prajñā is ever perfect,

11. As is their perfect liberation and

12. The auto-cognisance of their jñāna.

Three qualities related to enlightened activity:

13. Buddha's physical actions are always preceded by, accompanied by and followed by jñāna,

14. as are verbal acts and

15. every action of the mind.

Thus every physical, verbal or mental action is done in full knowledge of its every implication and in full knowledge that it has been properly carried out. This is the spontaneous outcome of the bodhisattva training in applying wisdom to the three stages of an act: when considering and planning it, while executing it and afterwards making sure that all has been done properly.

Three qualities related to buddhajñāna:

16. The jñāna which sustains their actions of body, speech and mind is completely aware of the past, i.e. there is no 'cut-off point' beyond which awareness is vague or non-existent.

17. Likewise their jñāna is unobstructed in its awareness of the present. No situation is concealed by distance, size or nature.

18. Similarly their jñāna is unobstructed with regard to the future.

These eighteen qualities are unique to Buddhas. Besides these, there are many other unique qualities, such as the immeasurability of the Buddha's body, the extremity of the head mound being out of sight (higher even that the gods' realms), the way in which the Buddha's presence immediately calms beings who are upset, and so on and so forth. The sūtras also mention that the Buddha's robes always hover four fingers' width away from his body.

All these are signs of the total completion of many lifetimes of practice, drawing the bodhisattva closer and closer to the perfection of natural reality: practice in which he or she also trains in bringing other beings, who have lost their way, into the path to true liberation and enlightenment. Śrāvaka and pratyekabuddhas do not have these qualities, as they have not properly developed these skills in guiding others.

254. *For great sages there are no mistakes, chatter, unmindfulness,*
mental agitation, various forms of ideation
or casual indifference.
Aspiration, diligence, recollection, perfectly pure and
immaculate prajñā, constant, perfect liberation
and jñāna of perfect liberation,
which is aware of all aspects of the knowable –
these are theirs
and these never suffer from any deterioration.

255. *All three activities, whatever they may be,*
are preceded by, accompanied by and followed by jñāna.
Their perfect awareness constantly and extensively
penetrates the three times without hindrance.
These having been made real, the Buddhas,
the Victorious Ones with compassion's magnificence,
achieve a perfect and fearless turning
of the great wheel of true dharma for beings.

The function of these eighteen qualities. This verse gives us a concise list of the qualities and explains that, having acquired them through enlightenment, Buddhas are able to turn the Wheel of Dharma for beings in a perfect and fearless way. As benefit for others, these qualities endow Buddhas with the greatest of compassion. As fulfilment for oneself, they confirm victory over the 'enemy', i.e. all the defiled, limited and imperfect things to be eliminated. Thus Buddhas are known as 'Victors' and these eighteen unique features are the final and complete manifestation of the qualities of true reality. Each reflects a corresponding area of purification practised during the bodhisattva path.

256. *Earth and so forth have properties of specific character;*
their nature is not that of space.
The intrinsic character of space, non-obstruction,
is absent in matter.
Earth, water, fire, wind and space
are equally common to all the worlds,
but not even so much as an atom
of the distinctive attributes of a buddha
is common to any of the worlds.

The first four prime elements each have their specific character:
- the earth element is substantial and resistant,
- the water element is fluid, cohesive and lubricating,
- the fire element is hot, burning, consuming and transforming and
- the wind element is dynamic.

The space element, however, is the quality of non-obstruction; a quality not possessed by the other elements and, furthermore, a constant quality, whereas those of the other elements are inconstant. Whereas there is a great deal of interdependence and interaction between the first four elements, the space element is unaffected by the others. Likewise, the eighteen unique qualities of a Buddha have nothing in common with the qualities of any other being. No other beings possess them and neither do Buddhas have any of the faults or limitations of ordinary beings, in this or any world.

The qualities of maturity – the relatively true kaya

1. THE THIRTY-TWO MARKS OF A PERFECT BEING

257. *Perfectly level and marked with wheels,*
his feet are broad and his ankles not protruding.
Long are his fingers and his toes, webbed.
258. *Soft is his skin and fine his youthful flesh,*
his body having seven elevated parts.
Like an antelope's are his calves
and like an elephant's are his private parts recessed.
259. *His torso is like a lion's*
and his clavicles not hollow but well-filled.
His shoulders are elegantly rounded;
rounded, soft and even are his arms.
260. *His arms are long and his perfectly pure body*
is surrounded by an aura of light.
His neck, like a conch, is rounded and without blemish
and his cheeks are like those of a king of beasts.
261. *Equal are his forty teeth. They are very pure, closely set,*
immaculate and evenly aligned;
the eye-teeth are perfect and excellently white.
262. *His tongue is long, unending and inconceivable,*
possessing the most perfect faculty of taste.
The spontaneously born has a voice
like the song of the kalavinka bird or like Brāhma's melody.
263. *The supreme of beings has beautiful eyes, like blue lotuses,*
and like an ox's are his eyelashes.

With its immaculate white treasure-hair,
his face is handsome to behold.
His head bears a mound
and his skin is pure, fine and golden.

264. *The hairs on his body are exceeding fine and soft,*
one from each (pore) and curling to the right and to the top.
His hair is impeccable and like a deep-blue gem.
As well-rounded as a perfect nyagrodha tree

265. *the ever-good and incomparable great sage has the strength*
of Nārāyaṇa in his firm body. These two and thirty marks,
vividly brilliant and beyond any concept's grasp,
are taught by our Teacher as those of a lord of men.

1. The feet are perfectly even and marked with dharma-wheels of a thousand 'spokes'. This is the outcome of the bodhisattva's proper taking, and keeping, of commitments, as well as his or her respect for teachers and the gathering of much virtue.

2. The feet are broad and the ankles do not protrude. This is the outcome of enacting innumerable virtuous deeds.

3. The fingers and toes are long. This is the outcome of giving protection to beings who would otherwise have been killed.

4. The digits of hands and feet are slightly webbed. This is the outcome of former peace-making.

5. His skin is soft and his flesh fine and youthful. This is the outcome of former generosity to the poor and hungry.

6. His body has seven elevated parts, i.e. the backs of the hands, feet and shoulders and the nape of the neck are all nicely full and rounded. This is the outcome of giving food and drink to the needy.

7. His calves are like those of an antelope, i.e. strong, solid and muscular. This is the outcome of a thorough mastery of all five branches of Buddhist learning.

8. His private parts are recessed, like those of an elephant. This is the outcome of always maintaining confidentiality.

9. His torso is like that of a lion, i.e. broad and majestic. This is

the outcome of looking after other beings with great ethical care.

10. His clavicles are not hollow but well-filled with flesh. This is another outcome of former generosity, especially that of giving medicines to the sick.

11. The tops of the shoulders have elegant curves. This is the outcome of right speech, which eased the fears and worries of others, and only used kind and appropriate words.

12. The arms are soft, round and even. This is the outcome of always being a friend for beings.

13. The arms are long, the hands reaching down to the knees. This is the outcome of always striving to fulfil others' expectations.

14. His perfectly pure body is surrounded by an aura of light. This is the outcome of relentless efforts to practice the ten virtues.

15. His neck is as immaculate as a perfect conch. This analogy refers to the resemblance between the three fine lines on the Buddha's throat to those of the spirals on a conch. They are a sign of the Buddha's perfect ability to teach all 84,000 aspects of dharma. They are also a specific outcome of serving the sick and providing them with medicines.

16. His cheeks are as magnificent as those of a lion. This is the outcome of never wasting the power of speech, through useless chatter, but instead using it to guide people into what is good and wholesome, and particularly into Buddhist practice.

17. He has forty teeth, twenty on each jaw. This is the outcome of treating everyone with equal kindness, as they have all been former parents. It is also the result of overcoming harsh speech.

18. His teeth are very white and beautifully aligned. This is the outcome of always speaking truthfully and so as to create harmony.

19. The teeth are immaculate and evenly aligned, i.e. they are without mark or defect and harmoniously aligned as far as their length is concerned. This is the outcome of giving away possessions and gaining a livelihood honestly.

20. The eye-teeth are perfect and brilliantly white. This is the outcome of former physical, verbal and mental actions being perfectly honest and straightforward.

21. His tongue is long, unending and inconceivable. The tongue, like the head-mound, gives the impression of endlessness to those who see it.[8] This is because the Buddha can declare the profound meaning of voidness, and it is the outcome of speaking sweetly and softly.

22. There is the most perfect faculty of taste. Everything that the Buddha eats has the most exquisite taste. This is the outcome of always providing solutions which were agreeable to beings and finding effective answers to their problems.

23. The Spontaneously Born has a voice as sweet as that of the kalavinka bird or as Brahmā. This is the outcome of always speaking in a pleasing, peaceful voice that proclaimed the truth, in a way which was relevant and meaningful to beings.

24. The Supreme Being has beautiful eyes, like blue lotuses. This is the outcome of always looking upon other beings with the loving concern of a mother for her only child.

25. The eyelashes are as handsome as those of an ox, i.e. long and beautiful and neatly separated (not glued in little bunches). This is the outcome of overcoming anger and hypocrisy in dealings with others.

26. With its immaculate white 'treasure-hair', his face is handsome to behold. The Buddha's face is very clear and radiant. Those who see it are deeply moved by its great beauty. It has the treasure hair, which is very long (more than one metre), white and curled into a tight swirl in the brow. This is often represented by a simple dot on the Buddha's forehead in paintings and statues. These signs are the outcome of always treating special beings, such as other bodhisattvas, with respect.

27. His head is adorned with a mound. In fact, those who look at the Buddha's head can never see where its upper part ends. It goes up and up, beyond the deva realms and out of sight. This is the outcome of devotion and service to gurus and other

teachers and bodhisattvas, while himself a bodhisattva.

28. His skin is pure and fine. This is the outcome of always striving to do good and to make the mind flexible and manageable.

29. His skin is golden-hued. This is the outcome of always serving the Buddhas and making offerings to them.

30. The hairs on his body are exceedingly fine and soft, one in each pore, spiralling to the right and upwards. This is the outcome of always meditating to make the mind manageable and applicable to all tasks, as well as of diligent effort in bringing the tasks to a proper conclusion.

31. His hair is impeccable and like a deep blue gem. This could have originally meant that his dark hair had a beautiful blue sheen, like dark sapphire, although it is sometimes taken literally and Buddha statues often have the hair painted blue. This is the outcome of always acting with loving kindness.

32. As well-rounded as a perfect *nyagrodha* tree, the Ever-Good, the incomparable Great Sage, has the strength of Nārāyaṇa in his firm body. This last mark applies to the whole body. The *nyagrodha* tree is well known for its harmonious proportions and straightness. Nārāyaṇa is another name for Vishnu, renowned for his strength.

All these marks shine with their own radiance and steal away the mind of the beholder with their beauty and sense of profundity, making one know that one is in the presence of the Supreme of Beings; in the presence of something beyond the grasp of one's mind. They were taught by the Buddha himself as beings the signs of an Enlightened One. Although some other great beings have several signs similar to these, at least in description, they are not the same. Nor are they complete.

2. AN EXAMPLE FOR THE THIRTY-TWO MARKS

266. *Just as the form of the autumn moon in a cloudless sky*
is seen in the azure waters of a lake,
so also are the form kāya of the All-Embracing
seen by the Victors' Sons in the perfect buddha maṇḍala.

The thirty-two marks described above are perceived by the bodhisattvas of the ten levels, who can experience many thousands of different Buddhas, each an expression of a particular facet of the one innate purity and each bearing these signs of perfection. The term *maṇḍala* means a central focus, accompanied by whatever is relevant to it. Thus, when the bodhisattva mind is focused upon the power of inner purity to purify karma, for example, the specific Buddhas relevant to purification manifest from mind's innate perfection, each accompanied by a retinue which expresses the supportive qualities which need to accompany effective purifcation. The various buddha maṇḍalas appear both in the bodhisattvas' meditation and inter-meditation experiences. The text returns to the example of the moon in water. The real moon in this example is enlightenment itself. The unperturbed, clear water is the mind of the bodhisattva and the reflection of the moon is the manifestation of these and other signs of perfection, as the sambhogakāya.

Scriptural Source

267. *One should know that these sixty-four qualities*
and their respective causes here follow their order
in the 'Jewel Discourse' – the Ratna Sūtra.

There are some slight variations in the description of these sixty-four qualities. Here they are presented following their order in the *ratnadarikasūtra*.

Recapitulation of the Examples

General attribution of examples

268. *Being invulnerable, undisheartened, peerless and unmoving,*
they are illustrated by the examples of a vajra, a lion,
space and the clear moon in water.

The ten powers of wisdom give clear knowledge of everything and leave no place for doubt. They are the reason for the Buddha's invulnerability and so are compared to a vajra, which penetrates all but is unharmed by anything. The four fearlessnesses are the reason for the Buddha never being disheartened, or feeling uncertain, and so are compared to the majestic confidence of a lion. The eighteen distinctive qualities, being peerless, are compared to space, which is like no other thing. The thirty-two signs of perfection are the constant expression of the innate qualities of unchanging enlightenment. Neither coming nor going but perfectly stable, they are the reflection of perfection, hence compared to the reflection of the full moon in still water, which occurs without the moon wishing it to happen but nevertheless faithfully reproduces some of the moon's qualities.

A further discussion of the examples

I. THE QUALITIES OF FREEDOM

269. *Of these, the six, three and one powers,*
have completely dispelled, respectively,
what is cognitive, meditative balance and those
accompanied by latent conditioning.

Thus they have pierced, destroyed and felled
those which are like armour, walls and trees.

> *Being firm, enduring, steadfast and invulnerable,*
> *these powers of the sages are vajra-like.*

The vajra as a symbol of the powers. Of these ten powers, the first six (see list earlier in chapter) dispel the cognitive obscuration, the following three dispel obstacles to proper meditative absorption and the final one dispels the defilements, along with any latent mental conditioning (habit). Thus, respectively, they pierce the weighty armour and defence-mechanisms of ignorance; they shatter the thick soundproof, sightproof walls of meditative limitation and they clear the forest of its trees of defilements which have grown out of the ground of ignorance, along with all the habits and reaction-patterns they have established.

> 271. *Why firm? Because they are enduring.*
> *Why enduring? Because they are steadfast.*
> *Why steadfast? Because they are invulnerable.*
> *Why invulnerable? Because they are like a vajra.*

It is therefore excellent to compare these powers to a vajra, because they are firm, enduring, steadfast and invulnerable. Why firm? Because these have the quality of changelessness, enduring in the face of the impermanent, ephemeral world of phenomena. Why, unlike phenomena, do they endure? Because they are the true essence of phenomena; their real, steadfast nature. Why is it steadfast? Because the light of this wisdom-nature is totally invulnerable to the darkness of doubt and ignorance, firmer than a rock, the one vajra nature of all things. The subject matter of this verse, as is often the case, takes on real significance in the light of meditation, when the meditator has reached a stage of actually experiencing the contrast between the phenomenal and noumenal aspects of experience.

> 272. *Being fearless, unconcerned and stable*
> *and possessing skill supreme, the lion of humans,*
> *the triumphant one, is likened to a lion because*
> *he is fearless in the midst of any gathering.*

273. *Having definite knowledge of everything,*
the Enlightened remain absolutely fearless of anyone.
Seeing clearly that even purified beings
are not their peers, they remain uninfluenced.

274. *Since their noble mind is constantly attentive,*
to each and every phenomenon, it has stability.
Having transcended the state of latent ignorance,
so difficult to transcend, they possess skilful mastery.

The lion as an example of enlightened fearlessness. These verses explain four qualities: fearlessness itself, unconcerned self-reliance, stability and skill:

- When the Enlightened teach and guide beings, they are not only without any anxiety or neurosis, such as a wordly counsellor may feel, but are completely without any concept whatsoever. They have no worry that the advice they give may not be the best, or that it may not work. This is because, due to the ten powers, the crystal clarity of their mind knows without confusion all the elements involved in the situation – not just at present but in the past and the future. This omniscience gives them majestic fearlessness, hence the image of the lion.
- For similar reasons, they are not concerned that someone else – even great bodhisattvas – may come up with better solutions or find flaws in their teachings. Buddhajñāna is reliable and independent. It is portrayed by the image of the lion which does not need some other beast to protect it.
- Such wisdom is stable, being a clear, direct, spontaneous and all-encompassing knowledge, and not something vacillating because based upon limited deduction or opinions. This is like the innate and supreme strength of the lion's muscles.
- Thus, whether amidst scholars, yogins, gods or any other being, the Enlightened are always fearless, natural leaders. This is also true when in the presence of the bodhisattvas, especially those of the very pure eighth, ninth and tenth levels, since enlightenment's lucidity recognises the subtle veils of latent

ignorance still remaining in those beings, in contrast to the total purity in themselves. Unswayed by others' views and opinions, they enunciate the deepest and most skilful of teachings. This is described through the natural physical skill of the lion.

275. *Worldlings, śrāvakas, those one-sided,*
the wise and the spontaneously arising,
have progressively subtler understanding,
as exemplified by the elements five.

Space as an example of the distinctive qualities. Beings each have their limits of understanding, especially when it comes to understanding the ultimate truth of existence. The text points to five levels of awareness. Beings steeped in worldly existence have many emotions and thoughts, clouding and colouring their understanding. They are compared to the earth element, as it is the densest. Less densely obscured are the śrāvakas, who understand the voidness of ego. They are compared to water. More subtle and less dense is fire, used here to denote the pratyekabuddhas, whose wisdom is further-reaching and starts to touch on the voidness of phenomena. Less blocked still is wind, depicting here the two-fold voidness understood by bodhisattvas. Unobstructed, unlimited and most subtle, like space, is the omniscience of the Buddhas. Their qualities are unique, unlike those of any of the four types of being.

276. *Buddhas are like earth, water, fire and wind,*
being sustenance for all the worlds.
They are like space, being beyond the characteristics
of both worldly existence and that which transcends it.

This verse employs the element analogy a little differently. Enlightened wisdom pervades all things and enlightened qualities are the foundation for all goodness in the worlds, just as the four changing elements are the prime qualities of all that is sustenance in the world, being respectively the matter, gravity, energy and movement found in all things. Enlightened qualities are the true nature innate to all things. This ultimate nature, however, must be distinguished from what is projected onto it: mental confusion (saṃsāra) and its resolution (nirvāṇa). Thus it is compared to space, of a totally different nature from the other four elements.

277. *Thus as two and thirty qualities are fashioned*
these aspects of dharmakāya.
Even so, they are as inseparable
as the colour, brilliance and shape of a gem.

Inseparability of these qualities. Although it is helpful for us to single out the various qualities described above – thirty-two in all – it would be a mistake to think of them as compartmentalised, separate things. The fractioning of enlightenment into any number of qualities is always a human, intellectual device. In reality, enlightenment is undivided and indivisible. The thirty-two – or however many qualities are discerned – are all facets of the one buddhajñāna. To bring this point home, the text gives the example of a gem. Its internal shapes are determined by where its various colours give way to each other. Colour itself is the brilliance so characteristic of gemstones. Is one looking at shapes? At colours? At different brilliances? Impossible to tell, since these are indissociable in the gem itself and only exist as 'separate' things in the analytical mind of the observer.

2. THE QUALITIES OF MATURITY

278. *These attributes which, when seen, inspire contentment,*
are known as the 'two and thirty' founded in kāyas two:
nirmāṇakāya and sambhogakāya
which makes dharma perfect.

These marks belong to the two form kāya. The thirty-two marks of the perfect being have a profound effect on those who see them, as well as on those who meditate upon them. They bring deep contentment. This is because they well from the deepest truth, being founded in the two form kāya. A superficial but interesting example may be to consider them like flashes an amnesiac has of his true identity, bringing a feeling of authenticity and relief. Since these marks are seen on Buddhas, they occur in a context in which dharma is being communicated perfectly.

279. *Those further from purity and those closer*
see these in two ways:
as being in the world or as the mandala of the Victors,
like the form of the moon, beheld in water or in space.

How these marks are perceived. Those 'further from purity' are śrāvakas and worldly individuals, who have the good karma to meet the Buddha's nirmāṇakāya. Those 'closer' to it are the bodhisattvas. The former experience the Buddha's nirmāṇakāya, manifest as a being appearing in their world. This 'reflection' of truth in their subjective reality is compared to the reflection of the moon in water. The bodhisattvas, however, experience the various mandala of the Buddha's sambhogakāya. Since these express much more immediately the true qualities of enlightenment, seeing them is compared to looking directly at the moon in the sky.

Notes

1   I am indebted to Goshir Gyaltsab Rinpoché for this explanation.

2   See 'Gems of Dharma, Jewels of Freedom', chapter 6, pps. 73–89.

3   The Buddhist analysis of mind and matter - one the three baskets of awareness.

4   Compassion, sympathetic joy and impartiality.

5   Tib: *lha'i mig*, literally divine vision, or clairvoyance

6   One cannot but help wonder if the crystal ball does not come from a deep primordial association of looking into the crystal clarity of the true sphere of reality, buddha nature, to find the answers one needs.

7   See "Gems of Dharma, Jewels of Freedom", chapter on the paths and levels.

8   As it is impossible to portray an infinite head mound, artists usually depict it as a large bump on the Buddha's head, but this is not how it appears to those who see the Buddha.

The Seventh Vajra Abode
– enlightened activity –

SUMMARY

a. Its Spontaneity

280. *Ever spontaneous are the All-Embracing One's actions,*
regarding the temperaments of those to be trained,
the means for training them,
the trainings suited to their dispositions
and their own movements in terms of time and space.

The two main points made in this chapter are that enlightened activity is spontaneous and unceasing. This first verse sums up its spontaneity as being entirely related to the needs of the person being helped, rather than some sort of definite action that Buddhas always perform. Enlightened activity is also unplanned and non-conceptual.

Some disciples like short, pithy answers to their questions, whereas others prefer long, detailed ones. Some need to feel cared for, whereas others take pride in their independence. There are all sorts of temperaments which solicit specific responses from the primordial purity of enlightenment, when it interacts with them.

Further, there are different means of training appropriate to different beings. Some are inspired to emulate good conduct through witnessing the peaceful, controlled behaviour of the Buddha. Others need to be impressed by the likes of miracles. Yet others prefer to receive large quantities of information, as formal teachings. Some are almost immediately ready to enter an advanced form of practice whereas others would be ill-advised to skip laborious preliminaries. Enlightened activity guides each and every one of them in the best way. Furthermore, it knows, without thinking, the best time and place to teach and thereby applies the appropriate teachings in a most effective manner.

b. Its Ceaselessness

281. *Endowed with a jñāna ocean,*
filled with a multitude of gem-like qualities
and with the sunlight of virtue and jñāna,
the buddhas have achieved all yānas.

282. *Without middle or end, exceedingly vast,*
buddhahood is all-pervading, like space.
Perfectly seeing that this treasure of unsullied qualities
is in every being, without the slightest variation,
the wind of their perfect compassion dispels
the complex cloud banks of defilements and false knowledge.

The second main point about enlightened activity is that it never ceases. The reasons for this are presented in terms of three analogies. First, buddhahood never runs out of resources and so knows no limit to the amount of help it can give. Thus it is compared to the vastness of an ocean, more rich in treasures, such as coral and pearl, than anyone could ever imagine. Secondly, its resources are of the finest quality, and therefore able to cope with all situations. This is explained through the example of the sun, which is able to bring all plants to maturity through its radiant light. The 'sun' in this instance is the perfection of the two accumulations (virtue and wisdom). Thirdly, buddhahood itself is all-pervading and without beginning, middle or end, like space. Like space, it is also deep and vast, since every yāna has been fully attained. Beings other than Buddhas have an attainment which is limited in duration, since it will one day evolve into something more profound.

Enlightened activity is also unceasing because its object, sentient beings to be helped, persists as long as time itself persists. There is not one being excluded from this help, because enlightened primordial wisdom recognises itself in all beings, and hence recognises the potential of each and every being to attain liberation. Whether they be practising the path or not, all beings are viewed as equal in potential. In the unawakened, the potential is present but obscured by 'clouds' of ignorance and transient impurity. Enlightened activity disperses these with the 'wind' of compassion.

2. FULLER EXPLANATION

a. Its Spontaneity

282. *Since thoughts of 'for whom', 'by what means',*
      'through which training', 'where' or 'when' do not arise,
      these masters of wisdom are spontaneous at all times.

It was mentioned, in the introduction to the last four chapters, that spontaneous action is hard for ordinary beings to understand. In everyday life, it is most often the case that the more something is intelligently thought out, and the more it is planned, the better the outcome. Action without thought is often catastrophic. However, in some ways, even ordinary beings can have a relative appreciation of a state in which thought impedes best action. Well-trained gymnasts, rock-climbers and the like need to rely on the experienced, split-second responses of their limbs. They could be put in peril by *thinking* about what they are doing. An airline pilot might well be better off bringing his plane in to land with well-tried intuitive expertise, rather than suddenly thinking out all the actions he has to do, the dials he must look at, the flaps he must lower and so on and so forth. Ordinary beings already have some degree of spontaneity.

However, Buddhas are not just ordinary beings. They have the two sorts of perfect primordial wisdom. Suchness primordial wisdom knows the truth as it is, hence it knows that to which beings need to be led. All-encompassing primordial wisdom knows each and every person and every thing precisely for what it is, hence knows from where they are to be led. This crystal clarity would be hindered, not helped, by thought, which would, at best, be a simplistic, dark echo of what it knows with complete lucidity.

283. *'for whom' – the temperaments of those to be trained,*
'by what means' – which of the many training methods,
'through which training' – which actions to use to train them
or 'where' or 'when' – on which occasion.

This thought-free spontaneity applies to all the teaching activities already mentioned above, i.e. there is no thought of *for what sort of person are these teachings being given?, which is the best technique to teach him or her?, on what path should this person be led?* or *when is the best time to teach this?* or indeed any other teaching-related concept.

b. Its Ceaselessness

284. *Buddha activity is unceasing, being devoid of concept*
regarding true freedom, freedom's support,
the result of freedom,
authentic possession of that result,
the obscurations which veil it,
and the necessary conditions for breaking through them.
285. *Genuine release is the ten levels,*
its cause is the two accumulations,
its result is supreme enlightenment,

an enlightenment which beings truly possess.
286. *Its obscuring veils are the endless defilements,*
subsidiary defilements and latent tendencies.
Great compassion is the condition for destroying these.

The ceaselessness of buddha activity is presented through six key terms, given in verse 284, and their meaning, given in verses 285/6.

- *True freedom* is the genuine release from saṃsāra attained in the first bodhisattva level and developed through the remaining nine levels. Buddhas first lead beings into the dharma path and this gradually enables them to free themselves. The freedom becomes irreversible with the first bodhisattva level.
- The *cause or support* of that freedom is the two 'accumulations', i.e. virtue and wisdom.
- The *result of the freedom* attained in the bodhisattva levels is the completion of their work when enlightenment is attained.
- The *authentic possession of this result* occurs at enlightenment, which is the total recognition of the primordial nature each being possessed from the outset, unknowingly. The recognition occurs because whatever obscured truth has gone.
- The *obscurations which veil it* are self-perpetuating root defilements (desire, aversion, pride, jealousy, doubt and ignorance), the twenty or so main subsidiary defilements and the tendencies and predispositions which all these create.
- The *necessary condition* for breaking through the wall created by these defilements is the great compassion of the buddha.

287. *These six points should be known as being respectively*
like an ocean, the sun, space, a treasure,
clouds and the wind.
288. *The levels are like an ocean of jñāna waters.*
Possessing the qualities of its ocean's gems.
The two accumulations are like the sun,
since by them all beings are sustained.

These six points are illustrated by the six examples listed in verse 287. The first two are developed in verse 288. The release achieved in the ten bodhisattva levels is compared to an ocean. The body of this ocean is constituted by its waters of primordial wisdom. It contains many gems, i.e. the qualities manifest within such wisdom. These are the qualities of the bodhisattva levels in general and, more particularly, the jewels of meditation, perfect recollection, intuitive cognition and so forth found in the tenth level. The two accumulations which cause this attainment are compared to the sun, which sustains all life in our universe and permits growth.

289. *Enlightenment is like space,*
being vast, centreless and without end.
The core character of beings is like a treasure,
being the very nature of utterly pure enlightenment.

Enlightenment, the fruition of the above, is compared to space since it is not a specific entity or creation. Thus it is beginningless, centreless and endless. Being immensely vast and profound, it is indescribable: not this space or that space but *the* space for everything. Possession of buddha nature is compared to having a treasure. If buried, the treasure still has all its own properties but these are of little use. When unearthed and used, it bestows unimaginable wealth. Just as, in order to unearth a treasure, one needs to dig through the dirt, so we have to dig through the dirt of the defilements in order first to find, and then truly take possession of, this wealth.

290. *The covering defilements are like hosts of clouds,*
being transient, pervasive and not entities.
Compassion is like a mighty wind,
being ever-present to dispel them.

The metaphor changes here – perhaps not inappropriately. At first, when one digs through the defilements, they may seem quite solid and removing earth may appear a good example for working with them. But, as time goes by, they are recognised for what they are, something transient, ephemeral and without entity of their own yet nevertheless very pervasive. Clouds are a good metaphor for this, especially if one thinks of the vast monsoon clouds of India. When the clouds are present, the light and warmth of the sun is greatly diminished. As they dissipate, its value is felt. Although blocking the sky, clouds are not the sky. Likewise, defilements block the mind but are not an intrinsic part of the mind.

What removes clouds? A great wind. The defilements are removed by the wind of enlightened compassion.

291. *Since their release is for others' benefit,*
since they see the equality of themselves and beings
and since their deeds have not been fully completed,
their activity is unbroken until saṃsāra ends.

Having established this sixfold profile of liberating activity, the text now explains why it is unending. First, one of the main motives for any Buddha's liberation is to be able to help others. This was their uppermost thought throughout their bodhisattva journey. Secondly, they recognise the sameness of themselves and others, inasmuch as all beings have the same essence as themselves and hence are capable of being helped to enlightenment. Their own commitment is to act to help beings until saṃsāra comes to an end, i.e. the end of relative time. This means that Buddhas are committed to altruistic activity until the end of time. During this period, the activity itself is unbroken, through the sheer extent of beings to be helped and the number of realms in which they live.

3. EXPANDED EXPLANATION THROUGH NINE EXAMPLES

a. Summary of the Nine Examples

292. *Like Indra, the drum, clouds, Brahma, the sun,*
a wish-fulfilling gem, an echo, space and earth
is the tathāgata.

Spontaneous yet perfect, non-conceptual, activity is hard to understand. This chapter gives us nine generous examples which do help us build up some picture of how it occurs, despite the inevitable inadequacy of any simile for enlightenment or its activity. Each of these similes will be most appropriate for one or another aspect of enlightened activity, but no single simile will be anywhere near appropriate for the whole.

The nine examples are the reflection of Indra, the invisible drumbeat in the heavens, monsoon clouds, the emanations of the god Brahma, the radiance of the sun, the power of the wish-fulfilling gem, an echo, space and earth.

b. *Explanation of Each Example*

1. INDRA

293. *Had the ground here the quality of flawless vaidurya,*
one would see apparent in it, through its clarity,
the King of the Gods accompanied by hosts of young goddesses,
294. *'Perfectly Victorious' – his resplendent palace,*
the divine abodes, other places with various wonders
and all the many kinds of enjoyment that the gods possess.
295. *Seeing these appearances, multitudes of men and women,*
living on the surface of the Earth, would exclaim:
296. *'Oh! May we also, before long, become like this divine king!'*
Having sincerely made such a prayer, so that it be realised
they would truly adopt virtue and persist in it.
297. *Though they may not appreciate*
that these are just appearances,
they would, nevertheless, through virtue, be reborn as gods
once they had departed from the surface of the Earth.
298. *These appearances are absolutely unintentional.*
They involve no movement. Nevertheless,
their presence on Earth is accompanied by great benefit.

The example: Through their particular karma, the inhabitants of a certain human lands have the precious gem *vaidurya*[1] instead of dirt as the ground upon which they live. In his Sanskrit dictionary, Professor Macdonell, Boden Professor of Sanskrit at Balliol and Fellow of the British Academy, says the term means *cat's eye*. This evokes a green rather than blue colour (Siamese felines excepted). There are green forms of *beryl* as well as blue and white ones and this would tend to support the argument for *beryl* as a translation. My personal conviction is that the gemstone in our world most closely related to celestial *vaidurya* is sapphire. The arguments for this would be its association with Indra (another name for sapphire is *indranila*), the use of Ceylonese sapphire (when obtainable) as *vaidurya* in Tibetan Medicine, its innate nobility and the frequent references to blue and white forms of this translucent stone. For safety, however, I have retained the Sanskrit *vaidurya*. instead of dirt as the ground upon which they live. This jewel ground, smooth and reflective, has the special power to reflect the normally-invisible palace of the King of the Gods, Indra. Thus ordinary beings can witness the splendour of *Perfectly Victorious* (the name of Indra's divine abode) and see the magnificence of Indra himself, all the pleasures he enjoys, his beautiful goddess consorts and so on and so forth. Apart from this, they woud perceive much of the lives of the devas in general.

This vision is very inspiring for the populace, who understand that Indra enjoys all these pleasures because of his former kindness, generosity and other virtues. They apply themselves diligently to virtue, with the hope and prayer of becoming one day like Indra. All their actions are based not upon a real journey to the heaven of Indra but merely upon this image apparent in the ground. Nevertheless, it is sufficient to make them practise many good things and there may be enough good karma to ensure their future rebirth as gods.

None of this happens through any intention on the part of Indra himself. Indra is Indra, busy with his own life in his own world. All that occurs is that the jewel ground acquires the magical quality of mirroring this in the human realm. He never leaves his paradise yet his image brings great goodness to the people of that land.

*299. In a similar way, beings with faultless faith and other (virtues)
   will, through practising these qualities,
   see the perfect buddha manifest in their minds,
300. endowed with the marks and meaningful signs.
   They will see him walking, standing, sitting, sleeping and
   enacting all the modes of conduct,
301. proclaiming the teachings of peace or, without speaking,
   remaining in meditation, performing various sorts of miracle
   and filled with magnificence and splendour.
302. Having seen this and felt aspiration for such buddhahood,
   they apply themselves to it most excellently.
   Through properly adopting its causes,
   the desired state is reached.
303. These appearances are completely concept-free
   and involve no shift.
   Though this be so, they bring great benefit to the world.
304. Ordinary beings are believed not to understand the fact that
   these are the manifestations of their own mind, yet
   to see such forms nevertheless brings them benefit.
305. Progressively, through what is seen, established in the yāna,
   they will see the inner true dharmakāya through eyes of jñāna.*

The meaning of this example: The mind of the bodhisattvas of the ten levels is the pure reflective ground, in which appears the image of the Buddha's sambhogakāya. Ordinary beings' minds are too rough and confused to give rise to such a reflection and, for the most part, humans have to follow the teaching entrusted by the Buddha to the saṃgha. Bodhisattvas' minds have the qualities of faith, diligence and intelligence and have been smoothed by a wealth of virtue. Therefore they see the Buddha walking, standing, sitting, sleeping and proclaiming the universal truth. They experience him as a radiant body of light, exceedingly beautiful and enhanced by the 32 marks of a perfect being, the 80 marks of attainment and so forth. The presence is so inspiring that they diligently pursue their path through the remaining levels. Ordinary beings with exceptional karma also see the body of the Buddha, in a nirmanakāya form. They experience him turning the wheel of dharma for the world.

The manifestation of the Buddha within the minds of all these beings is entirely without effort or intention on the part of the Buddha. It is the natural outcome of buddha nature being what it is, and of the purity of mind in an individual's mind being able to reflect something of this, in a material form. Even though these are simply appearances, they are so inspiring that they lead people into the practice of great virtue and this, in turn, will bring the result, i.e. 'seeing' the inner Buddha through the eyes of primordial wisdom.

306. *If all Earth were rid of fearful places*
and became flawless vaidurya,
lustrous and beautiful with all that jewel's qualities,
free from impurity, magnificent and of smooth, even surface,
there would appear, on account of such purity,
the various divine abodes and the form of the King of Gods.
By the gradual disappearance of such a ground's qualities,
these things would once again no longer be apparent.
307. *In order to obtain such a state,*
many men and women would turn to the 'precepts
of mindfulness', true generosity and so forth,
scatter flowers and do other similar deeds,
their minds full of aspiration.

Extension of this example: Although this example refers primarily to the smoothness of the ground as being the condition through which Indra's paradise appears, as a sort of reflection in a mirror, there is probably more to it than that, as far as the legend itself goes. As a simile, the purity of the ground, and likewise its magnificence and smoothness, are all relevant analogies for openness and virtue in the mind. This verse shows the transitoriness of the phenomenon. People are inspired to a very sincere and intensely motivated practice of virtue while its possible outcome shimmers before their eyes, but may lose interest when the reasons for the divine vision disappear. The virtues which the people practise, in the example, are those of making offerings of flower posies and garlands, observing moral rectitude such as acts of generosity, observing one or more of the eight *upavasa* precepts[2] *and so forth*.

282   Maitreya on Buddha Nature

> *In a similar way, in order to become*
> *the mighty Victor king, who had appeared in their minds,*
> *comparable to pure vaidurya,*
> *bodhisattvas develop their 'mind' perfectly,*
> *their spirit being filled with great joy.*

308. *Just as the reflection of the King of Gods*
   appears in the clear vaidurya ground,
   so also does the reflection of the king of sages' form
   appear in the clear ground which is beings' minds.
309. *For beings, the appearance and disappearance*
   of these reflections occur through their minds' condition,
   polluted or unpolluted.
   Similar to such manifestations of form in the worlds,
   these should not be taken as existing or extinct entities.

The non-reality of these images: Bodhisattvas joyously and diligently apply themselves to enlightenment because they are constantly in the presence of the Buddha's sambhogakāya, and are therefore constantly reminded of the goal they will attain. Having reached the ten profound levels, their mind is pure and smooth, like the *vaidurya*. For them, it is the irreversible condition allowing the image of the Enlightened One to appear in their awareness.

Unlike these, beings who have transitory experiences of Buddha's nirmanakāya, due to a blessed moment of good karma, will find that the experience comes and goes, as a function of their mind's purity. In either case, the Buddha perceived is an inspiring image only and not an existing entity which they are observing directly. It would be a mistake to take either of the Buddha's form kāya as such. Just as the appearance and disappearance of Indra's image in the *vaidurya* ground does not mean that Indra in person has arrived and then departed, existed and ceased to exist, so neither does the appearance and disappearance of the Buddha in beings' minds mean that a truly existing Buddha came to them and then departed.

2. THE DIVINE DRUMBEAT – Buddha speech

310. *Through the power of the gods' former goodness,
the dharma drum in the divine realms,
without effort, location, mental form or concept,*
311. *exhorts all the uncaring gods over and over again
with its throbs of 'impermanence', 'suffering',
'no-self' and 'peace'.*

The example: Devas are born into their state as a result of former good karma. Besides creating their sensorial delights and pleasant conditions, their karma also creates a very special phenomenon: the divine drumbeat. They hear the booming of a drum, and its throb makes them think of the Four Noble Truths, by echoing 'impermanence', 'suffering', 'no self' and 'peace'. Although there is the sound of the drumbeat, there is no drum anywhere. Thus there is no effort of a drummer hitting the drum, no location of the drum and no mentation on the drum's part, thinking, 'Now I must make such and such a sound.' Without its reminding message, these gods would easily lapse into idleness and insensitivity.

312. *Like this, the all-pervading is also without effort and the like,
yet buddha speech reaches all beings, without exception,
teaching the noble doctrine to the fortunate.*

Buddha speech, like the drum, is heard yet occurs effortlessly, without an entity creating it, without location and without preconception. Nevertheless, it has the power to reach out to both bodhisattvas and ordinary beings with enough good karma to experience it. They hear this speech pronouncing the Four Noble Truths and the Buddhist teachings.

313. *Just as the divine drum beats for devas,
through their karma, so also does the Sage's dharma speech
arise in the world, due to karma.
Just as its sound, without effort, source, form or mind,
brings peace, so also is peace procured by dharma*

without effort or the other things.
314. *The sound of the drum in the celestial citadel*
is the cause which both ends divine play
and also bestows fearlessness, to vanquish Asura armies
when, through defilement, war occurs. Like this,
that arising from such as formless meditation proclaims,
in the worlds, the way of the insurpassable path of peace,
to defeat, totally, sentient beings' defilements and sufferings.

The reason for either the dharma drumbeat or the Buddha's speech being heard is the same: good karma. Both have the effects of pacifying the mind and reducing laziness and defilement. Yet neither sound comes from something, somewhere, intending to be heard in that subjective way.

    The gods are attacked from time to time by the *Asura*, or Jealous Demi-Gods. Although the latter do not have enough good karma to possess the bounty of the gods, they strive vainly, in their ignorance, to attack them and steal their riches. The gods are obliged to fight them off and are generally victorious. Thus the divine drumbeat not only ends idle enjoyment of the fruits of their karma but also gives them courage when warding off Asura attacks. Likewise, the beautiful melody of Buddha speech, with its sixty qualities, stirs one from idleness, encourages diligence and gives courage in the battle with the defilements and the sufferings they cause. The wise guidance of enlightened speech carries this battle through to perfect victory.

315. *Universal, joyously beneficial and having threefold miracles,*
the Sages' melody is superior to the celestial cymbals.

316. *The mighty sound of the divine drum*
cannot reach Earthling ears,
yet the sound of Buddha speech
is heard in saṃsāra's underworld.

Superiority of Buddha speech: the spiritual sound of the divine drumbeat is not the only music to be heard in the deva realms. The gods get very sensually excited by the shimmering reverberations and angelic overtones of celestial cymbals. Buddha speech far transcends the latter, since it brings deep joy and benefit to beings, rather than lust. Furthermore, it is possessed of threefold miracles, i.e. those of body, speech and mind.

The divine drum, for all the benefit it brings, is a phenomenon confined to the god realms. Beings here on Earth and in other human worlds cannot hear it or be helped by it. Buddha speech can be heard in any realm, as soon as an individual's mind is ready. Thus even those who live beneath the earth, i.e. beings in the lower realms, receive Buddha's teaching from time to time.

317. *In the heavens, tens of millions of celestial cymbals resound to reinforce desire's fire, yet those whose identity is compassion give forth a single melody to extinguish, totally, suffering's fire.*
318. *The beautiful and pleasant music of cymbals in the heavens brings increased mental agitation.*
The speech of the tathāgatas, whose nature is compassion, turns the mind towards samādhi and stimulates reflection.
319. *In brief, it is said that the cause of happiness for those in each and every universe, in heaven or on earth, depends entirely upon that very melody, all-pervasively manifest in every world.*

Its miraculous activity: Gods work themselves into states of sensuous desire through the sounds of myriad cymbals clashing and resonating. Their passion is compared to a fire. Contrasted to this is Buddha speech. Its single, beautiful, truthful melody is enough to extinguish another sort of fire, that of suffering. Whereas the dramatic cymbals only serve to increase the mental agitation of the gods, pulling the mind to externals, enlightened speech brings peace and inspires one to reflect. Its natural depth also makes one value the benefits of profound meditative absorption.

When one considers the Buddha's speech in a very broad way, and in particular its long term effect, it becomes apparent that it is at the root of all goodness in every world, either in the form of proclaimed religions which teach natural morality, such as not to kill, not to lie etc., or as a basic sense of goodness. This is because it is the natural radiance of the pure and the ultimate, interacting with the relative and the impure. Although the religion we know as *Buddhism* is the highest and most perfect expression of natural goodness, in harmony with the absolute, it is not uncommon for our lineage teachers to express the view that many great religious teachers have been emanations of the absolute truth, or deeply in touch with it and expressing fundamentally good values, in a way and language suited to their times.

320. *Just as those with no hearing cannot experience subtle sound and even those with divine hearing cannot hear every sound, so likewise is the subtle dharma, the domain of very finest jñāna, to be heard by only those few whose mind is undefiled.*

Its subtlety: Those with defective hearing cannot hear very slight or subtle sounds. Even those who have mastered concentration meditation and acquired divine hearing cannot hear every sound. The 'profound' dharma teachings, i.e. those on voidness and especially on voidness as buddha nature, cannot be received in a defiled mind. Heard by few, they are only properly understood by those whose minds possess the very finest primordial wisdom, on account of their purity.

3. CLOUDS – the all-pervading compassionate mind

321. *In the rainy season, clouds continuously and effortlessly pour down vast amounts of water onto the earth and are the cause for good and bountiful crops.*
322. *Likewise, clouds of compassion, without any conceptualising, rain down the waters of the Victor's noble teachings and cause a harvest of virtue for sentient beings.*

The example: It is helpful to reflect that this example comes from India where the monsoon rains are a striking feature of the yearly cycle. When the monsoon breaks, millions of tons of water are poured down upon the earth. The rainfall is continuous, very heavy and completely effortless on the part of the clouds. In a matter of days and weeks, all nature bursts forth and flowers, plants, trees and crops come to their full.

The rain of blessing coming from enlightenment's clouds of compassion is equally generous and is also completely non-conceptual and effortless. The 'rain' in this case is the teachings of dharma, leading beings as quickly as it is possible along a path of practice which produces a harvest of virtue.

323. *Provided that the world is engaged in virtue's ways,*
the wind-borne clouds will cause a fall of rain.
Likewise the wind of compassion causes buddha clouds
to cascade their rain of true teachings
to increase virtue in beings.
324. *In the world, through great compassionate love and knowledge,*
the clouds of the Lord of All Sages abide amid space
unblemished by either that which changes or the changeless.
As their unspoilt essence,
they have samādhi and dharani waters,
which are the very cause for the harvest of virtue there.

Development of example: In bygone India, it was believed that rain fell as a good consequence of humankind's virtue. One should remember that rain, which can be a dreary nuisance in some countries, is very necessary and much-awaited in India; lives depend upon it. The monsoon rainclouds are borne in on the winds. Likewise, as a result of beings' virtue, the Buddha's compassion, which is like the wind, can bring in clouds of teachings which lead beings to the creation of virtue.

'That which changes' is worldliness, saṃsāra, and 'the changeless' is the arhat's state of peaceful quiescence, nirvāṇa. Neither of these affect the sky of dharmadhātu, whence come the compassion and teachings. The perfection of the eighty enlightened attributes of the bodhisattva is found therein, including such things as the perfection of *dharani*,[3] deep meditative absorption and so forth, which permit many diverse teaching activities to emanate from one simple essence, just as the simple power of water falling ripens various crops, fills the rivers for the fish, washes dirt from rocks and so on.

325. *Cool, delicious, soft, light water fallen from the clouds*
acquires many different tastes,
by contact with salty and other grounds.
Likewise the rain of the eightfold water of the sublime,
falling from the heart of that vastest cloud
of compassionate love,
assumes many a flavour,
according to beings' various mentalities.

Those to be taught: The rainwater in clouds may be soft, sweet-tasting and pure but it inevitably acquires the taste of the ground upon which it has fallen – a salty taste on salty ground, a bitter taste on bitter soil and so forth. Likewise, as the pure presence of dharma, referred to here as the Eightfold Path, is received in an individual's mind, it is interpreted automatically through the subjective conditioning of that person's mind, making sense to him or her. This is the great quality of a Buddha's teaching. Each person of faith in the presence of the Buddha feels that he or she is receiving a teaching that answers perfectly their needs and aspirations of the time. This is the outcome of their individual, relative mind encountering the infinite compassion of buddhahood.

326. *Those of appreciative faith, the middling*
and those with animosity
form three groups comparable to humans, peafowl and pretas.
327. *In the cloudless end of spring, men and these non-flyers suffer.*
In the summertime, when it rains, the pretas suffer.
This example is drawn upon to illustrate how,
depending upon whether there is a rain of dharma or not,
worldly beings will either aspire to it or feel animosity.
328. *Making a deluge of mighty raindrops,*
hurling down hailstones or thunderbolts,
clouds do not consider the small fauna
or those who run to the hills.

> *Similarly, clouds of perfect knowledge and compassionate love, with their very fine or larger drops, do not mind that some will purify their defilements while others tend to believe in self.*

Effortless application: Beings can react quite differently to the Buddha's teaching, depending upon their degree of faith or trust. These verses depict three cases: those of very great faith, who long for teachings and deeply appreciate them once received, those with some faith and respect and, finally, those who feel animosity towards the teachings. These are compared respectively to humans, peafowl and craving spirits. In the dry, electric period before the monsoon, humans suffering from the heat crave for soothing rain and feel deep appreciation when it comes, ripening their crops. Peafowl would quite like rain, and squawk happily when it falls. Through their own type of perception, craving spirits experience the rain as a fall of burning acid and detest it.

Monsoon rain simply falls. It does not think about the various beings it falls upon. Humans and peafowl enjoy it but some small animals, such as rodents, in fear of their lives, flee the rising waters and run for higher ground, where they hide in holes for safety. They hate the rain. The larger and smaller 'drops' of teachings which are poured down through enlightenment's compassion are respectively the *vast* teachings covering every aspect of the relative truth, and in particular those of the Buddhist path, and those of the *deep* teachings on ultimate truth, voidness. Beings react variously to these messages of truth: some are delighted and gratefully use dharma to purify their defilements. But others, who feel animosity and threat, persist in believing in their fantasies of persona. The natural radiance of truth from which spring dharma teachings is not concerned by these differing reactions, just as a mirror is uninvolved with the way people react to their reflections in it.

329. *In this saṃsāra of beginningless birth and death,*
  there are five sorts of sentient being.
  Just as there is no pleasant smell in excrement,
  there is no true contentment among those five.
  Their sufferings are like the incessant pain

*of burns, wounds, chemical scalds and so forth.
The clouds of compassion cause a mighty rain
of true dharma, which will soothe all these.*

Dharma is the ideal remover of suffering: In this saṃsāra, in which any individual's cycle of births and deaths has been happening since time without beginning, there are five types of beings: gods and demi-gods, humans, animals, craving spirits and those in hells. Although the first three sorts can experience periods of happiness, there is no true contentment in any of these states, and the price of the happiness they do enjoy is high. This point is made with great conviction through the analogy of excrement.

The happiness-to-suffering ratio in these five types of existence covers a whole spectrum. But there is always suffering. The gods spend the last years of their existence experiencing the decline of their beauty and power and beholding the spectacle of their future rebirth in lower realms. It is said that the mental pain, as they absorb the inevitability of this future fall, is unimaginable. The various sufferings in the five realms are compared to burns, wounds, chemical scalds and so forth, i.e. a range of burning pains. The Buddha's teaching soothes and heals this existential hurt, just as the flow of cool water soothes a burn, washes a wound and washes away the chemicals that bite into the flesh.

330. *Those endowed with prajñā have no longing
for even the highest celestial or human sovereignty,
having understood that divine death and transmigration
or humanity's constant searching are all 'misery'.
They have also seen, through prajñā and through following,
with faith, the tathāgatas' excellent teaching:
'This is suffering', 'this is its cause'
and 'this is its cessation' through 'understanding'.*

Bodhisattvas, especially those in the ten levels, have the wisdom to recognise the inherent shortcomings of worldly existence and have no desire for it at all. Knowing that even the most exalted human or divine states come as a package that includes suffering, they are uninterested in it. Instead, they value the insight into existence afforded by the Buddha's teaching which, via the Four Noble Truths, clearly outlines suffering, its causes, liberation from suffering and the path which leads to liberation. Bringing recognition of the existential situation which is summed up by the Four Noble Truths is at the very heart of the teaching activity of enlightenment. The Truths provide an overall framework into which all the remaining details of dharma fit.

331. *Just as a disease needs to be diagnosed, its cause eliminated,*
a healthy state achieved and the remedy implemented,
so also should suffering, its causes, its cessation and the path
be known, removed, attained and undertaken.

One well-known metaphor for the Four Truths is that of treating an ailment. Suffering, the disease, needs first to be accurately diagnosed. Secondly, the reason for the ailment needs to be understood and then eradicated. Thirdly, this can only be done fully and effectively if one knows properly what true health, liberation, really means. Fourthly, to achieve that end, the medicine needs to be taken according to prescription, until such time as full health is properly established.

4. BRAHMĀ – emanation

332. *Without effort and without departing from his Brahmā heaven,*
Brahma can manifest his presence in any divine realm.
333. *Likewise, never departing from dharmakāya, the great Victor*
effortlessly manifests emanations in any sphere, to the mature.

Today, television gives us an excellent example of how someone can appear in many places without ever departing from one central location. The easiest way to convey this notion in ancient India was by reference to the popular god Brahmā, who was reputed to be able to be seen in many other paradises while never leaving his own abode among the form-dimension gods[4] and without the slightest effort or movement on his part.

The real Buddha is the dharmakāya, which is the formless, true nature of mind. Without ever departing from this, formal expressions of enlightenment manifest and are experienced in the many 'worlds' of the relative mind, as either the sambhogakāya or nirmanakāya.

334. Without leaving his palace,
Brahmā manifests in the sense realm.
Seeing him there makes its gods
abandon pursuit of the sensorial.
Similarly, the sugatas, while never leaving the dharmakāya,
are perceived in every world sphere by those who are ready.
The vision constantly causes them to relinquish impurity.

Relevance of this example: The apparition of Brahmā in the deva realms of the sensorial dimension of existence is not without consequence. It apprises the gods there of higher states, which are infinitely more sublime than their own and the result of concentration meditation and goodness, rather than that of good actions alone. The presence of Brahmā turns their minds to higher things. Likewise the Sugata, the Buddha, can be perceived in the mind of someone with excellent karma. The consequence is to inspire people to aspire to higher things and to abandon the grossness and impurity which is binding them to their present state. Although the apparition of the Buddha has this beneficial effect, Buddhas remains at all time Buddha; the dharmakāya.

335. Due to the power of his former prayers,
and the gods' own virtue,
Brahmā appears effortlessly.
Forms of the Spontaneous appear similarly.

The cause of this: Brahmā's appearance in other realms is the result of a conjuncture of circumstances. One main cause is the impetus coming from Brahmā's former prayers of kindness, wanting to help other beings. Another factor comes from the gods themselves, whose fortunate karma, through past virtue, makes them receptive to Brahmā's presence. The coming together of these factors is enough to produce the image of Brahmā, without Brahmā himself having to make any effort at all to be present.

The Spontaneous One, the Buddha, appears in beings' minds through the ongoing impetus of his past connections with those beings and through the prayers he himself made, while a bodhisattva, to help them in the future, once enlightened. These factors combine with their own good karma, through past virtue, to produce an experience of the Buddha which appears to be a meeting with an external entity. When this happens, no effort is being made by the real Buddha, dharmakāya.

336. *Descent, entering the womb, going to his father's palace,*
enjoyment, solitary practice, the subjugation of negativity,
attaining enlightenment and teaching the path
to the city of peace,
having demonstrated these, the Great Sage became invisible
to those of insufficient maturity.

The twelve deeds: The supreme nirmanakāya is experienced by worldly beings as enacting the twelve major deeds of the Buddha, as explained in the chapter on enlightenment. It is a temporary phenomenon, since one of the causes for its presence is the personal karma of the Buddha's disciples and the group karma of a world. Whereas the perfect form of the Buddha is constantly accessible to bodhisattvas of the ten levels, the nirmanakāya is only temporarily glimpsed in the world.

5. THE SUN – wisdom's penetration

337. *When the sun shines, lotuses and similar flowers open.*
At the same time, the kumata flowers close up completely.
The sun has no opinion of 'good' or 'bad' that these,
the 'water-born' flowers, be either open or closed.
Also like this is the Sun of Beings – the Perfectly-Realised One.

Without thought or intention, the sun shines on one half of the Earth. Plants react to it differently. Many flowers, including the lotus (one name for which in Sanskrit means 'water-born'), open up to its warm rays. The *kumuta* flower, however, closes up in daylight. The sun has no opinion, good or bad, of these various flowers' reactions. It simply shines. Likewise the radiance of dharmakāya causes teachings to be given wherever sufficient karma opens a mind. Although past karma creates this encounter with a Buddha, it is the present mentality which determines how the individual reacts to the presence. Some welcome it, whereas others reject it.

338. *The sun, without ideation and by its own light's radiation simultaneously makes lotuses bloom and other things ripen.*
339. *Similarly, without ideation, the tathāgata sun pours forth rays of true dharma on those 'lotus' beings to be trained.*

Penetrating power: Just as the sun does not think or plan its radiation, or hold on to any ideas about what is happening, but simply radiates, nor does dharmakāya ideate. Nevertheless both the sun and the tathāgata have a powerful influence – the sun causing the flowers to open and harvests to ripen and the tathāgata's teachings penetrating the lives of beings, bringing them to maturity through the light of wisdom.

340. *Through the dharma and form kāya, the sun of omniscience rises in the firmament of the essence of enlightenment, to send forth its sunbeams of jñāna into sentient beings.*

How wisdom radiates: Perfect wisdom, omniscience in fact, is innate to the essence of mind. The two aspects of primordial wisdom[5] reveal themselves a little when the true nature of mind is first recognised and to an ever-increasing extent as one progresses through the ten bodhisattva levels. From a relative point of view, this is like the sun rising in the firmament. Just as sunlight reveals all the details of a landscape with sharp clarity, so does this wisdom reveal both the ultimate and relative natures of phenomena. Ultimate truth is dharmakāya, voidness, and relative truth is discovered in all its vastness through the form kāya.

*341. Due to this, the sugata sun appears at one and the same time
in countless reflections in all the 'water vessels'
which are sentient beings to be guided.*

Its manifestation is multiple: The single sun in the sky is reflected in many ways, according to the actual water it is reflected in and the tint of the vessel containing the water. Buddha is also experienced in manifold ways, as unique dharmakāya is reflected in the various 'vessels' which are beings' minds, in varying stages of maturity.

*342. Continually, from amid the sky of all-pervading dharmadhātu,
in a manner determined by the power of their own merit,
shines forth the buddha sun on the mountain-like disciples.*
*343. Just as the risen sun, with thousands of magnificent rays,
illuminates the universe, shedding its light in turn
on first the highest summits, then the lower, then the plains,
likewise does that sun, the Victorious One, shed his light
progressively upon the multitudes of beings.*

The true nature of beings, i.e. voidness or dharmadhātu, is like space; constant and all-pervading. How much of its innate wisdom is manifest depends upon the degree of maturity of beings. This is portrayed through the example of mountains. The highest mountain tops, fully exposed and with their pure white reflective snow, benefit most from the sun, receiving its rays first in the morning and enjoying them last at night. Mountain-dwellers soon get suntanned! The most elevated of beings have the fullest primordial wisdom.

Day and night still exists deep in the valleys, but mainly through the indirect light coming from the sky. Daylight there is shorter-lived, less intense and there are shady areas of landscape which are seldom illuminated. The valley-bottom analogy is used for ordinary beings and the way in which they benefit from the Victor's teaching. Between these two extremes one finds a whole range of both perception of light and benefit from it. A long walk in the mountains, starting in the dark, dank forests of the valley and working up to the summit, with its vast panorama, where one is surrounded by light and space, could be quite useful in bringing this example to life.

> 344. *The sun cannot radiate to the depths of space in every realm*
> *nor show the meaning of what is to be known*
> *to those obscured by the darkness of ignorance.*
> *The one identical with compassion shows beings the significance*
> *of that which should be known, clarity,*
> *through spectra of radiant multiple colour.*

The sublime nature of jñāna: the example of the sun has its limits. It cannot penetrate everywhere and it only sheds physical light. Buddhajñāna is available to all beings and can illuminate profound meaning, dispelling the darkness of ignorance and helping them free themselves from suffering. Interacting with various mentalities, it gives rise to a wonderful range of teachings, each relevant to the person involved. Just as the light of morning gives rise to each colour of the spectrum in a dewdrop, as one slowly moves one's head while admitting it, so do the dharma teachings each have their tonality, suitable to each being and to the various stages of the spiritual journey that any one of them goes through.

With knowledge, one comes to appreciate that all the vivid colours of the rainbow are due to the presence of white light, which can give rise to any one of them. As one matures on the path, the compassionate wisdom, innate to mind, reveals the one dharmakāya, voidness, in which *nothing whatsoever but anything whatsoever*[6] occurs.

> 345. *When the Buddha goes to cities, the eyeless see.*
> *They experience, through that seeing, the meaningful,*
> *free from the various aspects of what is not beneficial.*
> *Their intelligence illuminated by the light of the buddha sun,*
> *those blinded by ignorance, fallen into the ocean of existence*
> *and veiled by the darkness of preconceived ideas,*
> *see the essence they had not previously seen.*

Buddhism talks about five sorts of 'eyes', i.e. five types of vision: flesh eyes[7], divine eyes, dharma eyes, wisdom eyes and Buddha eyes. The first is the visual consciousness that humans, animals etc. enjoy. The second is a greatly enhanced form of this, in which meditational prowess extends the range of vision through clear cognition. Dharma eyes associate an understanding of the nature (impermanence etc.) of what is seen with the actual seeing and bring a wise, compassionate vision of existence. Wisdom eyes 'see' things from a perspective of voidness and the word seeing is more metaphorical than physical. One sees the truth of voidness with the 'eye' of inner wisdom, which operates whether visual consciousness is active in the moment or not. Buddha eyes know everything, through total primordial wisdom.

The 'eyeless' in this verse are ordinary beings. Blinded by their ignorance and preconceptions of self and other, they see reality from a limited and warped perspective and there is often little meaning to their lives. The radiance of dharma introduces them to the nature of things and they start to appreciate the meaning of impermanence, no-self, suffering and true happiness. In particular, they open to compassion. Their dharma eyes start to see. Beyond this, mahāyāna dharma introduces them to the illusory nature of perception and their wisdom eyes open to voidness and particularly to these teachings on buddha nature. They come to 'see' their own true essence.

6. THE WISH-FULFILLING GEM – the mystery of mind

346. A wish-fulfilling gem, though not thinking,
fulfils simultaneously all the wishes
of those within the sphere of its activity.
347. Likewise, Buddha does not think,
though those of varying aspiration hear various teaching,
when turning to the wish-fulfilling Buddha.

The fabulous wish-fulfilling gem has the power to make the wishes of those in its proximity come true. It is not a thinking, conscious entity but simply a gem with special properties. Meeting it is the result of very special karma but, even so, one needs to be within the radius of influence of the gem for its power to work.

People encounter Buddhas and their beneficent activity through the fruition of their good karma. They receive teachings and inspiration from the Buddhas, and this fulfils their wishes to purify their own minds and to bring help to others. This wish-fulfilment may not happen instantly but will definitely occur, the speed of this usually being determined by the individual's own diligence and faith.

Various beings gathered around a wish-fulfilling gem will have their different wishes fulfilled. Likewise, disciples receive the Buddha's teaching differently, even to the point of 'hearing' it in their own language. It addresses their particular needs and problems and is articulated in a way which speaks directly to their way of thinking. All the specific details of what they are taught result from their own openness in the presence of the Buddha. It is not as though the Buddha actually thought about teaching those details or actually pronounced them.[8] The process is extremely subtle and this is perhaps why the gem is chosen here, as the wish-fulfilling power of, say, a monarch, would not indicate so well the subtlety of the processes through which the interaction of the individual's mind with perfect mind brings about teachings of hinayāna, mahāyāna or vajrayāna, as appropriate.

348. *Such a precious gem bestows the desired wealth on others,*
perfectly, effortlessly and without any concept.
Similarly, effortlessly and however appropriate,
the Great Sage remains constantly in the world,
to help others for as long as it persists.

This verse repeats the now familiar themes of effortless and non-conceptual activity and makes the point that the Buddha remains constantly in the world, for as long as saṃsāra persists, acting to help its beings, which come and go. This is like the wish-fulfilling gem which is always benefiting someone even though, from the person's point of view, meeting it is a once-in-a-lifetime opportunity.

349. *Just as it is difficult for beings here desirous of such a gem
to find one, because it lies underground or in the ocean's depths,
so should one know it to be difficult
for beings here to see a sugata,
since they are poorly fated and in the grasp of defilements.*

Rare indeed is it to encounter a wish-fulfilling gem. They are often in caves or beneath the oceans, guarded by nāga or dragons. Furthermore, their presence is due to the good karma of beings and hence they are not to be found in times and places of bad karma.

Likewise it is rare indeed to encounter a Buddha, since the precondition for this is very good karma. Furthermore, beings are so wrapped up in their own defilements that often they cannot recognise Buddha through their blockages, which act like the ground or the ocean hiding the gem.

7. AN ECHO – mystery of speech

350. *The echo's sound arises due to others' faculties of cognition.
Concept-free, it is effortless
and abides neither without nor within.*
351. *Likewise, tathāgata speech arises due to others' cognitive faculties
and is concept-free, effortless and neither without nor within.*

These days we know that even a sound, let alone an echo, does not exist in its own right. When a hammer hits a gong, or a firework explodes, it sends out shock waves. These only become *sound* on encountering a human ear. Without a hearer, with eardrum, bones and nerves which respond to those frequencies of vibration, the gong itself is silent, as is the pyrotechnic device. In bygone times, the example of the echo was used to emphasise the subjectivity of sound.

To popular consciousness, it does seem as though a voice or a drum makes sound. Even were one to accept this as true, it is clear that the echo of that sound does not come from its primary source but depends on the location of the cliff-face, forest etc. which sends back the sound. It also depends upon the location of the hearer. When one asks oneself where exactly the sound of the echo is, one realises that it is neither where it seems to be coming from, nor is it uniquely within oneself. It justs *happens*, without effort, through a certain conjuncture of circumstances, and particularly depends upon the location of the listener. The reader is strongly recommended not just to savour this with the intellect but to actually go to a place of echoes, shout loudly and investigate where the echo actually *is*.

Likewise, the speech of the tathāgata occurs not externally but through the cognitive faculties of disciples. It occurs without concept on the Buddha's part and is located neither without nor within.

8. SPACE – the mystery of form

352. *Even though space is nothing whatsoever, non-manifest,*
not a mental object, without foundation, completely invisible,
without form and not demonstrable,
353. *It is seen as being 'up' or 'down',*
yet space is not like that.
Likewise nothing seen in relation to buddha
is like buddha at all.

Space is very obviously not a thing. It is invisible, without any cause or foundation and without any measurable properties. As there is no thing to be shown, it cannot be pointed to. It has no form of its own, although it is attributed form which it does not actually possess by beings who consider a hollow cylinder, for instance, to contain a cylindrical space. When deeply considered, 'space', as most people know it, is no more than a concept, refering to an absence of matter rather than the presence of some thing.

When there is a square aperture in a church wall, the intellect conceives of a square space occupying it. If the aperture is higher than the eyes of the observer, it is thought of as being high. Yet there is no thing, either square or high, occupying the wall.

Someone looking down from the clerestory may equally conceive of it as being a low space and, because of their angle of view, see it as rectangular or even as a narrow slit. There is no rectangular or low thing there either. The shapes are relative to what encloses the 'space' and its position depends upon the point of view of the observer. Likewise, beings define the Buddha in terms of their own personal experience of the form kāya, squeezing Buddha into the conceptual frameworks which limit their subjective minds and ignorant of the absolute nature giving rise to these relative images. Buddha is not at all the relative impression which they have. They see something when in fact there is nothing.

9. EARTH - application of compassion

354. *Everything which grows from the ground develops,*
becomes firm and grows
through depending upon the thought-free earth.
355. *Likewise, every root of beings' virtue, without exception,*
increases through dependence
on the thought-free buddha ground.

All animate and inanimate life on Earth depends upon the earth for its existence, whether it be plants which draw their sustenance from the soil or humans which depend upon the presence of the ground for stability of movement. Even though the nutrients in the soil enable the vegetable world to develop from tiny, fragile shoots into firm mature trees, bushes and plants, the earth itself has no intention to bring this much nourishment here and so much nourishment there. The earth does not make efforts to give to some plants and not to others. Its resources simply lie there, ready to be drawn upon once a growing things has the ability to ingest them.

Likewise, all the qualities manifest in specific beings are in fact manifestations of those present in the great ground of buddha nature, from which they have been drawn. The goodness, wisdom and purity of beings develops from tiny, fragile beginnings to the magnificence of great bodhisattvas. The growth depends entirely upon the presence of the true nature of mind: the wellspring of wholesomeness. Yet that true nature has no conceptual intention to bring benefit here or there. It has no partiality, expectation or plan. Thus the earth is chosen as this final example, showing how enlightened compassion applies itself, manifesting wherever someone's existence combines the circumstances creating openness to its infinite, inconceivable compassion.

a. Review of the Purpose and Significance of these Examples

356. *Since ordinary beings do not perceive action without effort,*
these nine examples were taught to annihilate disciples' doubts.
357. *These nine examples have been excellently and fully taught*
in a sūtra of a name which explains their purpose.
358. *The Wise, adorned with the great light of wisdom,*
born of such study, will swiftly enter all buddha domains.

Purpose and origin of examples: Most people find it hard to imagine perfect action which requires no thought. They may well feel dubious when hearing that Buddhas act with total perfection, in a way tailor-made for the individual yet requiring not the slightest thought or concept about that individual. The nine examples show non-conceptual benefit occurring very effectively in circumstances other than the play of enlightened activity: most of them are relevant to our world and can be checked and reflected upon quite easily. Furthermore, each example highlights a specific facet of enlightened activity and helps on get some feeling for the way in which it operates.

These examples come from a sūtra called the *the mahāyāna sūtra* known as *"the ornament shining with the primordial wisdom which pervades the spheres of all the Buddhas".*[9] As its title suggests (to those familiar with such titles), its purpose is to make clear, to those unaware of the reach of enlightened wisdom, just how far and how effectively that wisdom can interact with the confused minds of worldly beings. Such understanding fulfils a double purpose: its removes doubts and accelerates the bodhisattva's journey to enlightenment.

359. *This point has been taught through nine examples
such as Indra's reflection in vaidurya.
The meaning they illustrate excellently are:*
360. *Manifestation, speech, all-pervasiveness, emanations,
the radiance of jñāna, the 'mysteries' of body, speech and mind
and possession of a compassionate nature.*

Synopsis of the examples: Before entering into further reflection upon the examples, the text reminds us of the main focus of each one, as already indicated in the sub-headings of this chapter.

361. *All channels of effort have been pacified totally,
because their mind is free of ideation,
just like Indra's reflection and so forth
appearing in the stainless vaidurya.*
362. *Here, 'pacification of effort' is the proposition,
the 'mind free of ideation' is the logical justification.
The examples, Indra and so forth, help establish naturalness.*

Presenting effortlessness as a syllogism: What has been taught in this chapter about enlightened activity is summed up in these verses as a logical statement. The syllogism is:

> *predicate:* enlightened activity
> *statement:* it is effortless (or, as the verse explains, effort has been pacified, i.e. purified and removed for ever)
> *proof:* the enlightened mind is free of ideation
> *example:* this is like the reflection of Indra and so forth.

In ordinary life, we only experience action which requires physical or mental effort. Buddhahood occurs at the end of a path of practice in which the limitations imposed by dualistic thought are totally removed from the mind, thereby allowing all-encompassing jñāna and suchness jñāna to manifest. These provide total knowledge of all that is ultimate and all that is relative. Activity – which is interaction between ultimate and relative – becomes spontaneous and perfect.

363. *The point being made is that the Shower of the Way,*
who is beyond birth and death,
manifests effortlessly these nine; appearances and so forth.

Summary of effortlessness: The main point of this chapter is that enlightenment is a condition beyond birth, ageing, sickness and death but which nevertheless manifests nine facets of activity within worlds where birth and death exist. The nine – appearances and so forth – are the nine things listed above, through the examples.

364. *Effortless altruistic action, for as long as existence endures*
and like that of Indra, the drum, clouds, Brahmā, the sun,
the majestic wish-fulfilling gem, an echo, space or the earth,
is understood by the Great Yogin alone.

Significance of the examples: It might be easier for us to understand enlightened activity were Buddhas real beings, living somewhere other than our world and sending envoys from time to time to teach, rather like cosmic lords in a science fiction film. But as confusion and enlightenment each take place in the dimensionless space we loosely call 'mind', the play of pure action is impossible for us to imagine. It is not an exchange between two sorts of beings but the interaction of wisdom and confusion within the same space. What is really happening is only understood by the primordial wisdom of the 'Great Yogin', the Buddha. In order that ordinary people might grasp something of the spontaneity, effortlessness and non-conceptual nature of this interaction, the Buddha has given us these examples. One might think that just a single example would suffice but enlightened activity is so subtle that many examples are needed to highlight its different facets.

365. *Similar to Indra's jewel appearance is manifestation,*
like the divine drum is the perfect bestowing of instruction,
and like the hosts of clouds
are perfect knowledge and compassion
with which the All-Embracing pervades limitless beings,
up to the summit of conditioned existence.

The text again points to the meaning of each example. When one sees a Buddha, the image is really only a reflection in the temporary purity and openness of one's mind, and not a real person. This is like Indra's reflection. The teachings one receives are like the sound of the divine drumbeat, inasmuch as the cause for them lies in one's own condition and not in something external. The extent of wisdom and compassion within the enlightened mind is compared to monsoon clouds, vast yet formless. This vastness helps a great variety of 'ordinary beings' at each stage of their evolution. The highest stage of 'ordinary being' is called the 'summit of existence'.[10]

366. Similarly to Brahmā, they manifest many an emanation,
without ever departing from their untainted domain.
Like the sun, they radiate universally their jñāna light
and like the wish-fulfilling gem, perfectly pure is their mind.

The example of Brahmā gives some idea of manifestation without someone actually going somewhere. The impartial and universal radiance of buddhajñāna is portrayed by the light of the sun, filling the worlds. The mystery of the enlightened mind's purity is exemplified by the wish-fulfilling gem.

367. Like an echo, devoid of any verbalising, is the Victor's speech.
Like space, all-pervading, formless and permanent is their body
and like the earth, the universal ground for all medicinal herbs
that are beings' virtues, is the state of buddhahood.

Buddha speech is not pronounced by a Buddha, but heard by a disciple. The example of the echo helps us understand this. The Enlightened One's body is not something somewhere but a possibility of manifestation anywhere, and this is portrayed by space. The fact that the universal goodness of enlightenment is the ground for all virtue is shown by the example of the earth. The virtuous beings and their beneficent acts to which it gives rise are compared here to medicinal herbs, easing the sufferings of beings.

b. Review of These Examples, Showing The Sublime Nature

368. One sees the buddhas in this mind,
comparable to pure vaidurya,
through mind's purity, development of the faculty
of irreversible faith.
369. Since this virtue appears and disappears,
the forms of the Buddha may also appear and disappear.
However, like Indra, the Great Sage's dharmakāya
is beyond such arising and destruction.

That there can be manifestation without arisal and cessation: In ordinary perception, things arise, endure and finally disintegrate through the power of causality. Once circumstances have combined to create a phenomenon, its limited lifespan and final demise are inevitable. The manifestation of the Buddha is not like this, since it is not a creation, but a temporary and limited glimpse of something everlasting. The example of Indra's reflection helps one understand this. The temporary existence of the highly polished *vaidurya* ground enables beings to catch a glimpse of Indra and to see a little bit of his life. Likewise, the temporary presence of faith is the quality which enables one's perceptual faculties to glimpse the magnificence of primordial purity. As faith comes and goes, the mental image comes and goes but this is something quite different from a Buddha actually coming into being, enduring and ceasing. The dharmakāya, which has been temporarily glimpsed, is beyond that.

370. Like him, in a way which is effortless
and from this dharmakāya, which is without birth or death,
buddhas engage in activity, such as manifestation,
for as long as conditioned existence continues.

The activity is unceasing: Because the very nature of such manifestation is to be a partial reflection of the dharmakāya, which is beyond time and space, beyond birth and death, its presence can continue for as long as the relative world endures and without the slightest effort.

371. *Here follows a summarised meaning of the examples taught
in which, in order, dissimilarities are eliminated
from the former to the latter.*

Enlightened activity is superior to these examples: Although each example does help one understand a particular facet of enlightened action, it is merely an example and has many shortcomings. These will be pointed out, in their respective order, in the following verses.

372. *The Buddha is like that reflection, but not the same,
inasmuch as it does not have his melody.
He is like the celestial drum, but not the same,
inasmuch as it is not universally beneficial.*

Indra's reflection in the *vaidurya* ground is effortless, like enlightened activity, but it is a visual effect only. It does not convey the sounds of Indra's world. The image of the Buddha in someone's mind is accompanied by his sublime speech and so is superior to Indra's image. There is a need for an example of Buddha speech. This is the divine drumbeat. However, it too is inferior to enlightened activity, which is always beneficial, since the personal openness which gives rise to it also means it will have a useful effect. The divine drumbeat helps the deva at times but often goes ignored. Thus an example of far-reaching benefit is needed.

373. *He is like that vast cloud, but not the same,
inasmuch as it cannot remove useless seeds.
He is like Mahābrahmā, but not the same,
inasmuch as the latter does not engender lasting maturity.*

The monsoon rain clouds make all seeds grow; those of weeds as well as those of crops. Their rain cannot take away harmful seeds. Enlightened activity is superior since it gives beings the means to eliminate the potential for harm and evil from their minds. This raises the need for an example of solely beneficial activity, and Brahmā's presence is used. However, even though enlightened activity emanates somewhat similarly to Brahmā, it does so in a much better way, since it sets beings on the path to lasting benefit, whereas Brahmā's presence is only temporarily inspiring.

374. *He is like the form of the sun, but not the same,*
inasmuch as it cannot vanquish darkness for ever.
He is like the wish-fulfilling gem, but not the same,
inasmuch as its appearance is not that difficult to encounter.

Brahmā can only be experienced by the deva whereas the sun illuminates all the worlds in the solar system. Although the radiance of buddhajñāna may be like that of the sun in some ways, the sun cannot eliminate darkness for ever. Night follows day and the sun has to recommence its work every morning. Enlightened activity gives beings the means to remove their ignorance radically and eternally and sets them on a path of continual progress. This gives rise to the need for an example of uninterrupted activity, and this is shown by that of the wish-fulfilling gem.

This mighty jewel granting material wishes is rare but not that hard to find and, once found, is fairly easy to describe, as it is a solid object with form and colour. Enlightened activity is not a material thing and is not only rare but intangible. This leads to the need for an example of something immaterial: the echo.

375. *He is like an echo, but not the same,*
inasmuch as it arises through conditions.
He is like space, but not the same,
inasmuch as that is not the basis for goodness.

The echo has no location and is a product in the mind, created by conditions. Enlightened activity is superior to the echo, since it is not created by conditions and is something enduring. For an echo to be produced, a rock, an ear and many things are needed and, even then, it only lasts for a short while. This gives rise to the need for an example showing something lasting and unfabricated: space.

Buddha activity and space may be similar, inasmuch as neither is a compounded phenomenon, but the former is better because it gives rise to goodness. Space has no moral power. This leads us to the example of the earth, which supports a host of things.

376. *He is like the maṇḍala of the earth,*
being the supportive ground
for absolutely every single goodness in sentient life,
be it mundane or supramundane,
because the supramundane path
arises on the basis of the Buddha's enlightenment,
as do the paths of virtuous actions, concentrative meditation,
the limitless contemplations and the formless ones.

Like the earth, enlightened activity is the ground sustaining a host of different things. All that it supports is good. This may be the wordly virtue that arises from good moral behaviour and the practice of concentration meditation or it may be the supramundane goodness which comes through wisdom of voidness, compassion or the skilful activity of the bodhisattva path.

The four limitless concentrations can lead to rebirth in the deva realms, concentration meditation gives rebirth in the form realms and formless concentration meditation leads to rebirth in the form realms. All these are worldly states.

When the power of meditation is coupled with that of renunciation and wisdom of non-ego, it leads to liberation from saṃsāra. When coupled with compassion and full understanding of voidness, it leads one through the bodhisattva levels to enlightenment. These are supramundane states.

Be it the virtue of these wordly or supramundane results, all arises on the basis of enlightened activity guiding the beings of the world. It is the real basis for all goodness everywhere.

Notes

1   *Vaidurya* is a precious gemstone which has given rise to several translations, from the opaque *lapis lazuli* through *beryl* to *sapphire*. *Vaidurya* is mentioned in several sūtras as being the substance of one sort of wish-fulfilling gem. In the White Lotus and other texts it is said to emerge from the *ring.bsrel* relics of the Buddha. The palace of Indra is made, in part, of *vaidurya*. It is found in the *deva* or *nāga* realms

but not normally in the human realm, except by those of exceptional merit. Therefore, in some ways, it is pointless trying to equate it with a gemstone commonly found in this world. In Dharma-Master Hungchen Kara's work on the White Lotus, it is said to *resemble* blue beryl (i.e. aquamarine) in colour, but this does not mean that it is beryl.

2   *Upavasa precepts*: Not to kill, not to steal, not to commit sexual misconduct, not to lie, not to take intoxicants, not to eat after the midday meal, not to sit on costly, elevated seats or wear jewelry and not entertainment such as singing, dancing, playing instruments etc.

3   *Dharāni* is a profound topic, hard to describe in a few words. In a way, it is *mantra*, the power of absorbing the mind into a simple, prayerful essence which produces many consequences in the phenomenal world.

4   *Form-dimension gods*. There are three main types of existence: those based in sensorial experience, those in form meditation and those in formless meditation. Gods are to be found as the highest (in terms of environment) sensorial beings, or in divine states resulting from past form and formless meditations which achieved powerful results. Brahmā is a form god, through his past loving kindness and form meditation.

5   Suchness primordial wisdom and all-encompassing primordial wisdom.

6   A quotation from the last verse of Bengar Jampal Zangpo's *Short Prayer to Vajradhara*.

7   Called *water bubble* eyes in Tibetan.

8   The translators of this text had the privilege of serving HH the 16th Gyalwa Karmapa, who is seen as being the activity of the Buddhas. It happened on several occasions that people in group audiences emerged amazed that he spoke to them in their mother tongue and that he had talked about just the question that was occupying them at that time, when in fact HH only spoke in Tibetan.

9   According to Prof. Takasaki, this is the *sarvabuddhavisayāvatā rajñānālokālamkārasūtra*.

10 See *Gems of Dharma, Jewels of Freedom*, chapter on Paths and Levels.

Part Three
Conclusion

THE BENEFITS OF THIS TEXT

a. Its Inconceivability

377. *Buddha nature, the Buddha's enlightenment,
buddhahood's qualities and enlightened activity
are inconceivable things, even for purified beings,
as they are the domain of experience of their Guides.*

Having explained the final four chapters of his work, Asaṅga reminds us of what was said at their outset. The subjects of these chapters form, together, the cause for the manifestation of buddha, dharma and saṃgha. How and why this is the case is only fully appreciated by the totally enlightened, because the truth is beyond what thoughts can encompass. Even though ordinary beings can formulate some intellectual appreciation and very pure bodhisattvas have excellent understanding, only the Guides of Beings, the Buddhas, know the answer directly and fully.

b. Synopsis of Its Qualities

378. *The wise who trust this domain of the Buddhas
become vessels for multitudes of buddha qualities.
Genuinely delighting in a host of inconceivable qualities,
they surpass the virtues of every sentient being.*

Bodhisattvas may not have full understanding of these teachings but they may have great trust in them. The 'wise' in this case indicates bodhisattvas with intelligence, diligence and faith in buddha nature, as taught in this text. Such faith, and an aspiration to help all beings recognise the truth of their own minds, will make someone an ideal vessel for rapid awakening of the qualities of freedom and maturity that are proper to enlightenment.

To assimilate the meaning of buddha nature is to plant, in one's existence, the seeds of a future garden of delight, in which many qualities will flourish. When one plants a new tree, the roots must be firmly set in the soil. If this is done properly, a mighty, healthy tree can grow. Without the root, nothing will grow. To appreciate the presence of buddha nature in oneself and other beings is to plant a powerful root of virtue, which will give rise to many good things. To do this surpasses most other Buddhist practices, such as generosity, forbearance etc. This point will be developed in the following verses.

c. How it Surpasses Other Virtues

379. *One who hears but one word of this*
     and, having heard, has faith,
     will attain greater virtue than another who, striving for bodhi,
     offers golden lands adorned with jewels, equal in number
     to all the atoms in the buddhafields,
     to the dharma king, daily.

Generosity: Imagine two bodhisattvas, each with equal longing to attain enlightenment. The one studies this text, even a little of it, and trusts its meaning. The other is practising generosity and making considerable offerings, even to the extent of giving, really or mentally, as many golden lands as there are grains of dust in a buddhafield. Each land is adorned with precious gems and valuable substances. These are offered day after day to the Buddha. The bodhisattva with faith in this text has greater virtue and advances more quickly.

380. *One who hears but one word of this*
     and, having heard, has faith
     will attain greater virtue than that of the right conduct
     practised by the wise, longing for highest enlightenment
     and maintaining proper conduct of body, speech and mind,
     be it even for many cosmic aeons.

314   Maitreya on Buddha Nature

Right Conduct: Again, imagine two devoted bodhisattvas, longing and striving for perfect enlightenment. The one studies this text and trusts it, as above. The other maintains a very pure conduct, physically, verbally and mentally, not just for one lifetime but for many cosmic aeons. Even so, the bodhisattva with faith in this text has the greater virtue.

381.   One who hears but one word of this
and, having heard, has faith,
will attain greater virtue
than that of the meditative stability of others
whose dhyāna rids the three worlds of defilements' fires
and brings achievement of the divine state
of Brahmā's paradise,
even if practised as a way
to supreme, immutable enlightenment.

Profound Absorption: Again, imagine two devoted bodhisattvas, longing and striving for perfect enlightenment. The one studies this text and trusts it. The other becomes an expert meditator and has such stability and finesse of concentrative meditation that (s)he manages, with time, to remove all defilements and mental blockages associated with either the realm of the senses, the realm of mental forms or the formless realm. More than this, the meditation was all done with bodhicitta as its basis, and used as a means for enlightenment. Even so, the virtue which issues from this does not match that of the first bodhisattva.

d. Why it Surpasses Them

382.   Generosity brings affluence,
right conduct leads to higher states,
meditative stability removes defilements but prajñā removes
all defilements as well as what is cognitive.
Therefore this prajñā is a most excellent thing:
its cause is to study such as this.

Why is faith in this meaning so powerful? How can it surpass the power generated by generosity, right conduct or meditation? All these practices are causes, each bringing their respective results, and the result of trusting this meaning is by far the greatest. Generosity results in affluence for the giver. Right conduct generates rebirth in the higher realms of existence. Concentration meditation can remove defilements, once and for all. Wisdom – prajñā – not only removes defilements but also removes the cognitive obscuration, and is the finest of all the bodhisattva practices. It brings enlightenment as its result. Prajñā has many levels, and in particular three main levels related to the three dharmachakra. Studying teachings on buddha nature, such as these, reveals the meaning of points which are inconceivable for ordinary beings and would never be discovered by them in the ordinary course of events. Equipped with this knowledge, one will give rise to best prajñā.

e. Fuller Explanation of Its Qualities

383. *This presence, what it becomes, its qualities and accomplishing*
     that which is good: these four points are the domain
     of Buddha's perfect knowledge, as has been explained.

384. *Through faith in these, the fact of this presence,*
     it being the power and with qualities endowed,
     the wise are quickly ripe for tathāgata achievement.

One will Attain Enlightenment: This verse again stresses the fact that only Buddhas have full and true insight into what buddha nature is, what it becomes (enlightenment), the qualities of enlightenment and enlightened activity, accomplishing the good of all. Nevertheless, the words and concepts of this text give one a first approach. Because the Buddha, in his great compassion, has given these teachings, we can trust the fact that buddha nature is present within the mind. We can appreciate that removing whatever blocks its recognition will bring enlightenment, with its qualities and activity.

Trust in buddha nature teachings is therefore the first and foremost quality to develop. We can do this on an intellectual level and we can learn, under the guidance of lineage masters, how to trust buddha nature in meditation, through the matchless instructions of mahāmudrā. Faith will guide us to an appreciation of the potential present not only within one's own life, but also in that of each and every being. It can change the way in which we relate to ourselves and the way in which we relate to others. Someone who applies these teachings in both meditation and daily life will soon be able to cultivate the right sort of understanding and compassion. These are the two motor forces of enlightenment.

385. *Through faith, one believes this inconceivable domain present,*
       attainable by 'someone like me' and, once attained,
       to have such qualities and such endowments.

386. *Therefore bodhicitta is ever present in them, as a vessel*
       for the qualities of earnest aspiration, joyful endeavour,
       mindfulness, meditative stability, prajñā and the others.

It Fosters Bodhicitta: Faith in these teachings gives courage. Rather than seeing Buddhas and great lamas as another breed of being and feeling stuck with one's own lot, one can believe all beings to be potential buddhas. Since buddha nature is definitely present, somewhere in one's mind, all that is left to be done is to discover it. Far from being a distant thing, Buddha could not be any closer. We know that the infinite care and compassion of the Perfect One is within us, as well as a timeless peace and clarity that knows all things, endowed with the sixty-four qualities and the power to help beings throughout time and space.

Appreciating these last four chapters with the intellect is one thing: believing them profoundly is another. Conviction about buddha nature will bring great happiness and light-heartedness. It is the key to diligence – a word with an etymology meaning 'joyful enthusiasm' but to which common usage has given a sense of dutiful drudgery. In Buddhism, diligence means that one is so convinced of its benefits that one goes about it happily and with a great deal of enthusiasm and effort. Trusting buddha nature should bring effortless attention to the factors of Buddhist practice needed to bring one to maturity: bodhisattva aspiration, mindfulness, meditation, wisdom development and so forth.

387. *As this is constantly present, the Victor's offspring do not deviate.*
The pāramitā they establish, through virtue,
are perfected to become immaculate.

388. *Virtue, as the first five pāramitā, is brought to perfection*
by an absence of any triplistic thought concerning them.
They are completely purified by removal of their opposites.

Its Ability to Bring to Perfection: As recognition of buddha nature is constantly present in the ten levels, the bodhisattvas in those states cannot fall back into the illusion of saṃsāra. Such recognition, and its cultivation, is the sixth pāramitā, the prajñāpāramitā. There is a difference between the mere practice of generosity, right conduct and so forth, and practising the pāramitā of these same things. Generosity is simply giving. The pāramitā of generosity involves giving in the light of profound wisdom and pure compassion. It is a state of total openness and generosity because the truth of buddha nature, in oneself and all, is unmistakenly recognised. With nothing left to lose or gain, one can be generous indeed! Thus, with the support of this wisdom, all the pāramitā which the bodhisattvas bring to perfection through the ten levels will be quite stainless and perfect.

One main consequence of the bodhisattvas' recognition of buddha nature is a transcendence of triplicity, since the light of truth reveals buddha nature to be the true nature of all. In such bright light, the darkness of triplicity cannot survive. Triplicity is the triple illusion of self, other and self-other interaction. In other words, it is duality plus action. Dualistic thought habits – of I/other, a perceiving mind/a perceived universe, of subject and object etc. – still occur in the first seven bodhisattva levels. They are gradually removed by the mind resting in its true nature and providing the light of truth which progressively dries up the illusion.

As this process takes place, the pāramitā come to maturity because their opposites – avarice, lack of control, anger, time-wasting, a distracted mind etc. – disappear as the dualistic illusions which feed them disappear.

389. *Virtue born of giving is generosity.*
Virtue born of correct action is right conduct.
Forbearance and meditative stability
are both born of meditation.
Joyous diligence is a companion for all.

What Gives Rise to the Pāramitā: Removing duality and negativity, as described above, allows the true qualities of mind to fall into place and the pāramitā to manifest. This verse loses much of its sense in translation, from Sanskrit to Tibetan and then into English, as it is really explaining the terms *dana, sila* and so forth – the Sanskrit names of the pāramitā. *Sila,* the word for right conduct, for instance, literally means *coolness,* and shows the power of good conduct as being like the cool shade of a large, protective tree in the hot, passionate sunlight of India: an example which does not work so well in Scotland! The second line of this verse would have read something like *virtue born of correct action is 'coolness'.*

Giving one's possessions, time and attention is generosity. Acting according to the guidlelines established by the Buddha is right conduct. Meditation gives rise not only to meditative prowess but also to forbearance, hence the conquest of anger. Joyous diligence helps all these to develop.

390. *'Triplistic thoughts' are considered the cognitive obscuration;*
avaricious thoughts, and the like, the defilement obscuration.

391. *Other than prajñā, there is no means for removing these.*
Therefore prajñā is the best of all the pāramitā.
Its basis is study such as this; such study is supreme.

Removal of the Obscurations: As has been explained on several occasions in this commentary, the two main sorts of things blocking awareness of buddha nature are the defilement obscuration and the cognitive obscuration. The latter is the body of ignorant thoughts, that create illusions of a subject, an object and their interaction. The former are grosser developments of these, in which the illusory subject lusts after the illusory object, or detests it, envies it and so on and so forth.

Since both these obscurations are mental delusions, the only way to eliminate them is through clarity of mind, which sees the truth. This is prajñā. Other virtues operate within the domain of illusory manifestation, with an illusory giver practising generosity by being generous to illusory sentient beings or with an illusory monk practising right conduct by observing rules of illusory conduct. Only prajñā tackles the root of illusion itself and it is therefore supreme among practices. Of the six pāramitā, it is the one which carries the others to nobility and makes them pāramitā rather than mere virtues. The difference between mere generosity and the pāramitā of generosity is determined by the absence or presence, respectively, of prajñā. The word pāramitā conveys the notion of transcendence and perfection. There can be all sorts of giving, backed up by different types of motivation. A gift given in the light of prajñā, i.e. awareness of voidness as buddha nature in all beings, is the perfect form of generosity, carrying it to a level which transcends all others and creates immeasurable benefit. Furthermore, the obscurations which block enlightenment will never be removed by the other five pāramitā alone, no matter how diligently one practises them.

Real prajñā – direct awareness through meditation – arises from the prajñā of thorough reflection and this, in turn, arises through study under the guidance of lineage masters. This text conveys the highest teachings which the Buddha gave on voidness, and studying it is the finest of all studies, since it conveys the meaning of highest prajñā.

HOW THIS SHASTRA WAS COMPOSED

a. Why It Was Written

392. *Thus, on the basis of the trustworthy words of Lord Buddha,*
and of reason, I have given this teaching
in order to purify myself alone and, further, to nurture
intelligent beings – those having faith and virtue.

This *mahāyāna uttara tantra śāstra* was composed by Dharma Master Asaṅga as a direct result of the teachings he received from Maitreya. Maitreya's teaching was based purely on the words of the Enlightened One and set forth in accordance with the teachings of the *sūtra*. Asaṅga also relied upon logic and reason for clarifying any doubts he may have had concerning this subject matter. He confirmed the logical outcome of his reason through the direct cognition with which he was endowed as an accomplished yogin.

The reason for writing this text was the classical twofold motivation of the bodhisattva. Asaṅga wished to benefit both himself and other beings. The self-benefit comes through setting out the teachings as a sort of test of his own clarity concerning them and as a sacred act of writing down the truth. The benefit for others comes through apprising them of this hidden truth of buddha nature, illuminated by the instruction of Maitreya.

b. Upon What Basis

393. *Just as when, aided by a lamp, lightning, a gem,*
the sun or moon, those with eyes can see,
so likewise, by relying on the Great Sage,
who radiates the light of meanings,
terms, dharma and dharani,
I have now properly expounded this.

Why does the author need to apply his own logic when things have already been stated with authority by the Buddha in the Buddhist canon? Just as one needs something external, such as a bright light, to view an object properly, so also do we need the external light shed by the teachings of Lord Buddha. External light alone is not a sufficient condition to guarantee one seeing well: one also needs good eyesight. The ability to understand the points highlighted so expertly by the Buddha is ensured by the clarity of reason. Otherwise there is a serious risk of misinterpretation or of a highly subjective interpretation.

The verse gives several examples of different qualities of light which can serve as an external source of illumination, each with its quality and strength. Lamplight, sunlight, moonlight or the vivid but momentary brilliance of a lightning flash each have their own characteristics. Jewel light is that shed by a wish-fulfilling gem. One could take these various examples as indicative of the differing qualities of teaching given by Buddhas, bodhisattvas, erudite scholars etc. as the external source to whom we turn in our quest for learning. Asaṅga takes the Buddha himself as his guiding light, since the Great Sage (the Buddha) does not only explain the meaning of terms but also radiates the truth revealing the very nature of the phenomena (dharma) involved. He does so by resting in the highest *dharani:* remaining absorbed within the quintessential character of something, in such a way that other beings each receive word-based teachings about whatever is appropriate to their specific mentality at the time.

c. How to Recognise a True Buddhist Teaching

394. *Whatever has significance and is well-connected with dharma is a teaching removing the three worlds' defilements, showing peace's benefit: such is the Truthful One's teaching. What is contrary to this is something other.*

In turning to teachings as the external light illuminating one's path, one needs to be sure that they are authentic. The hallmarks of a true Buddhist teaching are that it be significant, that it accord well with the body of teachings given by the Truthful One, that it turn one away from the defilements and equip beings of the sensorial, form and formless realms with the means actually to destroy their own mind-poisons and, finally, that it emphasise the value and nature of peace. In other words, it should turn one away from saṃsāra and turn one towards nirvāṇa.

Although other teachings may be fascinating, interesting or cleverly constructed, they will not be considered a Buddhist teaching if they fail to meet these criteria. It is important to take note of this fact as our time has been predicted[1] as one in which charlatans abound and in which people are drawn in their hundreds to clever speakers, who lack the blessing of authentic lineage, yet overlook those with true meditation realisation or erudition, with but a handful of disciples appreciating them.

d. One Should Adopt Whatever Accords with That

*395. Whatever those of perfectly undistracted mind have expounded,
solely in accordance with the teaching of the Victorious One
and conducive to the path for attaining liberation,
should also be placed on the head, like the Buddha's own words.*

The śāstra were not given to us by the Buddha but by great Buddhist masters. Nevertheless, they are worthy of the same respect as the Buddha's own teaching, providing that they comply with the definition of a true śāstra. The Buddhist way of showing such respect to a sacred text is to place it upon the head. One of the main characteristics of a good śāstra is that it be written for the altruistic motives of strengthening dharma and helping beings, and not out of selfish motives, such as desire for fame.

e. Not to Assert Anything Other than the True Teaching

*396. Since no one of this world has more dharma skill than Buddha,
the Omniscient One who properly knows all without exception*

as being the supreme suchness, which others ignore, whatever sūtra were expounded by the Great Sage in person should not be adulterated; such would harm the true dharma through destroying the way of the Mighty Victor.

A true śāstra is an explanatory text which accords perfectly with the Omniscient One's teaching, generally known as the sūtra. A śāstra should never express ideas which go against, or adulterate in any way, the original message of the Buddha. Seeing all things clearly, the Great Sage explained them not only truthfully but also in a way which could give rise to a perfectly integrated system of study and practice. There is a certain majesty of raw truth in the original sūtra which is quite striking. The Buddha's teaching also has great integrity and the wonderful quality of limitlessness. Like layers of an onion, one level of understanding gives way to another and yet another as one approaches the heart of the matter. Any attempt to modify, dilute or give a partial interpretation of this original message would spoil its potency, limit it severely and make for an inadequate dharma path.

These days, as throughout Buddhist history, there is often a temptation to make dharma more palatable by giving it a partial slant – for example, trying to put it uniquely in modern psychological terms. In such an instance, it may appeal strongly to the few who respond to psycho-speak but immediately loses its universality and original 'flavour'. According to both Buddhist ethics and common sense, it is bad politics to try to go out to the audience and win them over. A good teacher will know, on the contrary, how to show the innate value of truth and make it shine in its own clothing, not disguised as something else. Whoever comes to it comes. Whoever has no feeling for it turns away. It is perhaps better that sheep be sorted from the goats at an early stage rather than many people being drawn into a pseudo-dharma by glib chatter, only to be disappointed later.

No one but the Buddha has the full picture, since only he sees all things as the nature of suchness, in its totality. Only from his perfect comprehensive clarity can the best of all teachings arise. Good śāstra simply gather together relevant parts of his sūtra, such as disparate teachings on karma, given in this place or that, and present them as a whole. Śāstra also develop and expound ideas which are only expressed with hermetic concision in the sūtra.

There is another point to be considered here. Not only should the Buddha's teachings not be mixed with other things — they should not be wrongly mixed with each other, or applied to the wrong situation. As explained in Chapter Two, on dharma, there are many expedient teachings guiding people along their specific ways. The advice pertinent to one person at a certain time will not be relevant to someone else, nor even, perhaps, to the same person at a later date. The instructions for a journey may commence with *how to pedal a bicycle to the station*, and continue with *how to board a train* and finish with *how to relax in an airplane seat*. There is no point pedalling in the plane and it will be fruitless to relax on the bicycle saddle and do nothing. Buddhism has some very profound teachings on relaxation and letting things pass, for advanced meditators. It also has pressing advice on strenuous diligence for beginners. Giving a beginner advanced instructions is not only fruitless but potentially harmful.

f. Exposing That Which is Contrary to the True Teaching

How One Abandons Dharma

397. *Those who are, through defilement, by nature ignorant*
revile the deeply-realised and despise their teachings;
all of which occurs through opinions. Therefore the mind
should never be confined in the impure prison of preconception.
Clean cloth may be dyed with colour; never cloth stained by oil.

Indirect Causes: Dharma can bring great value to a human life. To reject it is to harm and deprive oneself. Some people do reject it, through ignorant misunderstanding of the nature of reality. They take their own preconceived ideas to be truths and have nothing but contempt for those who express the real truth.

The popular view of reality in the Western world today is founded in the Cartesian scientific thought of the last century.

Whereas much of science itself has moved far beyond the dualist/phenomenal model of Descartes, and is in many ways converging with Buddhism, the majority of people on the famous Clapham omnibus (or the New York subway) may well think their out-of-date scientific rationalism to be a modern sensible view of reality and therefore consider Buddhism a lot of airy-fairy nonsense, just as they would consider a physicist's notions of curved space or multiple quantum realities to be far-fetched, once they grasped what the scientist was trying to put across. Moreover, any attempts to change their minds will just entrench them deeper in their naïve views. The same rigidity may be found in those with fixed fundamentalist beliefs in other faiths. The mind closed to reason is compared to oilstained cloth, which will retain its patch of stain no matter how much one dyes it. An open mind is like clean cloth, which takes on the new colour perfectly.

398. *Through lesser understanding, lack of aspiration for virtue,*
indulging in wrong pride,
a nature veiled by neglecting dharma,
mistaking the expedient meaning for the absolute – thatness,
greed's thirst, ideology's grip, the influence of truth despisers,
staying far from holders of the teachings and lower aspiration,
thus is the doctrine of 'the defeaters of the enemy' abandoned.

Ten Key Causes: Besides this indirect cause for rejecting dharma, there are ten specific causes for abandoning the doctrine of 'those who defeat the enemy':[2]

- *lesser understanding*, i.e. not enough intelligence to grasp the meaning of voidness,
- *a lack of aspiration for virtue*, in the form of little care for either helping others or improving oneself. This care-lessness acts like a general pollutant and fosters wrong views.
- *indulging in wrong pride*, through believing one has qualities or realisation that in fact one does not possess,
- *a nature veiled through neglecting dharma*, i.e. lack of exposure to dharma in previous lives,
- *mistaking the expedient truth for the absolute* or vice versa, and

thereby misconstruing the Buddha's teaching,
- *greedy thirst* is the longing for financial gain, prestige or power,
- *ideology's grip* is the power of rigid preconceptions, such as religious beliefs or political views,
- *the influence of truth despisers* is that of those who have rejected dharma and who try to sway others in their direction,
- *to stray away from those holding the teachings* is to lose the beneficial influence and guidance of good teachers and
- *lower aspiration* is to consider this life not primarily as a vehicle for dharma practice but for petty, worldly ends.

399. *More than fire, cruel poisonous snakes,*
murderers and lightning
should the wise fear the loss of these profound teachings.
Fire, snakes, enemies and thunderbolts only bring life to an end.
They do not take one to the fearsome state of worst torment.

How Not to Lose the Profound Teachings: Those with the great good fortune to have received these teachings and put them into practice need to know how not to lose them. The secret is in maintaining a fresh appraisal of their value. 'Familiarity breeds contempt' is an expression with a solid basis in human nature. It is remarkably easy to forget the preciousness of something possessed and to realise its value only once it is lost. Thus Maitreya advises us to fear the loss of the dharma far more than we would fear fire, cruel poisonous snakes, murderers or lightning. These are all truly fearful things but, at worst, things which can only deprive one of this life. Another life will follow: a good life if one has practised dharma. To abandon the teachings is a far more traumatic shock to the mind than one can imagine. The natural reverberation of this shock can carry the mind, after death when it is freed from the body, to the lower realms and, if the rejection is violent enough, to the lowest and most frightening states of paranoid hallucination, i.e. the hells.

400. *Even one who, through repeated association with evil friends,*
has had harmful intentions towards the Buddha
or who commits the most heinous acts of killing

father, mother or an arhat
or who creates divisions in the noble saṃgha will be quickly rid
of such things once sincerely reflecting upon this true nature:
how could there be liberation for one whose mind hates dharma!

How Even the Worst Mistakes Are Rectified by It: As these teachings are some of the most profound and meaningful that Lord Buddha gave, they hold great power. They are powerful enough to heal many of the wounds one has dealt the mind through bad karma. Therefore, even someone who has enacted what Buddhists consider to be the worst of all actions, i.e. the five heinous acts of immediate consequence after death, can repair their damage through penetrating the meaning of these teachings. The five worst acts are parricide, matricide, arhaticide, creating divisions in the saṃgha at the key time of its formation and plotting to bring physical harm to a Buddha.

The regular Buddhist teachings give four remedial powers for healing bad karma.[3] Reflection and meditation on buddha nature as voidness is a particular instance of the power of reliance and, in a subtle way, is all four powers wrapped into one. The mind lovingly and caringly directed towards truth can solve many things. How could there be liberation for a mind which cares not for truth? In fact, someone may have done terrible things but have a good chance of putting things right, through the intensity of their longing for good. Milarepa was a prime case in point. But someone who does not care for truth will remain involved with life's superficialities and may embark on wrong paths which lead to all sorts of lower states. One must always be on the alert for unhealthy attitudes, as they can cause more harm, in the long term, than just bad actions.

DEDICATION

401. *Whatever virtue I acquire through having properly explained*
these seven points – the jewels, the perfectly pure essence,
immaculate enlightenment, its qualities and buddha activity –

through it, may beings see the Sage of Boundless Life,
he endowed with limitless light. Having seen him,
once their stainless dharma eyes are opened,
may they then achieve supreme enlightenment.

Maitreya and Asaṅga dedicate, in this self-explanatory verse, all the virtue that they have generated by explaining to all beings the Enlightened One's teachings on buddha nature. Their wish is for us to experience Amitabha and Amitayus, the Buddhas of Infinite Light and Infinite Life respectively.

402. *On what basis, for which reasons, in which way,*
that which has been explained and those things in harmony:
these have been taught by means of stanzas four.

'On what basis' refers to the first two lines of verse 392, stating that this text was composed on the basis of the Buddha's own teachings and upon logical reason. The final two lines of that verse show 'for which reasons' this has been taught, i.e. in order to purify the author and other beings. Verse 393 shows 'in which way' this teachings has been given, i.e. by relying upon the Buddha's counsel and upon Maitreya's own understanding, using the example of the necessity of both light and good eyesight to see something properly. 'That which has been explained' refers to verse 394 describing an authentic Buddhist teaching. How to recognise such a teaching 'in harmony' with the Buddha's message is explained in verse 395.

403. *Two have shown the means for purifying oneself,*
then the causes for the loss and, through two stanzas,
an explanation of the result.

The 'means for purifying oneself' are shown in verses 396 and 397, which indicate respectively the need for not distorting the Buddha's teachings and for implementing them properly. That which causes people to lose the teachings is taught in verse 398 and the results of such a loss are explained in verse 399 and 400.

404. *In brief, the twofold result has been explained
in what is said in the last one: the surrounding maṇḍala,
forbearance and the attainment of enlightenment.*

The dedication, verse 401, shows the short-term and long-term results of understanding and applying these teachings on buddha nature. In the relative short term, one will emerge from the round of rebirth in saṃsāra and attain the bodhisattva levels. There, one experiences the pure lands of the Buddhas and will 'see' Amitabha and Amitayus, while at the same time recognising the true nature of the mind having those experiences. After traversing all ten bodhisattva levels, and with the dharma eyes opening to a fuller understanding of buddha nature, one will finally become totally integrated with that nature, in total enlightenment.

The original Sanskrit text was translated into Tibetan by the great pandita and scholar Sajjana, grandson of the Brahmin Ratnavajra, and by the Tibetan translator, the Sakya monk Loden Sherab (blo ldan shes rab), in the 'Incomparable City of Glory'.[4] *This new translation into English was completed on the auspicious day commemorating Lord Buddha's return from Tuṣita paradise in the ninth Tibetan month of the Earth Tiger year, by Ken and Katia Holmes in the Kagyu Samyé Ling monastery and Tibetan centre in Scotland. May it bring wisdom and happiness.*

Notes

1   By Padmasambhava, among others.
2   The 'enemy' in this case being the defilements.
3   See *Gems of Dharma, Jewels of Freedom* pps 130–137.
4   Probably present-day Srinagar

Index

ātman 70, 111
abhidharma 29, 39, 67, 196, 248
abhisamayālaṃkāra 41
abiding 115, 130, 132, 229, 234
   a. nirvāṇa 115
absence of self-entity 228
accumulation, stage of 169
achievement 187
actions 24
activity 45–47, 49, 86, 94–97, 114,
   116, 137, 139, 140–141, 157, 189,
   212–213, 217–219, 227, 231–233,
   235–236, 243, 248, 251, 255–256,
   271–278, 285, 291, 297–298,
   302–312, 315, 327
aeons 40, 42
   cosmic a. 56
affirmation 70
ageing 53, 88, 127, 131, 133–136,
   143–144, 199, 202, 208, 224, 236,
   304
aggregates 127, 171
aknstha 220
Akong, Dr, Tulku Rinpoché 19, 20
algebra example 38
all-embracing 208
all-embracing jñāna 243
all-encompassing jñāna 63, 79, 80–83,
   85, 119, 192, 303
all-encompassing primordial wisdom
   204
all-encompassing wisdom 159, 201
all-pervading compassionate mind
   286
all-pervasiveness 201
ambassador, Maitreya as 29
Amitabha 328–329
Amitayus 328–329
analytical primordial wisdom 189
Anandakirti 42
anger 168
Aṅgulimāla 63
ankles, of Buddha 260
antelope 260

apperception 62
application of compassion 301
arhats 88, 111, 114, 120, 143–145,
   147, 150–152, 166–167, 169, 180,
   198, 201–202, 208, 216, 229, 237,
   239, 244, 247, 250–251, 255, 287,
   327
arising 113, 120, 127, 131–132, 169,
   268, 284, 306
armour 251, 266
arms, of Buddha 261
artists example 148
Asaṅga 13, 18, 30–34, 41, 144, 312,
   320–321, 328
   Arya A. 30
asceticism 225
aspiration 60, 104, 256, 317
Asura 284
at peace 202
attachment 167
aura 221, 225
aura of light, of Buddha 261
authors, valid a. of śāstra 30
auto-cognisant 84
auto-cognisant jñāna 95, 256
auto-cognisant primordial wisdom 73
Avalokitesvara 230
avatamsaka 41, 64
ayonisomanasikara 152

bananas 161
basis, for achieving buddha nature 46
bee-keeper 156
bees 156, 167–168
beginningless 52, 165
Benares 227
benefit 51
benefit for oneself 202
benefit for others 199, 201, 203–204,
   252, 258, 320
   See also four fearlessnesses
Bengar Jampal Zangpo 112, 310
beryl 309

Index

birth 22, 53, 78, 84, 88, 108, 111, 118, 121, 131, 133–136, 142–144, 160, 166, 171, 181, 199, 201–202, 204, 208, 221, 229, 236, 247, 250, 279, 289–290, 304, 306, 309, 315, 329
bitch 32
blind 177
blo ldan shes rab 42, 329
Bodh Gaya 52, 190, 225
Bodhi Tree 41, 226
bodhisattva 29, 31, 33, 37, 41, 45, 52, 58, 60, 67, 79, 80–81, 83–84, 88, 96, 100, 102, 104, 106, 108, 111, 115–116, 120–122, 124–125, 134–143, 149, 151, 166–167, 170–171, 174, 176, 182, 184, 189–190, 196, 199–200, 202, 206–207, 212, 216–220, 225, 228–229, 232–235, 237, 240, 243, 245–253, 256–258, 260, 262–264, 267–268, 270, 275–277, 280, 282–283, 287, 290, 293–294, 301–302, 309, 312–315, 317, 320–321, 329
   b. actions 60
   b. saṃgha 82
bodhisattva Maitreya 13, 18
Bodhisattva Vow 247
body, of Buddha 260
bondage 69
   liberation from b. 69
Brahmā 262, 291–293, 305, 307, 308
branches of Buddhist knowledge, five branches 30
bridge between sūtra and tantra 40
btsan dri med shes rab 42
Buddha eyes 155, 210, 297
buddha nature 13, 16–17, 19, 26, 46–49, 57–59, 93–97, 99–105, 108–127, 129, 130, 132–135, 137, 139, 140, 142–147, 149–150, 153–169, 171–172, 174–180, 182–184, 191, 193–195, 199, 201, 210–211, 214–215, 219–220, 230, 232, 245, 255–256, 270, 276, 281, 286, 297, 301, 312–313, 315–317, 319–320, 327–329

basis b.n. 118
b.n., as tathāgatagarbha 37
result b.n. 118
Buddha speech 283–284, 305
   miraculous activity of B. s. 285
   subtlety, of B. s. 286
   superiority of B. s. 284
Buddha statue 162, 176
Buddha Within 13, 42
Buddha's robes 257
buddha-element 117
buddhahood 53–55
buddhajñāna 63, 73, 81, 85, 87, 100–102, 119, 184, 235, 251–252, 257, 267, 269, 296, 305, 308
   auto-cognisant b. 102, 122
   genetic quality of b. 102
Buddhas 78
   as refuge of mahāyānists 86
budh 204
buried treasure 160
butterfly effect 129

calves, of Buddha 260
canon, Buddhist 29
caste 222
cause refuges 48
ceaselessness 272, 274–275
celestial cymbals 285
centreless 52
cessation 67, 69, 73, 87–88, 114, 144, 207–208, 251, 253, 290–291, 306
chaff 157
chakravartin 244
cheeks, of Buddha 261
chicken 165
chicken-and-egg 165
child 163
cittamātra 30
cittamatrins 62
clairvoyance 155, 159, 270
clairvoyant god 158
clarity 36, 55, 80, 188
clavicles, of Buddha 261
clay 164, 167
   c. mould 164

clear light 80, 82, 188
clouds 181, 189, 192–194, 196, 243, 277, 286, 305, 307
clouds of ignorance 273
cognitive obscuration 53, 84, 193, 197–198, 204, 210, 216, 266
colour in a peacock's tail 247
compassion 23–26, 29, 32–33, 48, 52, 62–63, 68, 81, 101–108, 115, 117, 119, 123, 133–137, 141, 151, 155, 163, 179, 182, 189, 191, 195, 203, 216–219, 221–222, 226, 229, 231–232, 234–235, 239–241, 254, 258, 270, 272–273, 275–277, 285–290, 296–297, 301–305, 309, 315–317
compassionate love 50–51, 58, 62, 115–116, 151, 231, 252, 288–289
compounded 132
compounded nirvāṇa 145
concentration meditation 309, 315
concept-free 208
conch shell 165, 261
conduct 272
confidence 182
Confucius 21
confusion 55
conjurations 181
consciousness 22, 28, 41, 51, 62, 64, 100, 116, 127–129, 165, 178, 181–182, 199–200, 203, 230–231, 238–240, 297, 299
contemplation 205
continuum 40, 45
cosmic aeon 220
cosmic Buddhas 48
craving 55
   c. spirits 289
crazy wisdom 115
creation 52
   enlightenment is not a c. 59
crystal stupa 224
cultivation 167, 203
   stage of c. 170

dam pa tog dkar 241

dana 318
death 22, 53, 88, 127, 131, 133–136, 142–144, 199, 201–202, 204, 208, 224, 226, 231, 233, 236, 289–290, 304, 306, 326–327
deathless 202
debate 153
decay 202
deep 192
deep reflection 205
deep teachings 172, 212
Deer Forest 179
Deer Park 185
defilement 24, 37, 62, 68, 73–74, 76–77, 79, 81–82, 84, 89, 94–96, 106, 111, 123, 128, 129–134, 137, 147–148, 150, 153–159, 161–163, 165–169, 178–182, 210, 215
defilements when they are active 168
deluded consciousness 199
delusion 27–29, 36, 38, 58–59, 71, 74, 78–83, 94, 102, 106, 111–112, 114, 116, 121, 123, 125, 129, 130–132, 134, 136, 170, 174, 178, 181, 183–184, 192, 208, 212, 216, 235, 246, 319
denial 70
depth 188, 231
Descartes 325
desire 55, 167
desires 60
Deva 41
devas 54
devoid of other 42, 49
Déwachen 230
dhāraṇīrājeśvara 41, 63
dhāraṇīrājeśvarasūtra 30, 47
dhātu 99, 100, 103
dharani 287, 310, 321
dharma 14–16, 18, 20, 22, 26, 31–34, 38, 41, 45–49, 60–61, 64, 66–68, 70–72, 74–77, 87–88, 93–95, 97–98, 101, 103–108, 119, 140, 147, 151–152, 157–158, 161–162, 164, 166–167, 172–173, 176, 179, 182–183
   as realisation 68, 87

as refuge of pratyekabuddhas 86
as representations 67, 87
cloud of d. 140
definition 60
ten meanings 65
dharma drumbeat 284
dharma eyes 297
dharmadhātu 73, 80–81, 83–84, 88, 172, 191, 210–211, 214–216, 231, 287, 295
etymology 73
dharmadharmatavibhaga 42
dharmakāya 60–62, 100, 110–113, 119, 142–147, 150, 160, 172, 173, 178, 188, 191, 198, 200–201, 203–205, 211–212, 214–215, 218–222, 226–227, 230–231, 233, 236, 239, 246, 269, 280, 291–296, 306
all-pervading d. 101
etymology 60
relative d. 172–173
ultimate d. 172–173
dharmata 34, 125, 189
dhyāna 113, 120, 139, 151, 250, 314
digits, of Buddha 260
Dignaga 34
diligence 64, 256, 316
direct experience 206
dirt 167
Discerning consciousness from primordial awareness 64
Discerning dharma and dharmata 34
Discerning Middle and Extreme 34
disintegration 132
dissatisfaction 168
divine drumbeat 283–284, 305, 307
divine eyes 297
divine hearing 120
divine vision 120, 155, 250, 270
dkon.mchog 88–89
dog 33
dön 51
doubt 58
dragons 299
drastic change 202
dreams 181

dren pa 255
dualistic awareness 53
dualistic ignorance 197
dualistic perception 55
dualistic thoughts 66
duality 54, 60, 317
dukha 202

earth 18, 33, 63, 100, 104, 126–131, 141–142, 159–160, 165, 174, 180, 195, 217, 221–222, 227, 245, 258, 268, 276–278, 281, 285–287, 294, 301–302, 304–305, 309, 329
earth, man removing 32
echo 299, 305, 308
eclipse 193–194, 196
effortless application 289
effortlessness as a syllogism 303
egg 165
ego 70–71, 111
ego, voidness of 24
ego-belief 36
ego-delusions 59
eight conceptual fabrications 238
eight mental fabrications 230
eight upavasa precepts 281
eighteen distinctive qualities 146, 245, 265
eighteen elements 129
eighteen elements of consciousness 128
eighteen qualities unique to enlightenment 244
eighteen unique qualities 191, 255
Eightfold Path 288
eighth Gyalwa Karmapa 39
eighth Tai Situpa Chöji Jungné 35
eighty signs of perfection 220, 244, 280
element 22, 25, 29, 41, 100, 104–105, 116–118, 125–132, 178–182, 199–200, 212, 245, 258–259, 267–269
earth 22, 41, 258
fire 22, 41, 258
space 22, 41

water 22, 41, 258
  wind 22, 41, 258
elephant 260
elevated parts, of Buddha's body 260
emanation 291
embodiment as emanations 176
embodiment of perfect expression 176
embodiment of the essence 176
emptiness 26
endless 52
enduring nature 188
enlightened activity 46–47, 49, 96–97, 157, 231, 235, 255–256, 271–273, 278, 302–304, 307–309, 312, 315
enlightened qualities 35, 46–47, 49, 55–56, 81, 96–97, 169, 179–180, 183, 191, 230, 268
enlightenment 10, 21, 23, 26, 33, 35, 37, 40–42, 45–49, 57, 59–61, 64–65, 79, 88, 93–97, 101–102, 105, 115, 118–119, 136, 139, 142, 146, 157, 159, 182, 185, 187–193, 197–214, 217–241, 244, 252–253, 256–258, 264–265, 267, 269–270, 272, 274–278, 282, 287, 289, 291–294, 302, 304–305, 309, 312–316, 319, 327–329
ensuing wisdom 192
enthusiastic diligence 184
essence kāya 214
  five principal qualities 216
  intrinsic qualities 215
Ethic of Clarity 32
everlasting 202
exist, to e.: Buddhist definition 70
existence 71
  non-existence 71
existence and non-existence 71
  neither existence nor non-existence 71
experience 57, 68
  definition 57
explanation lineage 34
externals, depending upon 52
extremes, four 71
eyelashes, of Buddha 262

eyes of primordial wisdom 281
eyes of wisdom.
  See wisdom-eyes
eyes, of Buddha 262

face, of Buddha 262
faculties of beings 248
faculty of taste, of Buddha 262
faith 65, 177, 316
  hook and ring example 65
fear 57
fearlessness 57–58, 97, 106, 146, 148, 191, 244–245, 251–254, 265–267, 284.
  See also four fearlessnesses
feet, of Buddha 260
ficus tree, *f. religiosus* 190, 226
fifth Buddha 18
filth 167–168
fingers, of Buddha 260
fire 31, 56, 100, 120, 124, 126–127, 133, 138–139, 153, 226, 245, 258, 268, 285, 314, 326
first bodhisattva level 135, 275
First Turning 22–23, 25, 29
fish, as example of perception 28
five aggregates 112–113, 128–129, 136, 170
five branches of Buddhist knowledge 30
five branches of extraordinary knowledge 41
five branches of ordinary knowledge 41
five flesh-eating demons 243
Five Great Dharma of Maitreya 33
five heinous acts 327
five main mistakes 180
five poisons 196
five powers 120
five principal aspects of the sambhogakāya 217
five principal qualities of the sambhogakāya 219
five qualities 184
five skandhas 113

five sorts of eyes 297
five types of beings 290
five worst acts 327
five-thousand-year period 41
fivefold vision 221
flame 120
flesh eyes 297
focus 51
forbearance 64
form kāya 217, 231–232, 234, 246, 269, 295, 301
form realms 213
form-dimension gods 291, 310
formal mental activity 157
formless concentration 309
formless mental activity 157
four extremes 238
four fearlessnesses 146, 191, 245, 252–253, 265
four infinite contemplations 234
four limitless concentrations 309
four māra 226
Four Noble Truths 23, 66, 247, 283, 291
four philosophical extremes 66, 230
four qualities of fearlessness 244
four remedial powers 327
Four Truths 57, 179, 227, 249, 291
free from coarse sensations 209
freedom 81
   from defilements 81
   from impurity 188
   from inferior motivation 81
   from the cognitive obscuration 81
   from transient impurity 190
fruit 161, 198
   skin 167
fruition 193
frustration 168
full maturation of karma 247
function 199, 201
function, of buddha nature 116

Gampopa 16, 42, 102, 117, 213
Ganges 122, 191
garbage-heap 158–159

garbha 37, 189
gates of perception 127, 129
Gautama 50
Gems of Dharma, Jewels of Freedom 16
general characteristic 124
generosity 64, 313, 315
Ghanavyu-ha 64
goal to be achieved 46
God 16, 70–71, 94, 106, 112, 183, 210
gods 70–71
gold 158–159, 174, 197–198
   in rubbish 159, 174
golden ages 22
Good Aeon Sūtra 220
Goshir Gyaltsab Rinpoché 270
gotra 100, 172, 174
   explanation 118
grain 157, 168, 198
grains 157, 173, 197
Great Dharma of Maitreya, Five 33
great nature 231
Great Sage 321
great tree 197
Great Yogin 304
Greater Vehicle 179
greatness of nature 188
gtsug na nor bu 64
guru 138
   g.–disciple bond 138
Gyaltsabpas 42
Gyalwa Karmapa 220
gzhan stong 20, 42, 64, 215

hair, of Buddha 263
hair-cutting 224
head, of Buddha 262
head mound 257, 262, 270
hell-dwellers 54
hells 326
highest fulfilment 188
Highest Heaven 60
highest prajña- 104
highest truth 146
hinayāna 32
hinayānists 86

Hinduism 70
honey 156, 168, 197
  taste of 173
Hookham, Shenpen 13, 42
hostility 105
  to mahāyāna teachings 105
hovel 160, 163
hridaya 37
Hundred Thousand Dohas 195
Hungchen Kara 310
husk 167–168, 198
husks 157, 197

identification 182
ignorance 36, 55, 168
illusion 22, 24–27, 29, 35–36, 40, 57–58, 60, 74, 79, 81, 93–94, 101–102, 107, 109–110, 113, 118, 120, 135, 145–146, 165, 169-170, 174, 179, 180–181, 189, 199, 203, 209–210, 213, 224, 226, 228, 236, 240, 317–319
immaculate 209, 211
immature beings 78, 207
immeasurability of the Buddha's body 257
impartiality 234
imperceptible 209
impermanence 57, 115, 228, 283
impure beings 122
impurity 115
incalculable 211
incidental nature of defilement 132
inconceivability 69, 205, 312
inconceivable 211
  i. change 202
India 21, 50, 222, 287
indicator 153
indirect proof 153
individual, definition 78
Indra 46, 278≠279, 281–282, 305–307
Indrabhuti 227
indriya 248
Inferential proofs 153
Infinite Life 328
Infinite Light 328

innately-existing purities 192
insight 167, 203
  stage of i. 170
insight meditation 162
integration, stage of 169
inter-meditation 264
inter-sessions practice 201
interdependence 56
interlinked nature of things 28
interruption 202
intuitive cognition 276
invisible 209
iron bar, man rubbing 32

Jamgon Kongtrul Lodro Taye 63
Jamgön Kongtrul Yönten Gyamtso 35, 41–42
Jampal Bengar Zangpo 191
jealousy 55
Jewel in the Crown 61
jñāna 47, 62–64, 66, 74–75, 77–85, 95, 119–120, 149–150, 170, 184, 188–190, 192, 194, 199–200, 204–206, 214, 239, 243, 254–258, 272, 275, 280, 286, 294, 296, 303, 305
  all-encompassing j. 79–82, 83, 85
  definition 79
  ensuing j. 194
  inner j. 80–81
  non-conceptual j. 194
  thusness j. 79–82, 84
jñānakāya 205

kāya 60, 61
  definition 60
Kagyu 13, 16–17, 20, 35, 37, 151–152
  Karma Kagyu 41
Kagyu lineage 13, 37, 42, 177
  Karma Kagyu lineage 20
Kagyu mahāmudrā 35, 42
Kagyu masters 19
Kagyu Samyé Ling 16, 17, 20, 64, 329
Kagyu scholars 17
Kagyupa 42

Index

Kalachakra 222
kalavinka bird 262
kalpa 42
Kalu Rinpoché 219
karma 17–18, 24, 27–29, 37, 53–55, 58, 61, 73–74, 78, 81, 89, 94, 101, 110–111, 114, 121, 125, 129–135, 143–144, 147, 152–153, 166, 169, 181, 199, 202, 204, 213, 236, 243, 246–247, 249, 251, 264, 270, 278–284, 292–294, 298–299, 324, 327
    untainted k. 144
Karmapa 20
Karmapa Rangjung Dorjé 241
Karmapa, HH the 16th Gyalwa 17, 19–20
Karmapas 39, 42
Kashmir 34, 42
Katanka 224
Kaśyapa 222
Khempo Troru Tsenam Rinpoche 64
Khempo Tsultim Gyamtso Rinpoché 15, 19, 37, 151.
Khenchen Thrangu Rinpoché 17, 19, 20, 37
kleśa 24, 68, 73, 111, 125, 129–130, 135, 199, 202
knowledge of miracles 120
knowledge of others' minds 120
knowledge of past and future 120
kumuta flower 294
Kun.rtsob.bdan.pa 41
kusha grass 226
Kusinagara 52

laṅkāravātāra 41, 64
Lao Tzu 21
lapis lazuli 309
latent karmic traces 167, 169
lha'i mig 270
liberation 51, 256
light 207
lightning 326
lineage 14, 16
linear time 165

lion 245, 254, 260, 265, 267–268
Lion Buddha 220
Loden Sherab 329
logic 153
lotus 155, 167, 173, 193–195
    l. seed 195
Lotus Sūtra 229
lucid clarity 188, 191
lucidity 80, 82, 188
    great l. 82
Lumbini 52, 223

māra 226, 233
    m. of death 236
madhyamaka 30, 35, 42
madhyantavibhaga 42
magical illusion 181
mahābodhisattvas 84
Mahāmāya 222–223
mahāmudrā 35, 37–38, 42, 80, 95, 112, 177, 190, 316
Mahāparinirvāṇa 64
Mahāparinirvāṇasūtra 177
mahātma 112
mahāyāna 20, 30, 32–33, 45, 78, 81, 86, 104–108, 119, 134, 139, 150, 152, 172, 182, 190, 200, 218, 224, 227–229, 240, 249, 297–298, 302
mahāyāna dharma 218
Mahāyāna Treatise on the Ultimate Continuum 34
mahāyāna uttara tantra śāstra 45
mahāyānanottaratantraśāstra 37
mahāyānasūtralaṁkāra 41
Mahaberi 63
Mahamega 64
Maitreya 13, 16–19, 29–30, 32–34, 37, 39, 40, 45, 48, 51, 71–72, 93, 97, 100, 112, 125, 177, 179, 188, 220, 242, 320, 326, 328
    Maitreya, five teachings of 35
Maitripa 34, 42, 151
mangoes 161
manifest suffering 113
manifestation without arisal and

cessation 306
Manikuda 64
Mañjuśrī 41
Mañjuśrīmālatantra 41
mantras 40
marks 225
Marpa the Translator 42
mature love 184
meaning 51
meaning lineage 34
meaning-commentary 16
meditation 36, 64, 205–206, 264, 317
　m. jñāna 194
　m. phase 189
meditative absorption 104, 249
memory 255
mere peace 169
merely-mind tradition of Buddhism 30
Mīchö Dorjé 39
Middle Way tradition of Buddhism 30, 34, 38, 70–71, 100, 127, 147
Milarépa 42, 62, 185, 327
mindfulness 255–256, 317
miracles 272
mirage, as example of voidness 26
mistaken views 58
monastic ordination 224
monsoon 286–289
moon 193–196, 217–218, 246, 264, 270
　m. in water 264
mould 164, 176
mu stegs pa 151
mud 194
mud-born 167
murderers 326
mystery of form 300
mystery of mind 297
mystery of speech 299

Nārāyāṇa 263
naga 28, 299
Nagarjuna 41–42
Nalanda 31
nanny 108

Naropa 42, 151, 213
natural sequence, of seven vajra abodes 47
Négi, Acarya Tenpa 17
Neranjara 225
newly born baby 207
Ngog Loden Sherab 34, 37
nine examples, of spontaneous activity 277
nirmāṇakāya 188, 212–213, 217–218, 220–221, 226–228, 230, 232, 236, 280, 282, 292–293
nirvāṇa 111–118, 142–147, 150, 213–214, 226–229, 232–239, 255, 269, 287, 322
　non-abiding n. 116
no ageing 208
no birth 208
no death 208
no sickness 208
no-self 77, 108–112, 228, 283, 297
non-conceptual 52
non-conceptual primordial wisdom 189, 201
non-dual 62
non-dual wisdom 83
non-ego 36, 115
nyagrodha tree 263
nyams 64

obstacles 105
　four main o. 105, 106
obstacles to meditation 216
ocean 82, 118–119, 126, 131, 141–142, 230, 272, 275–276, 296, 299
og.min 220
oilstained cloth 325
omniscient jñāna 205
one taste of honey 198
one taste of voidness 173
oral tradition.
　See oral transmission
oral transmission 13
ordinary being 37, 78, 83, 121–122, 134, 136, 142–143, 150, 161, 166,

174, 176, 180, 200, 227, 232, 240, 245, 251, 259, 273–274, 279, 283, 295, 297, 302, 305, 312, 315
original canon 67
Ornament of Definite Realisation 34
Ornament of Mahāyāna Sūtra 34
Ornament of the Radiant Light 62
overstatement 210
ox's hoof-print 142

pāramitā 60, 64, 109–111, 113, 115, 147–149, 151, 181, 183, 203, 229, 232–233, 317–319
   p. of generosity 317
   p. of happiness 113
   p. of identity 111
   p. of permanence 113
   p. of purity 111
parinirvāṇa 227
path of integration 203
Path of Peace 67
paths 249
pauper 160
peace 24, 50, 52–54, 60, 62, 66, 68–69, 73, 77, 79, 82, 109–110, 117, 138–139, 143–147, 163–164, 169–170, 174, 198–199, 202–208, 211–212, 227–228, 236–240, 246, 251, 260, 280, 283–285, 293, 316, 321–322
peafowl 289
penetrating insight 38
Perfection of Wisdom, Transcendent 25
perfectly at peace 208
Perfectly Victorious 279
permanence 57, 202
personality 94
phase of accumulation 134
phase of integration 134
phases, ten, of Buddhism in world 21
phenomena, voidness of 24
pigeon 32
point of existence 51
possible and the impossible 246

post-meditation phase 189
potential 47–48, 59, 72, 94, 100, 102, 117–119, 126–127, 146, 150, 152, 161, 172, 174–177, 185, 195, 198, 213, 252, 273, 307, 316
potential as it innately exists 174
potential perfected through proper cultivation 175
potential to be perfectly developed 176
potential, fulfilling one's 51
poverty 160, 169
powers 52
prajñā 79, 103–104, 107, 115, 119, 150, 184, 205–206, 214, 254, 256–257, 290, 314–316, 318–319
   definition 79
prajñāpāramitā 25, 71–72, 185
pratyekabuddha 86, 106–107, 257, 268
   definition 107
predict the future enlightenment 229
predicting 212
pride 55, 183
prime cause 59, 97, 132
primordial wisdom 46, 53, 58, 63, 68–69, 73, 78–80, 84, 101, 110–111, 136, 147, 150, 155–156, 170, 172–173, 178, 182, 187–190, 194–199, 202, 204, 210–211, 215, 235, 238, 244, 273–276, 281, 286, 294–297, 302, 304, 310
principal causes 97
private parts, of Buddha 260
profound absorption 314
pure conduct 314
purity 37, 40, 48, 53, 56–58, 66–67, 69, 73–78, 81–85, 93–96, 103–104, 109–111, 120, 122–124, 129, 141, 144, 171, 187–204, 208–211, 214, 216, 226, 235–236, 240, 251, 264, 268, 270, 272, 281–282, 286, 301, 305–306
purpose of life 51

qualities of freedom 242, 245

qualities of maturity 242, 245

rab zhi rnam nges 64
rags 167
Rahu 193
Rahula 224
rang stong 19–20, 37–39, 42, 215
Rangjung Dorjé 35
ratna 88
ratnadarikasūtra 264
Ratnamega 64
Ratnavajra 329
realisation 14, 30, 39, 47–48, 50,
 56–58, 62, 68, 72, 74, 78–79, 87,
 97, 102, 114–116, 121, 134–136,
 139, 141, 169, 172, 177, 180, 183,
 208, 212, 217, 253, 255, 322, 325
 definition 57
realised beings 78, 82
realised saṃgha 81, 83–85, 88
recall of former states 250
Rechungpa 42
recollectedness 255
recollection 276
reflection 206
reflection of the moon in water 217, 246, 265, 270
refuge 43, 48–50, 55, 66–67, 77–78,
 82, 85–89, 91, 94, 142, 144–145,
 163, 233, 236, 247
 three r. 86
 ultimate r. 86–87
relatively true kāya 242
release from saṃsāra 275
religions 70
 monotheistic r. 70
 multitheistic r. 70
removal, result through 60, 97, 193
respect for others 184
result Refuges 48
right conduct 64, 314–315
rind
 See fruit
rishi 244
rjes.thob 141
rngog 42

Rokpa Trust 20
Rome, all roads leading to 39
root text 19
rope 80–82, 93–94, 102, 112, 118,
 129–130, 145, 170, 192, 203, 210
rotting rind 161
rtogs 64
rubbish 169
Ruegg 42
Rumtek 20

saddharmapundarikasūtra 181, 241
Sajjana 35, 42, 329
Sakyamuni, Buddha 16, 18, 21, 24,
 26, 29, 42, 48, 60, 131, 151, 190,
 202, 213, 220–222, 225–226, 243
saṃgha 45–49, 77–88, 93, 97, 137,
 249, 280, 312, 327
 arya s. 78, 82
 as refuge of śrāvakas 86
 realised s. 78
saṃsāra 73–74, 80, 82, 85, 94, 102,
 105–107, 109–110, 113–118, 121,
 128, 135, 142, 144, 156, 162–163,
 167, 170, 179, 188, 212, 214,
 228–229, 232–233, 235, 239, 250,
 255, 269, 275, 277, 284, 287,
 289–290, 298, 309, 317, 322, 329
samādhi 235
samādhirajasūtra 151
samapatti 139
śamatta 38
Sambhoga 217
sambhogakāya 143, 175–176, 188,
 198, 212, 217–219, 230–232, 236,
 244, 246, 264, 269, 270, 280, 282,
 292
sameness 114
 of saṃsāra and nirvāṇa 114
Sandhinirmanocana 64
sangs.rgyas 147
sapphire 309
Saraha 42
śāstra 26, 29, 34, 45, 67, 320, 322–324
Sattva 41
second phase 25

Second Phase of the Buddha's
    teaching 72
Second Turning 25, 29
secondary conditions 59
seed 194
seed of buddhahood 174
seeds 161
self 24, 36, 54, 57–58, 60, 62, 70, 80,
    82, 94, 107, 109–112, 115–116,
    121–123, 130, 170–171, 180,
    182–185, 192, 195, 210, 213–214,
    225, 228, 235, 240, 254, 267, 275,
    289, 297, 317, 320, 328
self-awakened 50, 55–56
self-blossomed 50, 55–56
self-cognisant 66, 70, 84, 172–173,
    214
self-confidence 182–183, 254
self-entity 35–36, 105
    belief in s.-e. 105
self-fulfilment 62, 63, 244, 253.
    See also four fearlessnesses
self-void 20, 42
self-wisdom 83, 205, 245
senses 157
Seven Vajra Abodes 45
Shamarpa Chöji Döndrup 35
Sharmapas 42
Shawripa 42
shell 168, 197
shen-tong 20
shengtong 19–20, 37–39, 49
short prayer to Vajradhara 240, 310
shoulders, of Buddha 261
sickness 23, 25, 38, 53, 88, 109, 127,
    131, 133–136, 143–144, 199,
    201–202, 204, 208, 224, 236, 304
Siddhartha 243
sila 318
six consciousnesses 238
six pāramitā 229
six realms of existence 78, 169
six types of beings 83
six types of clear cognition 141
six-tusked elephant 223
sixty qualities, of Buddha speech 284
sixty-four enlightened qualities 191,
    264
skilful means 229
skin, of Buddha 260, 263
smoke 153
snake 56, 80–82, 93–94, 102, 112,
    118, 129–130, 145, 192, 203, 326
snyoms 'jug 139
Socrates 21
soul 70–71, 111
space 18, 26–28, 40, 49, 52–53, 72,
    74, 80, 84, 96, 100, 103–104,
    124–133, 140, 144, 161, 188–192,
    198–200, 203–204, 210, 212–213,
    219, 231, 245–246, 258–259, 265,
    268–278, 287, 295–296, 300–301,
    304–306, 308, 316, 325
specific characteristic 124
spiritual seekers 117
spontaneity 61, 271, 273
spontaneous activity 271
spros.pa 112
    definition 112
sprul.sku 213
śrāvaka 86, 106–107, 257, 268, 270
    definition 107
Śrīmālādevī 41
Śrīmālādevīsūtra 63, 177, 207
stage of cultivation of insight 135,
    167, 196, 240
stage of meditation 240
stage of no more training 135
stainlessness 74
statue 164, 176
Sthiramati 34
ston.pa 65
strength 263
study 205–206
stupa 34, 42
sūtra 16, 29–30, 34, 39–41, 47, 62, 64,
    67, 220, 228–229, 257, 264, 302,
    309, 320, 323–324
subsidiary defilements 166, 275
suchness 81, 93–95, 97, 100, 121,
    174, 187–188, 204, 274, 310, 323
    tainted s. 94, 97
    undifferentiated s. 101
    untainted s. 93, 97

suchness jñāna 192, 243, 303
suchness primordial wisdom 204
Suddhodhana 223
suffering 22–23, 35, 38, 50, 52–53, 55, 58, 62–63, 68–69, 73–74, 79, 81, 85, 88, 94, 101, 104–118, 121, 125–127, 131–134, 144–147, 152, 159, 163, 168–169, 179, 184, 197, 202, 204, 208, 214, 228–229, 232, 235–236, 247, 252, 283–285, 289–291, 296–297, 305
suffering of change 113
suffering, Buddhist attitude to 22
Sugatagharba 93
Sukhavati 230
summit of existence 305
Summit of Goodness 221
sun 66, 190–196, 243, 272, 276, 293–295, 305, 308
sunlight 189
śūnya 26
supporting conditions 97
supramundane states 309
supreme nirmāṇakāya 227, 293
supreme yogin 216
Suvarnaprabha-sa 64
Svābhāvika 214
svābhāvikakāya 214–215
svābhāva 189
swastika 144, 152
sword 58

Tai Situpas 42
Takasaki 42, 310
tantra 20, 29, 39–40, 42, 45, 67
tantric Buddhism 17
taste of truth 157
tathāgata 37, 121–123, 140, 145–147, 149–150, 155, 161–162, 173, 198–199, 210, 245, 277, 285, 290, 294, 299–300, 315
tathāgatagarbha 16, 37
Tathāgatagarbhasūtra 63, 100
tathatā 100, 172
tattered rags 162, 170, 176
Teacher, as translation of ston.pa 65

teeth, of Buddha 261
temperaments of beings 248
ten basic obscurations 196
ten powers 141, 179, 191, 265–266
ten powers of wisdom 244
ten virtuous actions 203
tenth level 276
thatness 101, 122
third Gyalwa Karmapa 35
third phase 26, 72
Third Turning 26, 29–30, 101
thirty-seven factors of enlightenment 253
    See also four fearlessnesses
thirty-two major marks 191, 220, 244, 264–265 269, 280
three cosmic aeons 220, 226
three dharmachakras 35–36
Three Jewels 49
three pure levels 171
Three Rare and Precious Things 49
three realms 157
three root poisons 197
three types of beings 78
Threefold Collection 67
thusness 63, 79–82, 84, 98, 119–120, 147, 159
thusness jñāna 63, 80–82, 120.
    See also jñāna
thusness wisdom 159
Tilopa 42, 151
Tirthika 151
toes, of Buddha 260
tongue, of Buddha 262
torso, of Buddha 260
tranquillity 38
treasure 160, 197–198, 272, 276
treasure-hair, of Buddha 262
tree 198, 251
trees 266
tripitaka 42
Triple Collection 67
Triple Gem 49
triplicity 54, 60, 317
triratna 49
true taste of dharma 197
Truth of Cessation 66, 69, 73–74, 87

Truth of Suffering 125
  Truth of Origination of S. 125
Truth of the Path 67, 69, 87
Tsen Kawoché 35
tulku 213, 234
Turnings of the Wheel of Dharma 16, 22
Tuṣita 18, 33, 221, 329
Twelfth Tai Situpa 41
twelve deeds 221, 293
twelve gates of consciousness 128
twenty-one subsidiary obscurations 196
two accumulations 243, 273, 275–276
two extreme notions 215
Two Truths 57
twofold benefit 199, 201
twofold purity 66

ultimate element 179
ultimate reality 25
ultimate truth 63
ultimate truth kāya 242
ultimately true nirvāṇa 145
unceasing activity 271
uncompounded nirvāṇa 145
uncompoundeds 130
understatement 210
unequalled 211
unfathomable 211
unhindered 209
uninvolved 208
union of clarity and voidness 73
union of voidness and clarity 36
universal emperors 244
untaintedness 201
Upavasa precepts 310
Uttara Tantra 34–35, 37, 68

vaidurya 279, 282, 307, 309
Vaiśākha 226
vajra 42, 45–50, 58, 93–95, 97, 171–172, 226, 245, 251, 255, 265–266
vajra abode 42, 45–47, 49–50, 65, 77, 93–95, 97, 99, 172, 242, 271

vajra-like samādhi 171, 226
Vajrāsana 225
vajrayāna 17, 20, 53, 64, 73, 138–139, 149, 177, 182, 190, 227, 255, 298
valid sign 153
vasana 202
vast 192
vast teachings 173, 212
vastness 188, 231
Vasubandhu 32, 34
view 107
vijñāna 199
vimukti 201
vimuktikāya 201, 203, 205, 214
vinaya 29, 39, 67
vipyasana 38
Vishnu 263
visualisations 40, 182
voice, of Buddha 262
voidness 16, 24–30, 35–39, 47, 56, 60, 72–73, 78, 80, 82, 93, 98, 101–102, 105, 121–122, 124, 127, 134–135, 144–145, 149–150, 172–174, 179–183, 192, 195, 200, 210–212, 215, 217, 226, 228–229, 233, 262, 268, 286, 294–297, 309, 319, 325, 327
  v. as limitlessnes 27
  v. as wisdom 26
  v., omnipresence of 25
Vulture Peak 179, 227

walls 251, 266
water 26–27, 36, 68, 100, 103–105, 119, 126–133, 137, 142, 155, 160–161, 169, 184, 193–196, 217–218, 245–246, 258, 264–265, 270, 275–276, 286–290, 293–295
  w. spirit 28
water bubble eyes 310
water maṇḍala 128
water-born 155
waters of primordial wisdom 276
wheel, of dharma 22
wheel, of existence 22
White Lotus 310

wholesome 209
wind 100, 126, 128–130, 245, 258, 268, 272–273, 275–277, 287
  w. maṅdala 128
  w. of compassion 273
  w. of enlightened compassion 277
wisdom 13–14, 19, 26, 28–29, 36, 39, 45–46, 48, 51–64, 66, 68–69, 73–74, 77–88, 94, 101–102, 105–112, 115–124, 136–138, 146–147, 149–150, 155–156, 159, 169–174, 178, 182, 187–202, 205–206, 208, 210–211, 213–216, 220–221, 225–226, 229, 232–233, 235, 238–240, 243–245, 251, 257, 265–266, 268, 273–275, 286, 290, 293–297, 301–302, 304–305, 309–310, 315, 317
wisdom eyes 155, 158, 297
wisdom's penetration 293
wisdom, as voidness 26
wise 167
wish-fulfilling gem 19, 104, 198, 212, 217, 277–278, 297–299, 304–305, 308–309, 321
wishes 248
womb 167, 171, 176
worldly states 309

Yasodhara 224
Zarathustra 21

Also from Altea Publishing

Gems of Dharma, Jewels of Freedom
Ken & Katia Holmes

This, the principal textbook used in Kagyu Buddhist studies, comes from Jé Gampopa, the 12th-century Tibetan forefather of all the twelve main Kagyu traditions. A great scholar who subsequently achieved enlightenment, his book is a masterly overview of all the Buddha's teachings. This translation is the result of work over some seventeen years by Ken and Katia Holmes.

1994 • ISBN 0 9524555 0 1 • 320 pages • 230 x 155 mm • Pbk £12.50
Hardcover edition   ISBN 0 9524555 1 X   £17.50

Karmapa
Ken Holmes

Drawing on a quarter-century of experience close to the senior lamas of the Kagyu tradition, including the 16th Karmapa, Ken Holmes tells the fascinating story of the finding of the 17th Karmapa among the nomads of Eastern Tibet, exactly in accordance with instructions he left in a letter at the end of his previous incarnation. The book also includes extensive information on topics such as the Karmapa's uniqueness, his lineage, reincarnation, the land of Tibet and Tibetan Buddhism itself.

Pbk • ISBN 0 9524555 4 4 • £12.95 168 pp • Illustrated

Some other books, translations and edited transcripts by Ken & Katia Holmes

***Changeless Nature** – the root text*
Dzalendara and Sakarchupa
Way to Go (based on lectures given by the XIIth Tai Situpa)
Tilopa: some glimpses of his life (edited from lectures given by the XIIth Tai Situpa)
Compassion through Understanding